WEDDED WIFE

A Feminist History of Marriage

WEDDED WIFE

A Feminist History of Marriage

RACHAEL E. LENNON

Aurum

First published in 2023 by Aurum,
an imprint of The Quarto Group
One Triptych Place, London, SE1 9SH
United Kingdom
T (0)20 7700 6700

www.Quarto.com/Aurum

Copyright © 2023 Rachael E. Lennon
Design © 2023 Quarto Publishing plc.
Cover design by Terri Sirma
Text designed and set in Adobe Garamond Premier Pro by Jeremy Tilston

British Library Cataloguing-in-Publication Data
A catalogue record for this book is available from the British Library.

ISBN: 978-0-7112-6711-4
E-book ISBN: 978-0-7112-6713-8
Audiobook ISBN: 978-0-7112-6914-9

Printed and bound by CPI Group (UK) Ltd, Croydon, CR0 4YY
1 2 3 4 5 6 7 8 9 10

FSC
www.fsc.org
MIX
Paper | Supporting
responsible forestry
FSC® C171272

Love is giving, marriage is buying and selling. You can't put love into a contract.

– *MARGARET ATWOOD*, THE BLIND ASSASSIN

CONTENTS

CONTENTS

PREFACE

Do not marry at all ... You will be wiser not to chance it, it isn't worth the risk.

– SUFFRAGE POSTER, SIGNED 'A SUFFRAGETTE WIFE'[1]

Imagine being a fully grown woman and promising to obey another person. In all things. Until you die. Imagine being required to make that promise publicly, with no expectation of it being reciprocated. And then being forced to keep it.

A quick glance back at the history of marriage tends to lead us to agree with the suffragette who advised that, surely, 'it isn't worth the risk'. Marriage has a long, dark history of oppressing women and excluding diverse couples. In the 1970s, a feminist campaign was launched in Britain asking the question, 'YBA Wife?'[2] It asked if it were possible, or even desirable, for marriage to be redeemed.

In the UK, around 250,000 new marriages take place every year.[3] Half a million people join the club. Despite the fact that over 40 per cent of marriages end in divorce, half of the population over sixteen in the United Kingdom today are married.[4] Many more have been or will be. Though people are living single for longer, the vast majority still choose to marry at some point within their lifetimes. In the United States, around 48 per cent of adults are married today[5] and nearly two-thirds of all Americans have joined the institution at some point.[6] So, what is it that makes us return, generation after generation, to this institution?

My wife and I walked down the aisle together just three years after same-sex marriages started to be legally practised in England and Wales. Like so many couples, we did not spend a great deal of time deeply interrogating our motivations for marriage. Making the choice with the heart, rather than the head. Getting married provided an opportunity to commit to each other in a serious way.

There are not many choices that we make and imagine should last a lifetime. Not a lot that we expect to be or do forever. In the UK, we change jobs on average every five years.[7] In the US, every four years.[8] We move house roughly every twenty.[9] By the time I had married, I had already lived in thirteen homes. Similarly, people often have several relationships in a lifetime. Marriage, though, is a way of saying *this is different* to each other, and to everyone else. Of finding an anchoring relationship in a transient world.

Some motivations to marry are romantic, others more pragmatic. My wife and I made the decision to marry alongside the choice to become parents. Making a public and symbolic commitment before a deeply practical one. For my wife, being married meant that she would be acknowledged as the parent of our children when they were born, without jumping through legal hoops and navigating additional paperwork.

When we made the decision to marry, I knew I wanted a public celebration. A wedding. Eloping would have made much more financial sense for us at the time, but, unlike my fiancée, I was not very tempted. I had been a bridesmaid six times before my own wedding, a guest at countless others.

Weddings provide moments of connection beyond the couple at the centre, out into your community at that moment in time and back through time as you retrace and relive the experiences and choices of generations before. Girls are brought up to aspire to a wedding at every stage of our development. The expectation is profoundly limiting, it can be deeply harmful, and it's hard to totally shake off that level of social conditioning. Maybe it just got to me.

A wedding, however big or small, marks a change. It is easy to let the significant moments and relationships in our lives pass quietly, uncelebrated and unacknowledged. That was not what I wanted. For same-sex and queer couples, for people whose relationships have not been recognized before, public acknowledgement can bring a particular power and importance. There is a poignancy in publicly celebrating and rejoicing in relationships that have long been actively persecuted.

In 2004, the UK government passed the Civil Partnership Act. It sought to remove the financial, legal and technical inequalities faced by same-sex couples, unable to marry – couples prevented from accessing the wide range of benefits and rights enjoyed by opposite-sex spouses. However, very explicitly and deliberately, it avoided opening marriage to them. The hierarchy was clear and enshrined in law. Same-sex relationships were not deserving of marriage. A more clinical civil partnership was more appropriate.

Almost a decade later, in 2013, the Marriage (Same Sex Couples) Act was passed, acknowledging the rights of same-sex couples to hold a wedding, sign a marriage register and become a husband or a wife in England and Wales. I still so often introduce my wife, or the existence of my wife, to people who then refer to her as my partner, often straight after, in the same conversation. Like a correction. It feels like they have heard the queer bit and defaulted to 'partner'. 'Wife' doesn't quite sound right to them. It is all still very new.

When I made the decision to walk down the aisle, I felt a sense of walking in the footsteps of the people who had gone before me, of my family today and people long dead; of making the same choice; of drawing from the same traditions of our shared cultural inheritance. However, I was also aware of the lack of blueprint for weddings like mine, for marriages like mine. Of treading new ground and of forging new footsteps that more people might trace behind me.

Navigating the journey to marriage in this new territory was tricky. Waiting for the inevitable moment of misunderstanding in florists, venues and dress shops. *She*. 'My fiancée is a woman.' Being asked which one is the bride. Who gets the engagement ring? Who is being given away? Without a groom, who gives the speech? We were moving in and out of tradition and dealing with clichés and other people's assumptions. It was challenging – but liberating.

Marrying a woman allowed my wife and I to shake off some of the patriarchal expectations of marriage – though we still felt them. In the UK, marriage customs take many forms, drawing from a diverse range of traditions, but it is not difficult to find reminders of women's historic place in today's engagements, weddings and marriages.

We are continually seduced by nostalgia for the past. In marriage, particularly in the celebration of our relationships, we cannot resist looking backwards in the decision-making for our futures – to the proposals in classic novels, our grandparents' twentieth-century choices or Disney-influenced childhood fantasies.

Women continue to take a passive role in wedding ceremonies. The marriage register, the legal footprint of our relationships, recorded the 'father's profession' at every wedding until 2021, with no space for 'mother's'. In churches across the country, vicars, priests and deacons continue to ask, 'Who gives this woman to be married to this man?' Men, presumably, remain qualified to give themselves.

People choosing to marry today continue to navigate a problematic inheritance. In the UK, and around the world, people are forced into the institution without their consent. The unequal distribution of domestic labour within marriage contributes to entrenched economic inequalities. Women's sexual and reproductive freedoms continue to be defined by their marital status and intimate partner violence remains the reality of married life for far too many. We continue to struggle to define and refine what it means to be seen as a wife or a husband in the twenty-first century.

My motivations to marry were not without tensions and contradictions. I love community and shared experience. And ceremony. I love seeing and experiencing history and heritage in my contemporary life. And I'm a feminist, in a relationship with a woman. Resistant to the idea of doing things just because that is how things have always been done. Conscious that that is how inequalities perpetuate. So, what compels us to keep making this choice? Can we hold true to inclusive and feminist values and take the leap? And what does that even look like? How can we build on the past to redefine marriage for the future? This book explores these questions.

INTRODUCTION

Because I am female, I am expected to aspire to marriage. I am expected to make my life choices always keeping in mind that marriage is the most important.[1]

– CHIMAMANDA NGOZI ADICHIE,
WE SHOULD ALL BE FEMINISTS

The institution of marriage has enshrined the social, economic and political inequalities of the sexes into law for millennia. From the English monarch Elizabeth I to suffragist and socialist Sylvia Pankhurst, many women have chosen to reject the inherited expectations, assumptions and baggage that would define them as a wife. In European tradition, marriage has long oppressed people who expressed gender diversity and same-sex desire. The institution has seen barriers to the inclusion of people based on race, religion, disability and class. Yet, around the world, marriage remains one of the structures most consistently present across diverse societies. Throughout its long history, people have entered this very personal, political and ubiquitous institution on an enormous scale. We continue to do so today.

This book provides an intimate history. Centring my own journey to marriage as a bisexual, feminist woman from a working-class background in the UK, I explore the traditions, laws and customs that defined the choices of people who lived on these islands before me. I recognize the reach of these powers across centuries of colonial practices.

In this feminist examination, it is clear there is not one shared understanding of the history of marriage. Feminists have never come together and created a consensus on this age-old celebrated institution that has restricted the lives of so many women around the world. In 2020, Caitlin Moran wrote,

> *From my 45-year-old Witch Throne, where I have seen feminism ebb, flow and ebb again, I feel I should croakingly remind everyone, once more, about the most crucial, brilliant, sometimes frustrating thing about feminism: it's really not a science. It has no rules. It's still just an idea, created by millions, over centuries, and it can only survive if the next generation feels able to kick ideas around, ask questions, make mistakes and reinvent the concept over and over.*

Feminism is often misrepresented, maligned and misunderstood. There has been a history of elitism within organized movements; networks promoting white feminism and trans-exclusionary feminism continue to exclude people of colour and trans sisters. But, at its heart, feminism is about questioning, about looking again. And again. Challenging the assumptions, defaults and expectations we have grown up with. Unpicking the partial versions of the past that we have inherited and imagining new and fairer futures.

This book looks again at the assumptions that we inherit and the expectations we face as we decide to commit to a partner. I have centred the stories of women and those who challenged gendered norms. Women's lives and the lives of nonbinary people remain disproportionately hidden in our understanding of history. Some were actively persecuted, their experiences concealed and repressed. Most went unrecorded. Hillary Clinton descried that women do not get written out of history, 'they never get written in it'.[2] Voices of women and girls have been continually overlooked. For generations most women were illiterate. Within the UK, once married, many lost their legal status and so appear relatively rarely in official archives. However, through the customs, laws and traditions that shaped and restricted women's lives, we can see a clearer picture of the lived experiences of this under-represented majority. We can better understand what it meant to be defined as a woman or a wife. We can glimpse the realities of choosing marriage – and the risks of not.

As a curator of social histories, I have drawn together a collection of stories, moments in time and cultural traditions to create a whistle-stop tour of 500 years of modern marriage, within the United Kingdom and beyond. I have explored the lives of historic figures alongside fictional characters; well-known women alongside the marginalized and overlooked. In unpicking some of the cultural and social influences that shape our understanding of marriage today, I have aimed to highlight stories that might inspire us to think differently.

Marriage has never been static. We continue to look again, to question our inheritance and imagine new alternatives and fairer futures. For centuries, generations of women and people who expressed gender diversity were forced to defend themselves from injustices and deep inequalities. They fought to shape the institution of marriage that we have inherited today. This book is a celebration of their efforts, their sacrifices and their successes.

—

Marriages have existed in almost every society known to recorded history. There is something in it that we cannot quite seem to resist, but anthropologists tell us that no consensus, no agreement or one model of marriage has ever existed. There has never been one right way to organize our relationships and the foundations of marriage are not easy to pin down. Some claim that the life-long pairing of a man and a woman is part of the natural order of things, like the mating of males and females in the animal world. However, the vast majority of species are not organized two by two, as though ready to venture into the Ark. Even primates, our closest relatives, do not organize their societies around pairs. They group around females and their young, sometimes around one adult male and several females, and sometimes several adults. Rarely a couple.[3] And like Roy and Silo, the famous male penguin parents of Tango, in New York's Central Park Zoo, same-sex relationships are common across many species. Marriage has always been more complex than just an irresistible natural urge to pair off across the human race.

Others see the genesis of marriage as a trade-off between the sexes. They believe that the roots of marriage lie in the Stone Age; that women were poor and vulnerable and traded protection for sex, becoming 'hearth-keepers' while the men hunted.[4] Protection was an important element of marriage for millennia, but the nuclear family was not the central structure in early societies. Collective hunting and gathering among bigger groups was needed for survival, and women's foraging often provided the bulk of the food.[5]

This protective theory was often used between the 1950s and 1980s, particularly in the United States, to suggest that it was natural for men to go out to work as 'breadwinners' and for women to stay at home – Stepford cave wives. The Piegan, Blackfoot natives of North America, had a similar protective origin story to understand the roots of marriage – but in reverse. In their tale, the ancient Piegan men were very poor. Unlike the women, they did not know how to make lodges, they did not know how to tan their buffalo hides, they did not know how to cut dried meat and sew their clothes. The hungry and cold men gathered on a hill near to the women's lodges and waited for the women to choose husbands to take in.[6]

However marriage has developed, no consensus has emerged in the definition of the institution. Monogamy is by no means a given. For thousands of years, marriage was, for many people, an arrangement between a man and multiple women. Most of the world's major religions have embraced polygamy and polyamorous relationships and, from Jacob to King Solomon, men featured in the Torah, Bible and Quran have had anywhere from two to thousands of wives. Around the world, marriages have routinely taken place between a woman and multiple men. Among the Barí people in Venezuela, women took multiple husbands, believing it created greater security for themselves and for their children.[7] In communities in Tibet and India, for example, brothers have married a single wife to keep family lands intact.[8]

The concept of legitimate and illegitimate children, a status defined by marriage rules, has been central to some cultures and entirely alien to others. For millennia, matrilineal societies from North America to Asia have practised that children belong with their mother and their mother's family, inheriting their identity, status and resources through her, regardless of their paternity and any relationship commitment.

In areas of China, right up to the early twentieth century, women could marry a dead man to establish ties between the two families.[9] Couples, like those within the Gururumba people in New Guinea, have embarked on marriage with no expectation of ever cohabiting or working with their spouse.[10] In some small-scale societies, including communities in Sri Lanka, marriage was established by a man and a woman eating a meal alone together or a woman simply cooking for a man.[11]

Many native North American tribes formally acknowledged gender diversity and same-sex desire before European puritans violently repressed such practices. Queer relationships were accepted in pre-colonial Māori cultures. A legacy of European colonialism remains the persecution of queer relationships in some parts of the African continent today, but numerous African communities have practised same-sex marriages for centuries. In West Africa, 'female husbands' have been routinely recognized as the parent of their wives' children, providing them with their name, status and inheritance if a wife brought children into the marriage, or bore children afterwards.[12] Marriages between women have been recorded in more than thirty African populations.[13] Every populated continent has seen same-sex and queer marriages and relationships practised and celebrated.

In Europe, from the Middle Ages onwards, the Christian Church grew to dominate social structures and develop a monopoly on marriage. When this new set of rules and values were exported through centres of European colonialism, the diversity of history's marriage practices began to be repressed and obscured. Definitions of marriage were consciously rewritten in the emerging 'West'. Many of us grew up being taught that marriage is something between a man and a woman and that it is inevitable, natural and desirable, and that men and women have particular, different roles as husbands and wives. That is just how it has always been. But that is not, as we have seen, what history tells us.

There has never been a consensus as to what it means to be a 'wife'. In the UK, and across the West, many dominant ideas of marriage come from a narrow view of the relatively recent past. A history that has been routinely weaponized against women, used to reinforce gender binaries and perpetuate inequalities, injustices and bad habits.

Nothing about marriage is inevitable, natural or fated. It has not evolved organically. It is entirely constructed, but who constructed it? And why? Why do some practices persist and resonate for so many people today? And how can we redefine this ancient institution for the future? With no such thing as a truly traditional marriage, history gives us licence to shake off customs where they pull us in a direction that we do not want to go. Thus, marriage is, and always has been, what we choose to make of it.

SHE SAID YES

POPPING THE QUESTION

When you realize you want to spend the rest of your life with somebody, you want the rest of your life to start as soon as possible.

– FROM THE FILM *WHEN HARRY MET SALLY*, 1989

We begin at the end. From Shakespeare to Austen, *Cinderella* to *Love Actually*, the marriage proposal is the happy finale – the moment we have been building towards. The joyful resolution of everything that has gone before and the choice that will shape the future we do not see. We leave the characters we have come to know to walk off into the sunset with the promise of future wedded bliss, their lives defined by the joy and promise of this moment.

An engagement to marry is a key milestone in our lives; a serious commitment. Our partners, girlfriends and boyfriends become fiancée and fiancé, in a moment of transformation so romantic that we turn a little French. Across much of the world, we continue to be seduced by the idea that we can find 'the one' and that, when we do, marriage is a means to lock them in – to guarantee our very own happily ever after. In the United States, research suggests that 60 per cent of adults believe in the idea of soulmates.[1]

Proposing marriage today is big business. A proposal industry exists to help wealthy people ensure that when they become engaged to marry, the moment itself is everything they could have dreamed of. In 2018, a London-based company managed a proposal that cost £800,000.[2] The groom-to-be arranged for the couple's faces to be projected onto iconic locations in seven different countries, from the fairytale castle in Disneyland Paris to Niagara Falls.

In the UK, with nine out of ten couples cohabiting before marriage, proposals tend to follow previous discussions between partners and some level of planning towards a shared future.[3] However, there is a sense that engagement does not start there. That does not count. Engagement begins when a man pops the question. Preferably on one knee. In a romantic setting, at the perfect moment. Diamond ring in hand. *No pressure*.

It seems like an odd ideal for a twenty-first-century woman to mark the decision to marry in such a passive way. The idea of a 'traditional' proposal places binary and very different expectations on a couple looking to commit to a heterosexual partnership. Many people in same-sex and queer relationships simply find the expectations irrelevant and impossible to meet; expectations, rules and roles that remain surprisingly resistant to change. The roots of these traditions are fairly shallow and narrow. History is not full of men, century after century, popping the question down on one knee in a carefully choreographed performance. The proposal event is a twentieth-century phenomenon – but the myth endures.

It can be challenging for women to find active agency on this journey into their marriages. The legend of a leap year proposal is a relatively obscure custom said to date back to St Brigid of Kildare in fifth-century Ireland but is felt to have some relevance in the twenty-first century when the vast majority of opposite-sex proposals continue to be made by men. In 2010, the American romantic comedy *Leap Year* celebrated the concept that women are empowered to suggest marriage to a partner once every four years. In the UK, a 2019 survey found that just 16 per cent of engaged women had proposed to their fiancé – up from a mere 5 per cent nine years earlier.[4] The most popular day for these women to propose was found to be a Leap Day.[5]

Within the last century, when women have sought to subvert their role within a proposal event, the choice has seemed noteworthy. Actress Zsa Zsa Gabor proposed to all nine of her husbands. American politician Elizabeth Warren made a low-key marriage proposal to her husband in 2015, after watching him teach, and the story was widely reported in the national news. In 2021, Jodie Turner-Smith faced both misogynistic and racist backlash for proposing to her fellow actor Joshua Jackson in Nicaragua.[6] Exceptions seem to prove the rule, to reinforce the idea of a 'traditional' norm – one in which the default role for women is passive. Although men more commonly wear engagement rings in Sweden and some Latin American countries, it is still unusual for a woman to gift an engagement ring in the UK, US and most of the West. Yet it is expected for a man to do so.

Gender binaries play a role in today's romantic relationships from the very start. Research in the United States suggests that many young people still believe that, in opposite-sex relationships, it is a man's role to ask out a woman first.[7] Dating guides, books and publications aimed at women continue to discourage them from taking the first steps, for fear of seeming 'too eager'.[8] The idea that men bear unequal responsibility for paying for early dates still has not died.[9] Although lesbians do not date for free and gay men manage not to pay twice.

Decisions as to how our contemporary relationships progress tend to be taken together, based on the personalities of individuals and the dynamics of a relationship. For many couples, one partner might suggest that they move in together. There is likely to be a discussion. A decision is made, and actions are taken by the people in the relationship in the way that works for them. And then, as marriage approaches, we find ourselves, and those around us, tumbling, often awkwardly, into assigned gender roles, unable to resist the pull, like a magnetic force compelling us. Ready to adorn women with diamonds and manicured nails, and men with pats on the back and apathy as to flower arrangements. Few same-sex or nonbinary couples manage to entirely escape expectations within this very gendered reality. Having been barred from the institution until recently, some simply choose to reject it altogether. In their route to marriage, some adopt the roles traditionally assigned to a man or a woman in an opposite-sex partnership. Others try to navigate new paths.

When my wife and I decided to marry, neither of us proposed. There was no proposal event. No getting down on one knee, no anxious solo ring shopping or romantic event planning. No expecting, hoping or waiting and wondering. One of our many conversations about the future became more decisive. Although it does not sound particularly romantic, of course, it was. On holiday in northern Italy at the time, we bought two brightly coloured glass rings from a tourist shop on Murano, Venice – and wore them with silly delight. When we came home to London, we visited Hatton Garden, the jewellery centre, and designed a set of four matching rings together – the engagement and wedding combined. Not a traditional proposal event, perhaps, but an optimistic shared experience, nonetheless.

The importance of the proposal as an event has grown dramatically in recent decades as newspaper announcements morphed into Facebook status updates, Instagram photoshoots and TikTok videos. The dawn of the proposal story has given new life to nostalgic ideals. Just a few generations before social media shaped the look of our engagements, the dream of a Hollywood proposal was born. The movie industry brought idealized romances into millions of towns across the West and set the romantic standard with the aspirational personal lives of its celebrity actors.

A new advertising culture began to commodify the first steps towards marriage. In 1939, just 10 per cent of American brides-to-be wore a diamond engagement ring. The diamond specialist company

De Beers commissioned a new marketing campaign in 1947 to boost sales of their stones from South Africa, and a copywriter, Mary Frances Gerety, was credited with creating the slogan a 'diamond is forever'. By 1990, 80 per cent of US brides had a diamond engagement ring.[10] In Japan, diamonds rapidly monopolized the market by the 1980s. In 2011, a Shanghai wedding consultant, Lawrence Lo, reported that: 'Ten or 15 years ago, if you asked people what diamonds were for they would tell you they were used in power tools. Now China is one of the biggest markets for diamonds – especially for engagement rings.'[11]

However, the roots of these traditions run far deeper. So, what went before? How do our customs today connect back to previous generations and why do these practices persist? If my girlfriend and I had both waited to receive a proposal, we would never be married. A 'traditional' proposal could not resonate with us. What were the motivations, expectations and experiences of women taking the first step of this journey? Can marriage grow into an institution that begins with more women able to say more than 'yes'? Just how romantic are the traditions that we build on?

For most couples embarking on the decision to marry before the middle of the twentieth century, the agreement was unlikely to have been curated as a romantic experience in itself. Women who received a proposal would often have taken time to consider an offer and consult. Ambivalence in the reply would not have enhanced the Instagrammable romance of the moment. Whatever the motivations to marry, the stakes in the decision were high and the factors involved could be complex. The proposal of marriage may very well not have come from a man to a woman. In fact, it may not have involved the individuals expected to marry at all.

JUST THE TWO OF US

What's Love Got To Do With It?

– THE TITLE OF TINA TURNER'S 1984 HIT SONG

Until around 200 years ago, most societies around the world saw marriage as simply too important to leave up to the choice of two people.[1] From the Stone Age, relationship choices involved larger groups and were less about people fulfilling fairytale aspirations than about protecting the interests of families. Proposals were political and economic, and a major motivation was to find good in-laws. When survival was hard, no two individuals could survive alone together. They needed wider groups, and those units needed wider networks and allies.

As time went on, the stakes continued to grow. Around the world, as ancient empires developed increasingly complex social structures, who could marry whom became a question of huge power and consequence. From the earliest mighty states in the Middle East and North Africa, to kingdoms in India and China and empires in South America, rulers and elites relied on marriage to build allies and wealth, to recruit followers, reward friends and to establish legitimacy.[2] Later, in Europe, the Greek and Roman empires followed suit. Restrictions against women's choices grew, and the idea that women were the property of their fathers became widely accepted.[3] Daughters were assets in an ambitious parent's arsenal. And many parents found that they could not wait for their girls to be women to take advantage, should the right opportunity for advancement present itself.

For propertied families, marriage was an opportunity to consolidate wealth and power. It provided a vehicle for transferring money and the more wealth involved, the greater the stake of the relatives involved in the choice of partner. Exchanging money through marriage might have been subtle for some but, for many, there was outright bartering and open financial negotiation as wealth passed between families and new inheritance lines were created. For many couples, engagement was a time in which legally binding contracts were signed and sealed. Right up to the nineteenth century, dowries were still routinely exchanged between men in the transaction of betrothal among Britain's wealthy. Around the world, the transfer of money and resources continues to be negotiated between families as a decision to marry is made. In India today, the custom of women bringing wealth to their husband's family on marriage remains entrenched, despite having been illegal for over 60 years.[4]

In ancient Rome, parents could formally betroth their daughters from the age of seven, and marry them from the age of 12. Large age gaps were common, and a proposal was generally something one father did to another. Julius Caesar proposed a marriage between his daughter, Julia, and his ally, Pompey, when she reached her mid-teens. Pompey was 30 years her senior, older than Caesar himself. Their marriage was understood to be a relatively happy one until Julia died in childbirth in her early twenties, just as her father was invading Britain in 54 BC.

The choice of spouse for one's child was about more than wealth for the ruling elites. It was about politics and power, brokering social and political alliances. In Anglo-Saxon England, peace-weavers, the daughters of ruling families, were so-called to reflect the power of their marriages in creating ties of loyalty between potential enemies. The Old English poem *Beowulf* gives us a glimpse into the stories of two peace-weavers. Wealhtheow plays the ceremonial role of hostess, seeking to protect her sons through the limited diplomatic power she has. Hildeburh loses a son, brother and husband to the violent conflict that her marriage could not prevent. Leaving everything you know to enter your enemy's home must have felt like an impossible situation to the young girls making the journey.

The rich and powerful continued to propose marriage for their daughters, at very young ages, for centuries. On 5 October 1518, in a sumptuous room in Greenwich Palace, a two-year-old toddler stepped forward into a room full of attentive grown-ups. Dressed in gold, with a heavy jewelled cap on her small head, she accepted her first engagement ring.[5] The ring was handed to her from a man representing her new fiancé, the French dauphin. The future Queen Mary I's first engagement was to last just three years.

When she was six years old, Mary was engaged again: Spain looked like a better ally to her father, Henry VIII. Her next fiancé, the 22-year-old Holy Roman Emperor visited his prospective in-laws for six weeks to celebrate, enjoying his child fiancée's dancing for his entertainment. Mary's father popped the question again when she was 11 years old, signing another marriage treaty with France, this time for Mary to marry either Francis I or his son Henry. Which one was not particularly important to the engagement. The French envoys were frustrated to find the young girl not quite physically ready for marriage. They found her 'admirable by reason of her great and uncommon mental endowments; but so thin, sparse, and small as to render it impossible for her to be married for the next three years'.[6] Ultimately, it was the children of political marriages that prospective grandparents most desired and girls were expected to marry young to increase the likelihood of them producing heirs. *Male* heirs.

It was only when she acceded to the English throne that Mary could escape the control of others and choose to marry for herself. Following her father's infamous divorce of her mother, Catherine of Aragon, the very idea of betrothal, marriage and potential children for Catholic Mary had held such power that it was no less than potentially destabilizing to the nation. At the age of 37, the Queen found herself in an impossible position. As reigning monarch, she was expected to be the ultimate authority in her court. Her marriage to Philip II of Spain, in 1554, trigged English xenophobia: Philip was a foreign sovereign and male consort and, as a woman, Mary was required to submit unconditionally to any husband. Like her cousin, Mary, Queen of Scots, Mary I's power would be hugely compromised through her choice of marriage. Elizabeth I famously avoided the fate of both her half-sister and Scottish cousin through feigning interest in proposals for decades, without committing to any of them.

Childhood engagement was no surprise for Mary. Her own were superseded by her ancestors. Her mother, Catherine of Aragon, had been engaged at the age of three. Her dowry of 200,000 escudos was negotiated by ambassadors from Spain and England over several years, as valuations, payments and timings were challenged and examined.[7] Two generations earlier, Mary's great-grandmother, Margaret Beaufort, had been married to Edmund Tudor at the age of just 12. At 13, she gave birth to a Lancastrian heir, England's first Tudor king. Her young age increased the risks of childbirth and the particularly difficult birth damaged her health.

Once widowed, women from wealthy families could have more control over any future engagements. Margaret Beaufort went on to marry strategically twice more. However, for most economically privileged girls, the idea of choosing one's own husband, proposing marriage or even having a say in an engagement was far from the reality the first time around. Unmarried girls had few options. Until the Reformation, the only alternative for young women to submitting to a parent or guardian's choice of prospective husband, might be the celibate, childfree, confined life of a nun. By the middle of the 1500s,

Henry VIII had dissolved that option for so many. And, with the Church heavily invested in the marriages of the ruling elites, young girls disobeying their parents would not always have found much support there.

Although consent was legally required to marry, girls were judged able to give as much as required or desired at 12 years old. The marriageable age in Europe remained largely the same as it had been in ancient Rome – the formal age of puberty, established in the Roman Empire, 12 for girls and 14 for boys, remained the legal standard for marriage in Britain until 1929.

Today, child marriage remains common. Throughout the world, approximately one in five women are married before their eighteenth birthday – 650 million women today were married off as children.[8] In the US, there is no minimum age for marriage in nine states.[9] In others, it is legal for girls to marry as young as 14 years of age. Taboos surrounding sex and pregnancy outside of marriage remain strong among the Christian Right, and campaigns to end child marriage are resisted. In 1957, when 13-year-old Myra Gale Brown married her father's bandmate and 20-year-old cousin, Jerry Lee Lewis, he commented that, in Tennessee, 'you can get married at 10, if you can find a husband'.[10]

New research suggests that nearly 300,000 children, some as young as ten, were married in the United States between 2000 and 2018.[11] Most were girls married to adult men. Within the UK, until April 2022 when new legislation was introduced, 16 year olds – thought too young to vote, drink alcohol or drive – could marry in England and Wales. In Scotland and Northern Ireland, the age of consent to marry remains 16. The continued legalisation of child marriage is a legacy that has yet to be reformed in laws and customs around the world, from Italy to Iran, South Africa to Canada, and continues to leave girls vulnerable to pressure, exploitation and forced marriages.

In 2020, the Covid-19 pandemic inflicted economic hardship

globally, closing schools and reducing incomes around the world, particularly in areas already suffering from poverty and inadequate healthcare provision. The charity Save the Children estimated that over 10 million children, mostly girls, never returned to school, many marrying instead. It is predicted that the pandemic will cause an additional 2.5 million girls globally to enter marriage before 2025 – in addition to the 12 million girls forced into marriage every year.[12] In some regions around the world, complications from pregnancy and childbirth are the leading cause of death in young women aged 15 to 19.[13]

When it comes to marriage, parental consent continues to be privileged over the rights of young people, particularly girls. It is a legacy built on a deep tradition. The role of parents and wider family units in marriage proposals has been unquestioned in communities across the globe throughout the history of the institution. Although forced marriages have been criminalized in the United Kingdom, and much of the world, for centuries, in practice, the power wielded by parents and community leaders over children makes them difficult to prevent.

In 1624, just over 70 years after Mary I took the throne in England, Katherine Prescott, a 12-year-old girl in northwest England, was informed of her engagement to a 15-year-old neighbour. She told her father that she would 'leape into a worke pitt and drowne herself before she married William Bower'.[14] Poorer girls in early modern Europe were less likely to find a parent's choice forced on them, and at a young age. Working parents had less to gain politically by marrying off their daughters to allies or rivals, but families might still put enormous pressure on their daughters to marry for their own reasons.

Despite voicing her opposition, young Katherine Prescott found herself standing in a parish church with Bower, unable to prevent her wedding from going ahead. Her father, Henry, forced her to go through with the engagement by 'p[er]suasions, threat, and menaces' and his promise to withdraw financial support from his child.[15] Her objections were so clear that the minister and congregation encouraged him to give up the engagement. To no avail. She mumbled her way through the ceremony and was considered married. She was taken from the church and forced to cohabit with her 'husband' in her father's home. The determined 12-year-old managed to avoid consummation with the help of a young female servant by locking herself in her room. Having 'complained and made her moane and greefe knowne to divers persons with whome she was familier or durst speake', her situation reached the right people in Wigan and her suit was heard in the Chester court.[16]

It was clearly to the father's financial benefit that he acquired this young man, 'of a very good estate', as a son-in-law.[17] Child marriages were still practised throughout different classes at this time, but they were not the norm outside of the wealthy elite, as we can perhaps see in the congregation sympathizing with Katherine's plight. However, they did not interfere. Katherine had a 'want of libertie, frend, and meanes'.[18] Her father was the ruler of her small world: there was no meaningful state or social support for her beyond her family, of which he was the head.

This was not an arranged marriage, like those expected and experienced by many girls in the upper classes. Katherine was the victim of an openly forced marriage, something technically illegal centuries before this time. Although in violation of laws around the world today, marriages continue to be imposed on children and adults, with over a thousand forced marriages of British girls and women reported every year.

Around the time of Katherine's birth, Shakespeare dramatized the entitlement of parents to choose husbands for their daughters in his most famous story of doomed romance, *Romeo and Juliet*. Juliet is 13 when Paris proposes marriage to her father. Capulet tells his potential son-in-law: 'I think she will be ruled / In all respects by me. Nay, more, I doubt it not'[19] – and father of the bride and prospective groom happily schedule the wedding for three days later. On hearing of his daughter's resistance to it the next morning, Capulet violently silences her, threatening physical violence in his rage:

> *Hang thee, young baggage, disobedient wretch!*
> *I tell thee what: get thee to church o' Thursday,*
> *Or never after look me in the face.*
> *Speak not, reply not, do not answer me.*
> *My fingers itch.*[20]

A father's consent to a suitor suggested more than support. Capulet outlines the consequences of his daughter imagining that she has a choice in no uncertain terms.

> *An you be mine, I'll give you to my friend.*
> *An you be not, hang, beg, starve, die in the streets,*
> *For, by my soul, I'll ne'er acknowledge thee,*
> *Nor what is mine shall never do thee good.*[21]

Whether excited or terrified at the prospect of a parent's choice, for centuries some women and girls enjoyed little power in this life-changing decision. Entirely dependent on their families for protection, food, shelter, social standing and any comforts within their lives, many found themselves to be without a social safety net. For those able to enjoy the privileges of class and wealth, by attempting to defy a family's choice, they had a lot to lose and a long way to fall.

Today, some men continue to ask the permission of a woman's father before proposing to her. In the UK, a recent survey of 10,000 people found that over half of the women who responded (57 per cent) thought that men should request approval from the father of the bride before proposing.[22] While a prospective groom might politely inform a father today, a nod to a right for him to be involved, for so many men in the past this was the important proposal, and the conversation with the woman in question, the cursory nod to the right of consent. If it happened at all. It seems a strange reflection of how reluctant we are to let go of the traditional when it comes to weddings – that this practice continues in the West today.

BETTER TO MARRY THAN BURN – OR STARVE

If they cannot exercise self-control, they should marry.
For it is better to marry than to burn
with passion.

– 1 CORINTHIANS 7:9

Of course, for most people, engagements would not spark or end wars, forge or destroy alliances, build or diminish large fortunes. The rules surrounding the proposals of the wealthy just were not relevant to the poor. Working women had more say in their engagements than their richer peers. While upper-class parents were proposing political marriages for their children, in the lower classes social and practical concerns held sway.

In Europe, through the medieval and early modern eras, being a wife conferred status – and status was woven throughout the ups and downs of everyday life. Women were subordinate to their husbands, but they took on a role of authority over the rest of their household, as well as unmarried women in their community. In 1640, a bishop in Cheshire decreed that married women were allowed to sit in pews in church, but children and unmarried women were to kneel and sit in the aisles.[1] Around the world it has been on marriage that women have been seen to transition into adulthood. In ancient Rome, girls dedicated their dolls, seen to represent their childhood, to the family deities on the way out of the door to their weddings. In Hindu tradition, newlyweds move into the second ashrama, the second life stage, from student to householder, on their marriage. Today, many unmarried women continue to be titled *Miss*, as they were as children, their social status defined by their marital one.

Marriage opened doors for working women. Right up until the dawn of the Industrial Revolution, in the eighteenth century, most people in Britain worked in their marriages. Marriage was likely to be the most important career choice that they would ever make.[2] The Old Testament provides a description of an ideal wife and we see less interest in her relationship with her husband, her values or her personality, than in her proficiency as a worker: 'She considereth a field, and buyeth it: with the fruit of her hands she planteth a vineyard ... she perceives that her merchandise is good ... she layeth her hands to the spindle ... she looketh well to the ways of her household and eateth not the bread of idleness.' It is a job description.

For working women in the early modern era, to agree to an engagement without considering the financial situation on offer would be more than just frowned upon: it would be sheer folly. However, while finances were something to think about in the labouring classes, most women were free to do that thinking and make the choice of who and when to marry for themselves. Courtship was key. For many poor young women, their journey to marriage would not have been so very dissimilar to their descendants in the twentieth century: finding spaces to meet and test out potential interest, conspiring to spend time together away from the attention and notice of others; pushing social boundaries and dreaming of imagined futures.

Like today, once the working day was done, nightfall would provide opportunities for romantic possibility. Across rural areas of the United Kingdom, Ireland and New England, North America, courting young couples in the 1600s could even find themselves bundled up into a bed together to spend the night. A board might be placed between them and girls tied in a sack to prevent the youths getting ideas in the darker hours. The emphasis, of course, was on protecting a woman's chastity and the practice continued for well over a century. It is hard to imagine this being an ideal date.

It would be centuries until the dawn of dating in the way we think of it today – the word 'date' would not appear in use until the end of the nineteenth century[3] – but when parents or employers were in bed, young and single people might socialize indoors without supervision. Or chastity devices. There is evidence of even relatively middle-class young women escaping restrictions to spend time with suitors. In 1615, Susan White invited George Houghton to her mother's house late at night after her mother had gone to bed. Susan conspired with her sister and maid who 'prepared victuals ready and [they] gave as good entertainment to the said George as they could'.[4] Susan and George 'did sometime sit up till twelve or one of the clock in the night', after her sister and maid had also retired.[5] Her parents disapproved of the match.

In 1617, a merchant's daughter hosted a small party in her parents' house, while they slept, so that she could spend unguarded time with one of her father's apprentices. Joan Symonds arranged for a servant to cook treats for the group: two maidservants, two menservants, Joan herself and James Cartwright, smuggled into the house.[6] They reportedly stayed up until one or two in the morning, talking and kissing. Joan's father refused his consent for an engagement until James provided details of his suspicious finances, which he refused to produce.

Many women, in love and sexually supressed at home, circumvented family disapproval by eloping. It was a risky strategy. Joan resisted the temptation to run away with her father's apprentice. He would later threaten to 'publish her for a whore' if she did not marry him without her father's consent.[7] The involvement of her family seems to have protected the teenage Joan from making an irreversible commitment to a man who does not come across well in the record that survives, though probably not from the heartbreak.

Still, many women negotiated their own way into marriage without the support of families, inheritance or a dowry. Poorer women would go out to work, often as a servant, and earn the money they needed to start a new household themselves. In the 1600s, as the ruling elites were marrying off their daughters as children, the average age of a woman at her first wedding was twenty-six.[8] Around half of all young people worked as servants in someone else's home for a time. Employment provided an opportunity for flirtations, romance and sexual relationships, particularly in larger households.

Although women were still socially subordinate to men, the opportunity to go out to work and earn capital afforded some women more freedom of choice. A woman able to earn money in her teens and twenties would be in a stronger position on entering into an engagement than a girl entering a husband's house as a child and finding her primary means of influence might be reproductive. Courtship was an opportunity to negotiate the relationship, and influence the power dynamic, within your future marriage.[9]

Many women met a future spouse at work, spending time with them, committing to a monogamous liaison and starting some kind of physical relationship, before becoming engaged and saving together towards the costs associated with a wedding and marriage. It sounds familiar, but the similarities to what so many people experience today were likely to end there. For most women, choosing a partner was not likely to be simple. With almost no social safety net, poor women needed to be realistic when choosing their partners in order to give their new families a chance to thrive – and courtship brought challenges and risks. Society was designed to control any and all sexual desire in unmarried women. Women in the lower classes were vulnerable to manipulation and abuse by the men who desired them, and the men they desired.

In early modern Britain, as a young woman with an active sexual appetite, one's options beyond celibacy were to marry and have sex with your new husband or to decouple sex and marriage and risk losing any support network of family, friends and neighbours. Perhaps also income and the ability to participate openly in society. Women risked bearing children who they might need to support on their own – something simply impossible for many mothers, who were driven to abandon their babies. Whether their parents could support them or not, any child born out of wedlock would carry the stigma of illegitimacy throughout their lives. At a time in which damnation felt like a real and close reality, women were taught that they risked their very souls by such actions. Yet no such consequences were held over men of any class.

The Church was the arbiter and authority of marriage in European tradition from the ninth century until relatively recently, and used it to regulate sexual practices. Only sex between a man and a woman was permissible; between husband and wife. Unlike in other religions, including Hinduism and some Jewish denominations, sexual pleasure was universally frowned upon by the Catholic Church. As such, sex was permissible only for the purpose of procreation within a marriage – and, even then, in limited sexual positions. Women were daughters of the original sinner, Eve. More susceptible to lustful temptation, the rules and restrictions of marriage were the only way to control such appetites.

In reality, sex before marriage was common.[10] In the labouring classes, once marriage was on the table, social and sexual restrictions could be relaxed and many brides were pregnant by their weddings.[11] In rural areas, there were more opportunities to escape watchful eyes for a quick roll in the hay. Rates of children conceived before marriage tended to be high in the countryside.[12]

Across the eighteenth century, a wage economy grew and, across classes, it became increasingly difficult for parents to control the relationship choices of their children. The percentage of children born to unmarried parents doubled in England across the century.[13] For women who were sexually active and not engaged, pregnancy could be unimaginably challenging.

Under the 1733 Bastardy Act, poor, unmarried pregnant women who were financially unable to support a child, could be forced to appear before a magistrate and name the father. The man then had the choice of paying the parish for the child's upkeep, marrying the woman – if he was unmarried – or going to prison. In the 1780s, Parson James Woodforde recorded in his diary: 'it is a cruel thing that any person should be compelled by law to marry'.[14] He presided over many weddings with a groom in the custody of officers ready to take him to prison, should he get cold feet: '[I]t is very disagreeable to me to marry such persons,' he commented,[15] but surely still more disagreeable for the newlyweds?

Women had very little choice at all, their autonomy sacrificed as a consequence of their pregnancy. It is difficult to imagine the feelings of a young woman standing at the altar, committing herself for life to a man forced to be there, but pregnancy could be a strong motivator for marriage. For women in this position, options were bleak. A child might be offered charity from the local parish, which would likely take the baby away from its mother and offer only a basic level of support through its earliest years, and perhaps little care. With poverty widespread in Britain, and moral judgement harsh, the general welfare of mother and child were not a priority. Support was patchy and very limited and even this basic aid beyond the reach of many. Countless mothers and babies simply could not and did not survive alone in a society in which families were defined and built through marriage and headed by men. In the 1700s, it is believed that over a thousand children a year were abandoned on the streets of London alone.[16]

The taboo of sex before marriage was strengthened into the nineteenth century as authorities sought to control the sexual behaviour of unmarried people through women's personal morality.[17] An unprecedented emphasis on female purity and virtue developed. Internalized pressures and social shame left many women with few options but to become wives. For centuries, around the world, the dishonour attached to any sexual contact outside of marriage was perceived to be so great that marriage might be forced on women and girls as a consequence of abduction or rape. From the rape of the Sabine Women in early ancient Rome, to Hollywood's popular musical, *Seven Brides For Seven Brothers*, derived from the former tale, 'shotgun weddings' of kidnapped brides were celebrated, if not romanticized. In the 1954 movie, a group of young women in Oregon are forcefully abducted from their homes by a group of brothers who hold them captive over a period of months. The women marry their captors, at their fathers' gunpoint, in the romantic, happy ending, accompanied by joyful singing and dancing.

Today, 'bride kidnapping', the practice of a man abducting and often sexually abusing a woman he desires as a wife, takes place in communities across the world. A wedding can be seen as such a desirable consequence of sexual activity, that laws in twenty countries today allow rapists to escape prosecution for their crime if they marry their victim. Shame is attached to the woman who is then compelled to recognize a marriage to one of her attackers, particularly if she falls pregnant. Although internationally recognized as a sex crime, bride kidnapping continues to be how thousands of women and girls enter marriage.

Despite myriad pressures to marry across communities, throughout history, many women have chosen to live single lives. In the sixteenth century, it is thought that one-third to one-half of all European adults were unmarried.[18] In England, an estimated 30 per cent of women were unmarried in the Tudor period.[19] Before the dissolution of the monasteries, which began in 1536, a young woman might pursue a career and education within the confines of the celibate church. The most common choice of income for single women was domestic service. However, records survive of women independently supporting themselves in all sorts of ways, as weavers, spinners, laundresses and brewers.[20] Today, increasing numbers of women choose not to marry. Numbers of cohabiting couple families in the UK doubled between 1996 and 2016, and recent decades have seen a rise in the numbers of people who choose never to marry.[21]

The pressures on the decision to marry were sometimes overt, controlling, bullying and coercive, involving physical and sexual abuse. Sometimes, they were more subtle. For centuries, many working women found marriage the means to meet a need or achieve a new start – a barrier against hunger, the cold and loneliness. For many, it provided the hope for a different life.

THE USUAL INDUCEMENTS OF WOMEN TO MARRY

In vain I have struggled. It will not do. My feelings will not be repressed. You must allow me to tell you how ardently I admire and love you.

–JANE AUSTEN'S MR DARCY, *PRIDE AND PREJUDICE*

Towards the end of the eighteenth century, a cultural shift was taking place in Britain: love began to widely take precedence in people wanting to choose their spouse. It was an age of huge turmoil and change. Enlightenment philosophy had taken hold of Europe and individualism was on the rise. Imperialistic values drove the exploitation of people and resources by colonialists across the globe. Political revolutions were sparking new republics.

In England, new technologies accelerated the Industrial Revolution that was beginning to unfold. The middle classes were growing; young people were starting to earn wages that gave them the freedom to propose marriage without their parents' or employer's involvement. New social opportunities emerged for the young of relatively privileged families, with ballrooms, theatres, gardens and racecourses offering opportunities to meet potential suitors.[1] New questions were being asked, new ideas and philosophies were spreading across the continent and throughout the country: republicanism, abolition, individual rights

– the rights of men and the rights of *women*.

In 1792, Mary Wollstonecraft published *A Vindication on the Rights of Woman*. She argued that women were not naturally inferior to men. Their 'weakness' and 'femininity' were the consequence of their lack of education. She celebrated friendship and argued that marriage should be a partnership of equals – far removed from the cultural and legal reality of the time.

> *If marriage be the cement of society, mankind should all be educated after the same model, or the intercourse of the sexes will never deserve the name of fellowship ... Nay, marriage will never be held sacred till women by being brought up with men, are prepared to be their companions, rather than their mistresses.* [2]

In 1796, Wollstonecraft and fellow political thinker William Godwin became lovers. Both had criticized marriage and Godwin had argued for the abolition of the institution as a whole. Yet they married on 29 March 1797, when Mary became pregnant. The social pressures and punishments set up to induce marriage, it seemed, were too powerful to resist. Like so many others, they chose to publicly legitimize their child.

As new approaches to equality between the sexes were being debated by philosophers like Wollstonecraft, public interest in romance between the sexes was exploding with the new fashion for the novel. Marrying for love was becoming all the rage – to the alarm of the more conservative. In 1774, the *Lady's Magazine* published an article reminding the public that 'the idea of matrimony' was not 'for men and women to be always taken up with each other'.[3] It was for people 'to discharge the duties of civil society, to govern their families with prudence and to educate their children with discretion'.[4] I was pretty taken up with my girlfriend when we got engaged. I cannot say that I had the duty of civil society in my mind.

Jane Austen, who was writing her early novels around the same time as Wollstonecraft's marriage to Godwin, played with this tension in her literary works. Today, Austen is read as a conservative force by some and a progressive by others, her novels set against problematic, dark histories of slavery, colonialism and class oppression. Her writings on English marriage, largely across the aristocratic and middle classes, reveal the collision of the practical proposals of the century just ending with the changes posed by the century to come. Her stories not only often end with decisions to marry – they are full of proposals, the moments on which the lives of her characters turn; the crossroads of all crossroads for many women of the age.

More than 200 years later, Austen's stories continue to set a romantic bar in popular culture, but the social and economic pressures on middle-class women to marry are always present in Austen's narratives. In one of her most famous novels, *Pride and Prejudice* (1813), it is difficult to overlook the fate of 'plain' Charlotte Lucas. Presented with a proposal from the 'ridiculous' Mr Collins, who three days earlier had professed his undying love to her friend, Elizabeth Bennet, the 27-year-old Charlotte finds the offer relatively appealing.[5]

Charlotte is financially dependent on her parents, who would not expect to support all their children through adulthood. She lives in their house as she has since birth, with, we can only imagine, little privacy, autonomy or stimulation. She cannot earn money for herself; she has not been raised or trained to generate any income through skill or labour, and she and her family would lose their social standing if she tried. A seemingly unimaginable choice in Austen's world. On desiring to leave this situation, her only option is to marry. Charlotte Lucas is not starving or likely ever to starve, but she does not want to spend her entire life as a financial drain on her family, celibate and living like a frozen child at home, 'an old maid', ridiculed and increasingly poverty stricken, like Miss Bates in *Emma* (1815).[6]

By the end of the eighteenth century, marriage for practical considerations was beginning to seem distasteful. People continued to marry largely within their own class, but purely mercenary motivations were starting to be frowned upon. Austen expressed disapproval of Charlotte's choice to marry through her heroine, Elizabeth, who derides Charlotte as having 'sacrificed every better feeling to worldly advantage'[7] – eighteenth-century language for she's a 'gold-digger'.

In her novels, Austen celebrated only proposals made, and accepted, for love and affection. Most of her proposals are written as the wrong choice for her female characters and she can be more than a little judgemental about them. Sex with Mr Collins seems a punishingly high price to pay for some autonomy and authority. It is difficult to disagree with the assessment that 'Charlotte, the wife of Mr Collins, was a most humiliating picture!'[8]

It is only Austen's most famous heroines who resist the temptation to marry under practical and social pressures. Elizabeth Bennet is proposed to three times in the course of *Pride and Prejudice* and, while the men undertaking the proposal confidently expect a yes, they, instead, receive a refusal. Both Mr Collins and Mr Darcy are incredulous that Elizabeth should feel empowered to refuse them. As Mr Collins indelicately states, 'it is by no means certain that another offer of marriage may ever be made to you'.[9] The reality is further expressed in Austen's Gothic novel, *Northanger Abbey* (1817): 'man has the advantage of choice, woman only the power of refusal.'[10] Some would say, just as the tradition remains today.

On a cold evening in 1802, Austen herself accepted the proposal of family friend Harris Bigg-Wither. She was twenty-six years old, a year younger than Charlotte Lucas. Like her sister, Cassandra, and six brothers, Austen was dependent on a father who had a relatively modest income: Bigg-Wither was heir to a local estate. This was possibly her only chance of marriage, of financial stability, of having a household of her own and of sex and motherhood. By the following morning, though, she had changed her mind and called off the engagement. It seems that she could not bring herself to make Charlotte's choice.

Austen's worlds are small ones, but they shed light on the opportunities for middle-class women in Britain at the turn of the nineteenth century. Austen struggled with the economic reality of a marriage market that had defined women's options for so many years, setting the parameters of what was acceptable. She wrote to her niece that: 'single women have the dreadful propensity for being poor – which is one very strong argument in favour of matrimony', but concluded, 'anything is to be preferred or endured rather than marrying without affection'.[11]

An emphasis on affection would define the engagement choices of the next century. As the idea of marrying for love began to take the public imagination by storm, new generations of young Victorians could look to their monarch for inspiration. Although the royal wedding of 1840 was arranged according to family ties and elitist principles, it was Victoria's romantic choice. She represented to the world marriage to her 'dearest, dearest dear Albert' – and later widowhood – as one of idealized love. Victoria and Albert seem like they could well have jumped out of the pages of a nineteenth-century romantic novel.

Nuptial fever gripped Victorian Britain and it was not all about the Queen. The married state became idealized like never before, and generations of women were increasingly encouraged and expected to marry younger. In 1928, while enjoying an affair with fellow writer Vita Sackville-West, Virginia Woolf published *Orlando*, a novel in which the eponymous character is born a man in Elizabethan England and lives through 300 years of British history. At some point in the seventeenth century Orlando become a woman. When experiencing the Victorian era, Orlando feels a 'tingling' on the 'second finger of her left hand'.[12] Marriage becomes inescapable. 'It now seemed to her that the whole world was ringed with gold. She went into dinner. Wedding rings abounded. She went to church. Wedding rings were everywhere.'[13] The pressure to marry becomes too much and Orlando quickly accepts that there is nothing they can do but 'yield completely and submissively to the spirit of the age, and take a husband'.[14]

The Victorians made marriage the centre and focus of their lives in an unprecedented way. When entering into an engagement, emphasis shifted from in-laws, status and security to the bride and groom themselves. The couple began to take centre stage as 'the spirit of the age' took hold. The increased level of importance on the new family unit placed pressure on young women considering marriage. Did they love their fiancé enough? Did they love you? Were they willing to reframe their entire lives around one partner?

In 1838, Charles Darwin approached this question with a characteristically scientific approach, making a pros and cons list of marriage before he popped the question. He balanced the limitations on his travel, the 'freedom to go where one liked', with the comforts of a marital home and the 'charms of music & female chit-chat'.[15] Considering the potential for 'children – (if it Please God)', alongside the 'conversation of clever men at clubs', Darwin felt marriage would be 'good for one's health – but terrible loss of time'.[16] Though nothing to the time lost by so many new brides expected to relinquish all personal pursuits as they took up their marital duties.

Darwin captured well the motivations of many men of his class to marry. The romanticized, male-centred ideal of a family home won out. 'Only picture to yourself a nice soft wife on a sofa with good fire, & books & music perhaps,' he commented.[17] Who could resist 'a nice soft wife'? He proposed to his cousin, Emma Wedgwood, in November 1838 and wrote in his journal 'The day of days!' They were married less than three months later.[18]

As courtship changed in Britain, new customs developed around an effusive male role, declaring passionate love for the object of his adoration. Writers of this next century embraced the sublime act of falling in love in their poetry and novels, as well as their lives. The famous correspondence of poets Robert Browning and Elizabeth Barrett in the run up to their elopement exudes the romance of the age: 'I love your verses with all my heart, dear Miss Barrett ... so into me has it gone, and part of me has it become, this great living poetry of yours ... I love these books with all my heart – and I love you too.'[19] In the 1840s, author Nathaniel Hawthorne wrote to his fiancée, Sophia Peabody: 'Where thou are not, there is a sort of death.'[20] Following their wedding, they began to keep a diary together, taking turns at making entries in the same shared notebook.

An ideal proposal scene began to take hold, one where the declarations of a man's love would be received by a woman who would demur, perhaps hold out, cautiously expressing affection.[21] Emphasis on the female virtues of silence and chastity grew. By the Victorian age, fashionable outpourings of a man's affection might be accompanied by a physical show of their adoration as they bent down to one knee. Centuries earlier, in medieval courts, a man might have genuflected to a woman to express fealty, or loyalty, in the same way that they might show religious respect and piety. It was the kind of trope enjoyed in courtly romances like the twelfth-century *Romances d'Aventure* – the knight offering himself to a lady. Like the medieval subjects of Pre-Raphaelite paintings, middle-class Victorian society revelled in the nostalgia.

For women, the choice to marry and the journey to becoming a wife would not be the same. Practical considerations remained important, families continued to feel entitled to some involvement and elitist class lines endured, but expectations had profoundly shifted. The idea that one should be in love with one's fiancé had become not just widely established, but accepted.

POLITICAL PROPOSALS

It not only is a complete undermining of the principles of family and marriage and the hope of future generations, but it completely begins to see our society break down to the extent that that foundational unit of the family that is the hope of survival of this country is diminished to the extent that it literally is a threat to the nation's survival in the long run..

– REPUBLICAN CONGRESSMAN TRENT FRANKS
ON GAY MARRIAGE, 2011[1]

By the middle of the twentieth century, most young people in Britain would not only aspire to be in love with a fiancé but expect to be. Although you now might very well choose to marry someone just because you love them, not everyone could marry for love, even when that love was between two consenting, single adults who wished to make that choice.

Around the world, people have found their marriage options to be restricted by class, gender, sexuality, religion, race or disability. The twentieth century saw political battles on each of these fronts and it was only in 2020 that people in all parts of the UK achieved access to marriage equality on these terms. Cultural barriers, not just legal hurdles, have been put in place to prevent marriage. In 2001, future Prime Minister Boris Johnson compared a marriage between two men to the idea of three men marrying a dog in his book 'Friends, Voters,

Countrymen'. Senior Conservative Councillor James Malliff reflected in 2011 that, were the government to pass a Same Sex Marriage Act, they 'may as well legalise marriage with animals.'[2] Comparisons to bestiality have been used for centuries to dissuade people from committing not only to a same-sex partner, but a person from a different cultural background, class, race or ethnicity.

Same-sex and transgender unions are an ancient feature of the institution of marriage. Many African, Asian and indigenous societies have recognized and celebrated same-sex and nonbinary relationships. In Europe, at least two Roman emperors, Nero and Elagabalus, held weddings with men. However, as the Christian Church grew in power from the fourth century through the Middle Ages, they became strictly forbidden. European colonial expansion restricted and homogenized marriage definitions around huge swathes of the world.

Over the last few centuries, queer people in the West have navigated restrictive, heteronormative rules of marriage in various ways. Some have avoided the institution entirely. For many, marriage to an opposite-sex partner provided an opportunity publicly to be seen to conform. For others, marriage created a template, a model that they might adopt and adapt to celebrate their romantic relationships and build their lives around them.

It was not easy to access this exclusive and privileged way of life. Before the middle of the eighteenth century, it was relatively difficult and frowned upon for two women to be seen to set up a household. Without a man, who was the head of the house? Women in love with other women, who hoped to share their life together in one union and home, faced practical and social barriers. Roles were tightly defined along gendered lines; nonbinary identities and gender transitions were not recognized.

Until the middle of the eighteenth century, British weddings were largely unregulated, however, and many queer marriages thrived. In the 1730s, two teenagers reportedly moved to London to start a new life together. They found work and a home and began their marriage as husband and wife. They had both been born biologically female. Mary, a sixteen-year-old domestic servant, had transformed into James How and the couple lived as married publicans in the East End of London for decades. James became an active member of the community and a leader in public life, as a foreman of juries and overseer of the poor. They kept their secret for more than thirty years before James was extorted for money from someone who recognized them from their childhood.[3]

Jen Manion has traced the lives of several people in the UK and US who were assigned female at birth and later transed gender and married women.[4] History glimpses these marriages only when their secret has been discovered. Through entering the married state, these couples opened up lives together for themselves as 'husbands' and 'wives' that would have been unattainable otherwise. As grooms, 'female husbands' were able to access legal, social and economic positions supposed to be reserved for men.[5]

As the eighteenth century progressed, restrictions and prejudices around gender binaries remained widely entrenched, but it was becoming much easier for two women with some financial means to share their lives together. In 1778, Lady Eleanor Butler and Sarah Ponsonby used their financial advantages to flee their family homes in Ireland and settle together in Plas Newydd in northeast Wales. Sharing a household, home and a bed, the 'Ladies of Llangollen' called each other 'my sweet love' and 'my better half' and when the famous lesbian diarist Anne Lister visited them, in 1822, she reflected that their relationship was surely 'not platonic'.[6] The couple were able to embody the model of marriage in their life together – though not the formal institution. An acquaintance of Lister's observed that 'they must be 2 romantic girls … it was a pity they were not married'.[7] She did not mean to each other. The Ladies of Llangollen shared their lives for more than 50 years and are buried together near their Welsh home.

By the turn of the nineteenth century, women who shared their lives in affectionate partnership were seen as enjoying 'romantic friendships'. Largely accessible to white, economically privileged women, they offered some freedom to pursue long-term queer relationships. Though they were, of course, never thought to be sexual. Victorian women of a certain class were understood to have virtually no sexual desire at all. Romantic friendships seemed unthreatening to the leaders of the time who viewed them as more of a practise at a marriage with a man than as an alternative.

Lost to history, details of their proposals, their mutual promises, almost never survive. There was no roadmap for women embarking on lifelong commitments to other women. And, for many, saving mementos, copies or evidence of these private proposals would have brought risk at a time in which sexual acts between women were deeply repressed and sexual acts between men were illegal. Without a footprint, these intimate moments leave no tradition for women today to pick up and pass on as we take the leap towards a same-sex commitment.

The most explicit account of a woman pursuing a model of marriage with another woman before the legalisation of same-sex weddings in the UK survived despite the odds – left in cryptic code in the walls of a house just outside of Halifax in West Yorkshire. The diaries of Anne Lister reveal details of her many romantic and sexual relationships with women. In them, she charts her journey to find a wife. Lister had exchanged vows and rings with two other women before Ann Walker, the woman with whom she shared her life, from 1832 until her death.

Lister's pursuit of Ann was, in many ways, a conventional nineteenth-century, middle-class courtship. Lister was looking for a sexually monogamous, committed partner with whom she could pool resources and cohabit until death. Writing explicitly of Ann's wealth as a major attraction, Lister wanted to make a 'good match' as understood in early nineteenth-century terms – and that meant financially advantageous, as well as affectionate.[8] As she pursued her courtship and considered proposing, she noted that they got on 'very well together' and hoped that affection and attraction would grow. On proposing marriage, she gave Ann time and space to consider before making the commitment, writing in her diary that 'I am easy about it and will prepare either way'.[9]

On 10 February 1834, her proposal was accepted. Lister recorded that her new fiancée agreed 'to consider herself as having nobody to please and being under no authority but mine'.[10] Two days later, after a long night of 'capital' sex 'so that little time for sleep', they decided to exchange rings 'in token of our union as confirmed on Monday'.[11]

A century after the informal commitment solemnized between Anne Lister and Ann Walker, Virginia Woolf attended the London wedding reception of writer Sybille von Schoenebeck and Terry Bedford. Born in Germany, the daughter of an aristocratic father and a Jewish mother, von Schoenebeck had spoken out against the rise of the Nazi party and, in 1935, found herself in England. Unable to renew her German passport, her bank accounts at home had been frozen and she faced deportation by an unsympathetic UK government back to Nazi Germany, so a friend suggested that marriage was the way to secure her safety.

Von Schoenebeck enjoyed multiple relationships with other women throughout her life, including a twenty-year relationship with American novelist Eda Lord. Recalling her wedding reception, she later remembered, 'Virginia Woolf came up to me, took mine into her exquisite hand ... This, she said, is a very queer party. I can't understand anything about it; one day you must come and tell me.'[12]

The bride took her new husband's name and published her later works as Sybille Bedford. But it was understood that her husband, an ex-boyfriend of one of W.H. Auden's menservants, would live an entirely separate life. In the same year, 1935, Auden himself married a German Jewish bride, actress and writer Erika Mann, securing her safety from

Nazi persecution through British citizenship. The couple met only briefly before their wedding.

Unconsummated marriages of convenience have a long history in the queer community, undoubtedly saving many lives. For centuries, for many women, they created the ability to set up an independent household that would have been unattainable were they not seen as a 'wife'. Marriage might provide freedom from family control, and sometimes space to pursue other relationships. Until well into the twentieth century, women from wealthy families found that walking down the aisle provided access to sometimes large amounts of money – resources designed to be settled on them only in marriage.

As the twentieth century progressed, queer people began to more openly seek formal, public marriages within their romantic relationships – to pursue the right not only to live their lives as a husband or a wife but to be formally recognized as one. Two hundred years after Mary and James How shared their life in Poplar, another couple pursued a married life together in London's East End, only to be hindered by strict gender laws. In 1954, Jean Lee walked down the aisle of St Luke's Church to formally marry her partner, Vincent (previously Violet) Jones. On the discovery of the sex assigned to Vincent on birth, the couple each received a fine of £25. Vincent said of his wedding: 'We both love each other and when everything is put right we intend to get remarried. We shall have a public ceremony. We have nothing to be ashamed of.'[13] Despite the many risks of pursuing public recognition of their relationship, the couple persisted in seeking the married state.

In 1970, a UK judge made it more difficult again for trans people to choose marriage. In 1963, April Ashley, a model and trans-equality campaigner had married aristocrat Arthur Corbett. When their marriage broke down, her husband sought to avoid maintenance payments to Ashley through an annulment, rather than a more expensive divorce. The judge ruled that the marriage had never existed on the grounds that April had been assigned male gender at birth and it was not possible to legally change sex. It was not until 2004 that trans people were given legal recognition of their gender in the UK. Married people hoping to legally transition require the consent of their spouse to do so – the 'spousal veto' can prevent legal recognition until the finalization of a divorce. For many trans people hoping to marry, reliance on birth certificates in the UK means that marriage remains inaccessible.

In 2004, same-sex couples were given largely the same rights and responsibilities as married heterosexual couples through civil partnership. It would be a further ten years until, in 2014, same-sex couples could finally marry in England, Scotland and Wales. People in Northern Ireland would have to wait until 2020.

Just a few months before my own engagement, in 2016, I caught the bride's bouquet at a friend's wedding in Hertfordshire. My girlfriend bounded over, excited. An American guest politely asked if we were allowed to get married here and I thought: 'Shit. That's a reasonable question. Yes. Only just.' Just one year earlier, the US Supreme Court had judged, in *Obergefell v. Hodges*, that the fundamental right to marry must be recognized for people in same-sex relationships across the nation. Hundreds of thousands of weddings later, at the time of writing, this hard-won victory remains fragile, actively threatened by the political right and the Supreme Court itself.

The question as to whether consenting, unmarried adults have the right to choose their spouse has long been politicized in America, with legal barriers established to prevent marriages on the grounds of race for centuries. Within the British Isles, interracial marriages were never formally criminalized, though social barriers were endorsed and felt by many.

Marriages have taken place between people from different racial backgrounds for centuries in the UK. Although men and women undoubtedly faced racism in their day-to-day lives, in some working-class communities interracial marriages were, as historian David Olusoga finds, 'a seemingly unremarkable feature of life'.[14] In 1512, Henry VIII gifted a wedding outfit to his African trumpeter, John Blanke, a fairly typical gift for the time.[15] In the eighteenth century, while the profits of trafficked, forced and enslaved labour created massive wealth for the establishment, the anti-slavery activist Olaudah Equiano married Susannah Cullen in England in 1792. There are similar such examples – Jamaican-born Francis Barber, servant and friend of Samuel Johnson, married a local English woman in 1776 and Dido Elizabeth Belle, the daughter of an aristocratic father and an enslaved mother, accepted the proposal of steward John Davinier and married in 1793.

However, as the twentieth century dawned, while marrying a person of a different class was becoming more acceptable, marrying from outside of one's own ethnic group was becoming increasingly politicized. With the shadow of war, ethnic tensions and increasing migration, interracial couples found that social challenges averted weddings that were technically possible in law. Eugenics was on the rise and interracial families were condemned in public and political life. In the 1920s, the Foreign Office required marriage registrars in the United Kingdom to read a warning statement to white British women who registered their intention to marry 'Hindus, Moslems, African Negroes' and 'Chinese' men.[16] The statement informed them that they would lose British 'protection' following their wedding.[17]

A 1914 Act had stated that 'the wife of a British subject shall be deemed to be a British subject, and the wife of an alien shall be deemed to be an alien'.[18] Women entering into engagements with foreign nationals faced losing the citizenship rights of their birth; they were refused passports and treated as aliens themselves at home following their marriages. Many brides were left stateless through their choice of partner. The loss of nationality was a deliberate attempt from the government to deter women from entering into 'mixed marriages ...

which are in the women's case nearly always most undesirable'.[19] British men were subjects in their own right; British women's very nationality was dependant on their marital status.[20]

Sir Cecil Hurst, legal adviser to the Foreign Office, defined Britain's position in 1923: 'Our law in this country ... is founded on the principle that husband and wife are one, and that one is the husband.' Chrystal Macmillan, barrister, suffragist and women's rights activist, campaigned for decades for reform, both in the UK and internationally. In 1931, she proclaimed: 'there is no reason why the rights of a woman in connection with nationality should be curtailed because of marriage any more than are those of a man.... The right to nationality in one's own person is the most fundamental political right.'[21]

It was not until 1948 that British women were able to retain their nationality on marriage.

The problematizing of interracial marriages reached a peak in the 1930s with the Fletcher Report describing Liverpool's interracial couples as 'disharmonious', 'immoral' and 'promiscuous'.[22] By the time the US military brought an unprecedented Black population to England – 130,000 African American GIs were stationed in Britain in the 1940s, following US involvement in the Second World War – the British government was keen to support segregation where possible.[23] Not everyone complied. Many British people were to reject the racism promoted by the political classes and forge friendships, flirtations and relationships with Black American GIs in the latter years of the war. Relationships between Black soldiers and white locals shocked many white Americans serving in their segregated army who saw it as their responsibility to intervene on seeing Black troops and white girls socializing. Harassment and violence ensued. General Eisenhower wrote to Washington explaining the cause of tensions in September 1942: 'To most English people, including the village girls – even those of perfectly fine character – the negro soldier is just another man.'[24]

In the postwar years, around 70,000 British women accepted proposals from American servicemen and travelled to the United States under the GI bride scheme.[25] In 1947, Margaret Goosey, an English shoe worker from the Midlands, travelled to Virginia to marry her boyfriend, GI Thomas Johnson. They were arrested and separated – their marriage unrecognized. Thomas was Black and, despite his military service, sent to the state industrial farm. Margaret was imprisoned for six long months and then deported.[26] When her case was brought to the attention of the British Parliament, the government refused to intervene. Around 2,000 British women at home gave birth to babies with Black GI fathers. White commanding officers in the US military routinely refused permission for the fathers to marry, ordering the servicemen to leave their children and the new mothers behind.

At the end of the Second World War, interracial marriages were still banned in the US in over twenty states. Policies first introduced by British lawmakers in the seventeenth century were to endure in North America for 300 years. The legacies of British and European colonialism saw anti-miscegenation laws passed around the world well into the twentieth century. In 1918, the Aboriginals Ordinance was passed in Australia, restricting marriage between indigenous and non-indigenous people – the Act built on powers for local states to control the marriages of indigenous Australians, as well as to take control of their children.

The Prohibition of Mixed Marriages Act was passed in 1949 under apartheid South Africa.

In 1948, the wedding of Ruth Williams, a 25-year-old, middle-class clerk, in London, attracted the attention of both the British and South African authorities. Her choice of groom was Seretse Khama, son of the leader of the Bamangwato people, in what is now Botswana. The high-profile statement of their interracial wedding both threatened and outraged the neighbouring South African government, which was in the process of instituting apartheid. British authorities supported South

Africa's brutal system of racial segregation and controversy ensued. The marriage was reported as front page news around the world. Following attempts by the British government to prevent the wedding from going ahead, the English clerk and African prince married in a London registry office, having been denied a service in the Church of England.

The British government interfered in their marriage in support of South African policies over the next decade, exiling Khama from his homeland for six years. Their marriage was to endure despite international attempts to compromise it. Following a period of exile in London in the 1950s, Ruth was to live the rest of her life in Botswana, first as Queen of the Bamangwato people, and later as the First Lady of the newly independent Botswana. She had four children with her husband and their marriage endured for more than thirty years until Seretse's death in 1980. Ruth was buried alongside him in 2002.

The British fashion for eugenics waned in the 1940s, as the consequences of such policies in Nazi Germany became clear, but the racism at the heart of the enthusiasm for the eugenics movement continued to bubble away through the rest of the century. In 1958, riots broke out in England when a small number of white men objected to a white woman and Black men chatting to each other in a bar in Nottingham. Violence quickly escalated across the city and spread to London. In part, because two young people of different racial heritages chose to have a drink together. In the 1960s, the infamous politician Enoch Powell and his supporters promoted the idea that an interracial couple and their children had no place in British society.

The social and legal changes of the 1960s and 1970s profoundly changed the way marriage would be debated for the following 50 years. In 1967, the US Supreme Court ruled against anti-miscegenation laws still present in the South. It declared that marriage was 'one of the basic civil rights of man'.[27] Activism around same-sex marriage stepped up. In 1970, Richard Nixon conceded the demand for interracial marriage but said of same-sex marriage: 'I can't go that far – that's the year 2000.'[28]

In the second half of the twentieth century, as marriage began to be widely discussed as a human right and debated as a political question, more women began to openly reject the institution. If marriage was primarily an expression of love, then what value did it add? Was it not redundant? Surely it was better to avoid a practice that had long embedded homophobia, transphobia, racism and the inequality of women and men in law. Across the twentieth century, waves of activists debated connections between the institution of marriage and the inequalities suffered in wider society. Through their campaigns, the choice of whether to marry or not, and the institution itself, began to transform.

———

For centuries, and in diverse cultures around the world, women's opportunities and obligations were dictated by the choice to become a wife. The pressure surrounding the decision of whether to marry, and, if so, who, was enormous. Until a century ago, the choice would likely inform their work and career and determine the home and community in which they lived. A decision often shaped by family and wider stakeholders, a woman's marriage would fully define her social and legal status until recent decades. For many of history's women, the choices they faced on engagement might dictate the activities they undertook from the moment they got up in the morning to the moment they retired to bed, and the time spent in-between.

The decision of whether to marry today is pretty much unrecognizable from the one faced by so many of our ancestors. Waves of feminists and activists fought to strip back the role of marriage in our lives; to empower women with choice. Across much of the West, the consequences of these hard-won reforms have been to create a new model for an institution that can be bolder in letting go of its problematic past; to transform marriage from something essential into something *desirable*;

to open up the option to more people from diverse backgrounds today.

Marriage remains a choice that we continue to actively shape; an imperfect institution that perhaps more women might one day choose to enter into by saying more than 'yes'.

THE BIG DAY

A MANOEUVRING BUSINESS

'Maria was married on Saturday ... The bride was elegantly dressed and the two bridesmaids were duly inferior. Her mother stood with salts, expecting to be agitated, and her aunt tried to cry. Marriage is indeed a manoeuvring business.'

– JANE AUSTEN, *MANSFIELD PARK*

I have been a bridesmaid six times. I have been involved in the weddings of siblings and friends since my early twenties. Yet, when it came to planning my own wedding, I was not quite prepared for the scale of the task: the challenge of keeping the budget down, balancing the expectations of families and friends, resisting consumerist standards, navigating gendered norms and the pressure of creating nothing less than the best day of our lives. As a creative idealist and people-pleasing perfectionist, with an obscenely high London rent and upcoming fertility bills, it was tricky. Wedding planning provided a shared experience for me and my soon-to-be wife and it created opportunities to spend more time with friends and family in the run up to the big day. It was a fantastic project, an outlet for imagination and self-expression – and it was a manoeuvring business.

Every choice in our weddings can feel loaded with meaning as we set the boundaries of our relationships for the future; often looking back behind us as we take this big step forward. It is a challenge not to stumble over the gendered baggage that we have inherited on the way. I defy anyone to plan a wedding without encountering the idea of the 'traditional'. A traditional wedding is a tricky aspiration. It is not static. In every time and place and culture traditions evolve. They are fluid, flexible, intangible and ever changing. So which ones do you choose? Which family's traditions, which community's customs, do you follow? How far back do you go? Who gets to define what traditional means for you? Can we detangle ourselves from the problematic and uncomfortable bits of our history and cultural inheritance? From the expectations around us, the social norms and civil requirements? And how? How can we resist the deep nostalgia that pervades nuptial celebrations and empower ourselves to commit to a future while bringing only the best from the past?

From the earliest moments of celebrating an engagement to the final hours of the wedding day, we find ourselves confronting expectations that have trickled through to us from previous generations. Since childhood, we are taught to read the symbols, signs and coded language of the ephemera that define weddings. Set colour palettes and particular styles, rings, choices of music and flower compositions. There is poetry in the continuation of the legacies that we inherit from the past. In walking in the shoes of your parents, and grandparents and their grandparents. Of sharing an experience across time and place. I love the rhythm of tradition, the ease and comfort of falling into the familiar roles, and words, and actions that we inhabit in these significant moments of our lives. The customs that come to us provide us with a roadmap to help navigate these transitions not only at times of celebration but also at times of potentially overwhelming change and times of grief. However, I also know that there are some traditions, lessons and experiences that I do not want to pass on to my children. That I have been lucky to not share with my grans. That they were relieved to not share with their

Victorian grandparents. Customs have always evolved.

In the big white Western wedding, many of the practices that we have inherited through the decades and centuries are legacies from a dark past; traditions that have lingered on from the grim realities of entrenched gender, class and racial inequalities. The quickest of glances back at the history of marriage would make anyone want to resist traditions that are justified by the idea that 'that's just how it's done'. Many of the customs we think of as traditional have shallow roots. Contemporary practices are packaged and sold as long-standing tradition – like the proposal stories celebrated today, many of the expectations that we inherit for our weddings emanate from the second half of the twentieth century, just a few generations ago.

As couples navigate various perceptions of 'traditional', they find the journey complicated by a wedding industry that has successfully transformed the experiences of the uber wealthy into the must-haves for all. Desirables transformed into essentials. The minefield of event planning is then populated with family and friends, celebrants and officiants, vendors and venue teams. The many stakeholders in *your* day. My wife and I were lucky to have two families ready to support us and the choices we made. Across much of the world, the ultimate decision to walk down the metaphorical aisle continues to move slowly away from the families and communities of a prospective bride and groom. However, there is a level of investment that has not gone away. Sometimes expectations are unspoken, resting in shared cultural assumptions, and sometimes spoken very loudly.

In the United States, the average cost of a wedding in 2019 was nearly $30,000.[1] According to the same survey, couples in Canada, Spain and Italy all spent an average of more than $20,000 in the same year.[2] The UK average cost of £19,000 increases to £31,974 when engagement and wedding rings, honeymoon and other secondary expenses are taken into account.[3] As the spend on weddings bounces back from a dip during

Covid-19 restrictions, many couples rely on financial help from parents and families towards the cost of their celebrations. Even here, the legacy of a gendered past lives on, with higher expectations still falling to the bride's family in some communities. In a past where brides were expected to be 'given' in marriage, and to have little autonomy or independent means, a bride's parents were the natural choice of host for the day, picking up the bills along the way. Templates for 'traditional' Western wedding invitations can still encourage couples to top the bill with the names of the bride's parents. 'Mr and Mrs William Astor request the pleasure of your presence at the marriage of their daughter, Miss Helen Astor, to Mr James R Roosevelt'.[4] Leading with the parents just feels odd and this template certainly was not designed with couples like mine in mind.

It is not possible in most of the world for a couple to get married without asking others to fulfil supporting roles on the day. Even the smallest of civil ceremonies still require witnesses. Although Quaker ceremonies are self-uniting, formed between the couple and God and not arbitrated by an officiant, most spiritual and religious services are led by particular people empowered to create the union, and have dedicated roles for a cast of others to play. Both religious and secular traditions encourage a couple to involve close family, friends and those around them. In Hindu weddings, the bride and groom stand under the mandap together with, not only the priest, but usually their parents. Both bride and groom name their father, paternal grandfather and paternal great-grandfather in many Hindu services. In Chinese wedding teas, for 1,500 years, newlywed couples have been serving their parents together. Prayers are said for, and by, the wider families and congregation across a wide range of religious weddings, from Christian Orthodox to Muslim ceremonies, Hindu to Catholic and Jewish services.

Ceremonies are rarely made up simply of an officiant, the couple and the guests celebrating the union. Wedding parties group family and close friends into designated roles, with particular responsibilities that define their experiences, seating and even their outfits. The primary factor in assigning these roles remains gender for most. It is the groom, his ushers and best man who most often welcome guests to a ceremony in a church. They take responsibility for the wedding rings; bridesmaids take care of the bridal bouquet and any veil or train. Brothers or uncles might accompany a Hindu bride. Guests are likely to be segregated by gender at a nikah, with Muslim men usually taking the active roles. Across religious and cultural practices, when asking who is best suited to take on a wedding responsibility, the gender of potential candidates is often the first determining factor.

In opposite-sex weddings, the labour of pseudo-professional event planning, project management, admin and decision-making is widely expected to fall to women. Expectations of a groom and male relatives are relatively light. One top tip in a 2021 wedding magazine encouraged brides to 'Involve Your Significant Other: Don't feel like you're in this wedding planning process alone. Consult with your partner along the way; their opinion is bound to be invaluable ... even if they're only involved in some aspects.'[5] Another tip was to 'take some time off together'. Reading the article, it was not clear to me what the groom was taking time off from. The idea of a man leading the planning of an opposite-sex wedding is so ridiculous to so many people that *Don't Tell the Bride* is an international reality TV franchise. It allows viewers from the UK to the US, Scandinavia to Australia, to watch the often car crash choices of people who have not been socialized and raised to undertake this kind of labour – in the way women struggle to avoid from childhood.

In the run up to the big day, gender looms large, with parties of segregated people coming together to celebrate and prepare. From kitchen teas to mehndi ceremonies, bachelorettes to bridal showers, brides are expected to take time to surround themselves with women and family ahead of impending marriage. A mehndi ceremony begins the wedding itself and involves a combination of acts of preparation, with the application of the bride's henna and acts of celebration, like formal dancing. Kitchen teas and bridal showers provide brides with gifts as they take the leap and transition into their marriage. The harbingers of the big white wedding in the West, these separate parties are anticipated elements of nuptial celebrations – and a recent phenomenon. Gatherings of people known as hen and stag dos were taking place in mid-nineteenth-century America as single-sex gatherings but rarely anything to do with a wedding. A stag party might involve fishing or hunting in celebration of a birthday. Hen parties involved more genteel activities deemed suitable for women – though, in 1907, a newspaper in the United States reported: 'in what is vulgarly called a hen party, cigarettes and liquers [sic] are handed round and partaken of just as though men were of the company.'[6]

It was not until the 1960s that hen parties and stag dos, now seen by many as both essential and traditional, became an inbuilt feature of wedding preparations in the United Kingdom and across much of the West. In the decades that followed, they transitioned from being moments of preparation and relatively quiet celebration to whole weekends dedicated to the bride-to-be, often decked out in a costume, adorned with a sash and a plastic tiara, sometimes months before the big day. Pre-wedding pranks in China, as well as pranks on the big day, have been getting so out of hand that the government has made official efforts to crack down on them.[7] Originally designed to relax the couple, for some, choices have escalated to the point that the police have had to intervene.

For many, pre-wedding parties have been a chance to let your hair down. Particularly for men, they have been celebrated as a 'last night of freedom', a free pass on misbehaviour before being tied down, by the metaphorical ball and chain. Today, for many people in long-term, committed relationships, mourning the loss of sexual freedoms through infidelity is a fairly uncomfortable way to celebrate impending nuptials. However, hen dos and stag dos endure as largely same-sex gatherings, perpetuated by a massive industry telling us to make the most of these moments and opportunities. To treat ourselves. Although they have evolved beyond their original functions, pre-wedding parties today make space to centre relationships that can be complicated by geography or career and family responsibilities.[8] They acknowledge a shift in priorities that marriage can bring. As their purpose has changed, perhaps so too can expectations around the format and guest list.

It is difficult for nonbinary, trans and gender-queer people to navigate these, so highly gendered, traditions, and for these parties to avoid perpetuating artificially gendered stereotypes. It is easy to slip into bad habits, encouraging set gender roles and priorities and actively excluding those who do not conform. For people expressing same-sex love and gender diversity, where do you start navigating binaries like this?

Chimamanda Ngozi Adichie has reflected that:

> *The problem with gender is that it prescribes how we should be rather than recognizing how we are. Imagine how much happier we would be, how much freer to be our true individual selves, if we didn't have the weight of gender expectations.*[9]

While uncomfortable for many guests, navigating binary expectations is particularly tricky for people who find themselves pressured to conform to either male or female rituals that do not fit their gender identity while planning their own weddings. Not everyone getting married defines themselves as a bride or a groom. Some of these traditions, these habits, are barely a couple of generations deep – but it can feel like a big deviation to challenge and to move away from them.

Constructed ideas of gender permeate every aspect of weddings and wedding ceremonies. From the very entrance of a bride in European tradition, she leans on others. In May 2018, international news was agog to discover how Meghan Markle would navigate the aisle of St George's Chapel in Windsor Castle when her father was unable to attend her wedding. Pundits, journalists and commentators expressed concern at the pressure the responsibility might put on her ceremonially inexperienced mother. A lack of experience that had not seemed to cause concern for her father, the default choice. Meghan Markle travelled to her royal wedding with her mother before 'walking herself' halfway down the long aisle until being met by her soon-to-be father-in-law, Prince Charles – who, as a very ceremonially experienced man, was perfectly positioned to take her arm and lead his soon-to-be daughter-in-law the rest of the way.

Customs around wedding processional order vary wildly but, as a wedding party enters the ceremony, the order can be strictly defined as combinations of parents, officiants, groomsmen, bridesmaids, flower girls, ring bearers, best men and maids of honour join the ceremony. However, for the entrance of the bride, the big question often remains ... who is giving her away? Although Meghan might have been allowed to 'walk herself' down the aisle in Windsor, she could not reach the groom alone – she was 'given' to her future husband by Prince Charles. In a nikah, the bride's male guardian, usually her father, offers her to the groom. The kanyadaan is an important moment in Hindu ceremonies. The father of the bride places his daughter's hand in her soon-to-be husband's, in a cross-cultural gesture of blessing, approval and handing over.

My sister's wedding was one of the first I had attended. I remember my dad being asked to stand, take my sister's hand and place it in her fiancé's. 'Who gives this woman to be married to this man?' 'I do.'

It was not easy telling my dad that he would not walk me down the aisle. My fiancée and I walked in together. It felt like the most natural choice for us. Two brides. How else do you do it? And really not a reflection on him at all, but it was hard to resist the idea that I was taking something from him – his entitlement to that role.

Navigating expectations defined by gender lines is a minefield for LGBTQIA+ couples. And very liberating. You can find yourself without a default person to take on the roles and responsibilities expected of either a groom or a bride. At a wedding between two women, you can discover that the template is missing not only a groom but his best man, his ushers, the mother and father of the groom. You will also find that you have duplicated of-the-brides. The format does not quite fit, and the pressure of expectation is eased. Defying expectations in the process of wedding planning can be challenging. Facing surprise and confusion. 'Sorry, so which one of you is the bride?' Over-enthusiasm, over-compensating and constant correction. 'No she's not my sister, she's the other bride.' 'I'm marrying a woman.' 'Her. She's a she.'

Civil weddings are still adapting to the reality of a ceremony not always centred on one man and one woman. I crossed out the word 'groom' at least once on the paperwork my fiancée and I filled in for the registrar before my wedding. Formal religious customs rarely adapt more quickly. Of all the siblings in my Catholic family, I was the only one who happened to marry a Catholic, and the only one not allowed to marry in my family's parish church.

The wedding templates that we have inherited were designed around deeply binary ideas of what it means to be a woman or a man, a wife or a husband, a bride or a groom. In much of the West, as we challenge the idea that the life and work of a person should be defined by either their gender or their sex, the allocation of responsibilities on that basis is uncomfortable and problematic. Yet the assigned roles of 'bride' and 'groom' continue to be defined very distinctly for people getting married.

Nonbinary weddings fall entirely outside of these templates. In the United States, 1.2 million adults, 11 per cent of the LGBTQIA+ population aged 18 to 60, identify as nonbinary in their gender.[10] A 2021 UK government survey of 108,000 LGBTQIA+ people found that 6.9 per cent identify as gender fluid.[11] An Ipsos survey conducted in 27 countries found that 2 per cent of all respondents rejected a binary cis gender identity; 3 per cent of all respondents in Germany and Sweden and 4 per cent of Gen Zers.[12]

With greater public expression of diverse genders and sexualities, perhaps we can all more confidently challenge, question and deconstruct the roles and labels we inherit as we commit to a partner. Whatever our gender, and that of our partners, would not gender-neutral traditions serve us all better?

With gender so central to wedding tradition, the smallest choices in same-sex, trans and nonbinary weddings can feel radical. Subversive. Without a blueprint it is easier to pick and choose the customs and practices we take forward; to pave the way for questioning and moving beyond uncomfortable, unhelpful traditions. To give the past a vote, but not a veto.

As we step forward into our marriages, we can all feel empowered to shape the roles that feel right for us and for our relationships. To make choices that align with our values, and the foundations on which we want to build our futures. Choices that learn from the lived experiences of our history – acknowledging the good, the bad and the ugly. It feels right to share moments with the past and to acknowledge and appreciate our inheritance – but not to limit ourselves by it.

MAKING IT OFFICIAL

Come, Friar Francis, be brief; only to the plain form of marriage.

– **WILLIAM SHAKESPEARE,** *MUCH ADO ABOUT NOTHING*

At the heart of the wedding day is the moment of transition – officially sanctioned transformation – when the marriage contract is sealed. Defining the moment of change, pinning it down, controlling and articulating when it happens, has been a source of huge power in any community. Deciding who can create it, and for whom, has been even more so. Weddings have been political footballs for millennia. The social and spiritual battles of the past, lost and won centuries ago, continue to dictate the choices of couples planning their services today.

The ceremony itself is often the point on the journey to marriage that couples planning their weddings can control least. It is the element for which the expectations of others are transformed from informal assumption to formal requirements. For some, wedding ceremonies are primarily spiritual moments, sacraments and rites led, blessed and authorized by religious leaders. For others, weddings are secular legal contracts, sanctioned by a state. Throughout history, religious and state authorities have jostled for control. Women's needs and desires have been routinely overlooked by authorities consistently made up of men. Authorities who worked for centuries to deliberately restrict and strip back a broad diversity of wedding practices.

However, people have always found their way around restrictions imposed upon them. Weddings have varied dramatically depending on the wealth, class, geography, age and religion of the couple, the attitude of their families, their personalities and the politics of the day. In Britain, a diversity of wedding definitions and practices has always flourished – from the big and performative to the quick and easy, the spiritual to the secular, the by-the-book to the close-enough.

Most people were financially excluded from the elaborate services of the wealthy, and many from accessing legal weddings at all. They got creative. People in poverty, excluded minority religious, racial and ethnic groups and same-sex couples each created their own customs. For century after century, ceremonies took place in living rooms, barns, municipal buildings, prisons, fields and diverse places of worship. Although our ceremonial choices can feel dictated by set formula today, the lack of widespread and longstanding customs can empower people to look again at the blueprint of the 'traditional' wedding that we have inherited. To step outside of our time.

For many of history's working couples, creating a marriage was fairly simple. Authorities were consistently less invested in the practices of the poor. In Britain, from the medieval period to the middle of the 1700s, weddings were built on a tradition of consent. 'It is clear,' wrote Thomas of Chobham in 1216, 'that a man and a woman can contract marriage by themselves, without a priest or anyone else, in any place, so long as they agree to live together forever.'[1] What better witness could be required than God? Among poorer communities in Europe, there was a shared understanding that all a wedding ceremony needed was the verbal agreement of two eligible people, in the present tense. Consent to marry in the future tense was a betrothal. Consent to marry in the present tense was a wedding. If the intention to marry was followed by sex, that created a marriage too.

Planning a wedding was easy. Too easy. If a marriage could be created so simply, how could parents and guardians avoid inappropriate matches for their children? How could vulnerable young women, deliberately raised in ignorance and judged entirely by their sexual choices, be protected? How could the paternity of children be prioritized and assured? Inheritance and wealth passed down hereditary lines as husbands took ownership of the property of their brides. How could the wealth of families be controlled? Expressing yourself to be a husband and wife remained the definition of a valid wedding in England for centuries, but the authorities had means of encouraging couples to hold more formal, regulated ceremonies.

Medieval priests who were caught marrying people outside of the regulations could face suspension from their role and income for three years. In 1215, the Fourth Lateran Council, a meeting of leaders of the Catholic Church in Rome, declared that 'we absolutely prohibit clandestine marriages'. In an effort to tighten up the definition of a wedding, three things were necessary: the bride had to have a dowry, banns had to be published beforehand and the wedding had to take place in a church.

Between 1200 and 1342, more than 30 sets of Church statutes were created in England to define a wedding, in an attempt to standardize practices.[2] As these persistent efforts suggest, marriages outside of the rules remained common, particularly among the poor. No church in England succeeded in fully regulating wedding services or achieved the monopoly they were looking for.

Alongside the varied customs of the poor, a diversity of religious practice thrived beyond the control of the Christian Church. Muslim and Hindu ceremonies and celebrations have deep roots in these islands, and records of Jewish weddings in England go back nearly a millennia.[3] However, from the 1100s, formal marriage in Europe had become intricately intertwined with Christianity. For medieval and early modern couples, a wedding was a holy moment and understood to be a sacrament by many.

The Catholic Church's understanding of a wedding as a holy sacrament has not changed in the centuries since. Despite Pope Francis' previous statements of support for same-sex civil unions, the Vatican, when asked whether the Church has the power to bless same-sex relationships in 2021, responded with a resounding no. 'The blessing of homosexual unions cannot be considered licit. This is because they would constitute a certain imitation ... invoked on the man and woman united in the sacrament of Matrimony.'[4]

Many Catholic clergy support welcoming same-sex couples into their communities. An empathetic deacon offered a marriage blessing to my wife and me when we married. The Vatican's proclamation is a clear decree banning such blessing. 'It is not licit to impart a blessing on relationships, or partnerships, even stable, that involve sexual activity outside of marriage (i.e., outside the indissoluble union of a man and a woman open in itself to the transmission of life), as is the case of the unions between persons of the same sex.'[5] It is only within the sacrament of marriage that sex should be practised and permitted: sexual acts with the design of conceiving children.

The essentially medieval definition of a marriage endured. In the 1500s, as bishops in Italy were first explicitly defining a wedding as the creation of a holy sacrament, the Reformation pushed ahead in England. The core of Western wedding practices today dates from the sixteenth century, as Catholicism and Protestantism battled over the very soul of Europe.

Thomas Cranmer, the first Protestant Archbishop of Canterbury under the Tudors, built on medieval wedding practices and translated them into English in his *Book of Common Prayer*. The vows he wrote into his service required the groom to promise to love, comfort, honour and to keep his wife. The bride promised to love, honour and keep, but also to obey and serve. 'Obey' stuck.

Forcing women to obey a man, within a Church, and with the very real threat of eternal damnation, is no small exercise of control. Even Queen Victoria, with the excessive privilege she was born to, as the most powerful woman in the world, felt it necessary to promise to obey her husband on her wedding day. In her journal, she reflected on the power of such tradition, particularly over young women being forced to make this promise as part of a holy sacrament, within a spiritual space. 'The Ceremony was very imposing, and fine and simple, and I think ought to make an everlasting impression on everyone who promises at the Altar to keep what he or she promises.' There would be four centuries of women, generation after generation, solemnly promising to obey men before the Church of England began to omit 'obey' from the official service in the twentieth century.

Cranmer's wedding service remains remarkably familiar: 'To have and to holde from this day forwarde, for better, for wurse, for richer, for poorer, in sickenes, and in health, to love and to cherishe, til death us departe.'[6] The familiar and iconic language was exported around the globe through British colonialism. From Cranmer's set template, wedding ceremonies in the English language continued to be tightened, tweaked and tested, reformed and rewritten, according to the politics of the day.

A generation after Cranmer helped to establish the right of Henry VIII to marry Anne Boleyn in the new Church of England, Puritans began a campaign to dismantle the Church's hold on marriage, laying the foundation of the modern civil ceremony. This service was stripped back. By 1653, Thomas Cromwell's government passed a Marriage Act that established a secular 'Registrar' role for each parish. The Registrar was to be informed of intentions to marry at least 21 days before the wedding. After three successive announcements, a certificate was issued and the couple could come before a Justice of the Peace, and at least two other credible witnesses, to be declared man and wife. Although it wasn't to last long in the seventeenth century, the whole process sounds remarkably like the route to my civil ceremony in 2017. Between 1653 and 1657, this Act excluded religious authorities altogether, and declared that 'no other marriage whatsoever ... shall be accounted a marriage'.[7]

It is hard to imagine that compliance to the regular, dramatic changes to the rules over these centuries was widespread. On 10 October 1655, the famous English diarist Samuel Pepys exchanged unofficial wedding vows with Elizabeth Marchant de Saint Michel, in front of a clergyman and they began to live together as husband and wife. Nearly two months later, on 1 December, they participated in another wedding, this time in front of a Westminster Justice of the Peace, and were legally married. Six years later, on 10 October 1661, Pepys wrote in his diary: 'So home, and intended to be merry, it being my sixth wedding night.'[8] Every year, the couple celebrated their wedding anniversary from the autumn date of their religious ceremony, leaving the 1 December unmarked.

Governments and Churches sought, one after the other, to define what a wedding should be, passing hundreds of decrees, doctrines, laws and statutes. Their leaders looked down on private, informal weddings and tried to prevent them but struggled to overcome their perceived legitimacy. Outside of the wealthiest classes, from the medieval period to the 1750s, a wedding was what you could get away with within the customs of your local area. The tradition of consent endured and couples marrying outside of the rules continued to pose a problem for the authorities. Private weddings created challenges when one party wanted to get out of the marriage or if a spouse died; they were an obstacle for parents looking to protect and control their children; they challenged the idea that marriage was a sacrament to be ordained through the Church; they were an untaxable, missed income stream for the state. They continued in various forms, no matter what action the authorities took.

Across these centuries of clandestine wedding days, some women and girls found freedom. Independent choice in times when a woman's preference was a poor currency and parental consent an important element of wedding planning. Some accessed expediency. People might seek informal weddings to circumvent publishing banns and marry quickly, perhaps because of pregnancy. They might be escaping previous entaglements, betrothals or other private weddings that would prevent a marriage. Some women faced exploitation, married with uncertain legal standing, without the support of family and friends.

Many customs and traditions of the informal weddings that endured century after century, have been lost. Among working communities, handfasting or trothplight ceremonies were simple services used, generation after generation, to signify either a betrothal or a marriage as couples literally tied the knot. The distinction between engaged and married could be a very fine line. In areas of Scotland, handfasting ceremonies were used to facilitate one-year trial marriages, after which time the couple could choose either to part ways or commit to staying together. Walter Scott featured a handfasting trial marriage in his 1820 novel *The Monastery*, set in the Scottish borders of the 1550s.

Local variances in informal ceremonies, and the simplicity of the service, could cause some confusion. In 1562, in a parlour in northern England, Elizabeth Bird and Morgan Edmund held hands and said to each other, before witnesses, 'I take you for my husband' and 'I take you for my wife, with all my hart, & I will marry you, by my faith and trouthe.'[9] They kissed and 'pointed a day to marry' in a Church. Then Morgan fell sick and was unable to attend the Church wedding. So, were they already technically married? No one seems to know. The story appears in Chester's ecclesiastical court after Elizabeth, thinking he was dead, went on to marry someone else. She is recorded in the court records as saying that in her conscience she thought she was Morgan's wife.[10]

Four-and-a-half centuries before my wife and I married in the English border county of Northumberland, Janet Ferry was married there to Martyn Hugh, by her grandfather. 'One Lancelot Ettes, a very elderly man, dyd hanfast them.'[11] In 1573, 'said Martyn and the said Janet dyd willingly take hands together, and aither of them 2 dyd pleight their faith and trueth to the other, as man and wyff, byfoor God, after the country manner'.[12]

The 'country manner' of weddings lasted longest in Scotland and northern England, where attempts to stamp out informal ceremonies seem to have been resisted longest. In 1633, near my home in Durham, William Emmerson held a wedding in his own barn and was married 'by a strainger, with whom he was not acquainted'.[13] Simple ceremonies, taking place in your own home, would have been accessible weddings, as cheap or expensive, as long or short a celebration, as you wanted and could afford. These home weddings continued from the Middle Ages until the eighteenth century.

For couples looking to avoid the local church, there were alternative venues for a more official setting than your living room or barn. From the 1500s to the middle of the 1700s, prisons in England provided an organized, though perhaps less romantic, wedding service. Penitentiary chapels were the venues for thousands of clandestine marriages. As early as 1502, the Commissionary Court of the Bishop of London shows records of dubious weddings in the most famous of London's prisons, the Tower. The now World Heritage Site is a wedding venue again today, for couples spending tens of thousands of pounds on formal celebrations. In the 1630s, Archbishop William Laud explained that 'in the side of the White Tower, by the King's lodgings' sat a chapel 'where these disorderly marriages are made'.[14]

In 1632, the Court of High Commission charged the Lieutenant of the Tower with:

> *The great mischeifes growing by clandestine marriages in manie*
> *places of this kingdom ... especiallie they have observed this disorder*

*in the Tower of London, to the great hurt and undoing many times
of the marryed persons, and to the great greife of their parents and
friends, and against the canon and ecclesiastical lawes.*[15]

Prisons declared themselves outside of the juristiction of the Church
and the phenomenon of the Fleet wedding grew. In the seventeenth
and early eighteenth centuries, incarcerated clergymen might marry
thousands of people, without much fear of consequence. Crackdowns
simply spread the trade beyond the chapel into the wider Fleet area,
with profits from the weddings extending to local taverns and alehouses.

In 1719, a broadsheet complained that 'multitudes' of honourable
and reputable Families have been greatly injured, and many of them
utterly ruined, by Clandestine Mariages, solemnized in Taverns, Brandy
Shops, Alehouses, and other Houses, within the Liberties of the Prisons
of the Fleet.'[16] By 1740, over 6,000 marriages a year were taking place
around the Fleet prison. Over half of all Londoners may have been
marrying in this unlicensed way at this time.[17]

In 1753, the government intervened. The Clandestine Marriage Act,
or Hardwicke's Act, validated the Church of England's near-monopoly
on marriages across England and Wales. Leaning heavily on Cranmer's
almost 200-year-old *Book of Common Prayer*, it set out strict definitions.
Couples must have their wedding in a church or chapel, be married by a
Church of England minister and meet strict restrictions, including the
times of day at which a wedding was permitted to take place. Hardwicke
became the unlikely wedding planner for almost all couples marrying
across England and Wales, creating a legacy that would continue to
shape international wedding planning more than two centuries later.
People were left with little choice around how to arrange their day. The
penalties for not complying with Hardwicke's vision became much
harsher, with offending clergymen threatened with transportation and
marriages declared void.

The law did not apply to Scotland, where expressing consent and proclaiming personal vows in front of witnesses remained valid. Border villages began to see a boom in weddings as English couples with some means, who may once have been tempted to head to the Tower or the Fleet, began to head north. The most famous of these venues remains Gretna Green, just two miles over the border.

Robert Elliot, one of the first men to run the village's famous Blacksmith Shop described the wedding ceremony of Gretna Green's visiting couples:

> *The man is then asked, 'Do you take this woman to be your lawful wedded wife, forsaking all other, [and] keep to her as long as you both shall live?' He answers 'I will.' The woman is asked the same question, which being answered the same, the woman then produces a ring which she gives to the man, who hands it to the priest; the priest then returns it to the man, and orders him to put it on the fourth finger of the woman's left hand, repeat these words, with this ring I thee wed, with my body I thee worship, with all my worldly goods I thee endow in the name of the Father, Son and the Holy Ghost, Amen. They then take hold of each other's right hands, and the woman says 'what God joins together let no man put asunder.' The priest says 'forasmuch as this man and this woman have consented to go together by giving and receiving a ring, I, therefore, declare them to be man and wife before God and these witnesses in the name of the Father, Son, and Holy Ghost, Amen.'*[18]

There was no promise to 'obey'. By the eighteenth century, bridal obedience had been a longstanding feature of officially sanctioned wedding practices but would have been easily discarded in more informal ceremonies, where the only real aim was for the couple to be married at the end of it. Entrenching gender inequalities and enforcing religious doctrine were not a priority for lovers on the run or for the people selling these informal wedding services.

Jane Austen, born two decades after Hardwicke's Act, featured Gretna Green in several of her novels. Its intrigue and romance made it into Agatha Christie's mysteries in the twentieth century – and to TV and film in the twenty-first century, from documentaries on the still-thriving trade to dramas such as *Downton Abbey*.

As demand grew, newspapers published scandalous announcements of wealthy young couples fleeing to Scotland together. In February 1815, the *Western Luminary* reported:

> *Another fashionable couple have eloped ... The Lady must have emerged in great haste from her bed chamber, having no covering but a flannel petticoat and a great coat. They ... proceeded northward from Stafford, for that celebrated spot, Gretna Green. The parties were unknown.*[19]

The elopement, the choice of this woman to opt out of the sexual rules imposed on her, might very well have been a positive and empowered one for this anonymous person on the run. However, making this long journey, half-dressed and in secret at the beginning of the nineteenth century, makes her seem very vulnerable to many of the threats and injustices faced by women at the time.

In Austen's *Pride and Prejudice*, Lydia Bennet writes, in a note left for a friend: 'I am going to Gretna Green ... for there is but one man in the world I love ... I can hardly write for laughing.'[20] The sheltered, inexperienced fifteen-year-old is 'easy prey' to a weak, manipulative older man who persuades her to leave her support network on the pretext of a Scottish wedding, with no intention of travelling to Gretna Green and seeing it through. She is understood to be 'ruined'. Her perceived value in Georgian society plummets and it is only through Mr Darcy's interference and the payment of a large sum of money that the groom is bribed into a 'patched-up wedding' later, a simple wedding, without her close family present. Middle- and upper-class women who married after sex were expected to forgo the pomp and celebration afforded to their sexually inexperienced sisters. In Christian tradition, wedding ceremonies have long been a means of rewarding or punishing sexual behaviour in women.

Society judged marriage between Lydia and Wickham the best-case scenario for the very young woman, still a child, following her scandal: for Lydia to be married to the man that used her, 'ruined' her and deceived her family and friends, rather than to remain unmarried within her stable, loving family. When rules and definitions are tightened, those falling outside of the norms are left more, not less, vulnerable.

Although the Hardwicke Act defined wedding ceremony options for huge numbers of people in England and throughout its colonized territories, some communities remained unrecognized and excluded. They continued to find their own way, carving out ceremonial customs, creating and passing down wedding traditions in parallel to the legally recognized ones. Marriage has always been about more than the creation of a legal contract and marriages have long existed outside of formal structures.

Nearby the fictitious Lydia and Wickham, as they hid in Austen's nineteenth-century London, secret wedding ceremonies were taking place in Molly Houses across the city. Molly Houses were the precursors of today's queer clubs. Usually brothels, they were often tailored to people assigned male at birth who expressed same-sex attraction and gender diversity. They provided liberating social spaces and hosted elaborate marriage ceremonies in dedicated 'chapels' for decades. Couples would participate in a wedding ceremony, drawing from the customs of the time, and then usually 'consummate' their marriage.

In February 1726, a raid took place at Mother Clap's Molly House in

Holborn. A constable, Samuel Stevens, infiltrated the building, visiting and constructing evidence before the raid. He later testified:

> *I found near Men Fifty there, making Love to one another as they call'd it. Sometimes they'd sit in one anothers Laps, use their Hands indecently Dance and make Curtsies and mimick the Language of Women – O Sir! – Pray Sir! – Dear Sir! Lord how can ye serve me so! – Ah ye little dear Toad! Then they'd go by Couples, into a Room on the same Floor to be marry'd as they call'd it.*

Over thirty people were arrested. Three men were put on trial and sentenced to death.

The weddings of London's Molly Houses served as a sexual pursuit for some, but it is likely that they also held emotional weight for couples who performed the rituals that were denied to them outside of these spaces. The performative ceremonies played with the signs and symbols of weddings that were instantly recognizable from the legally sanctioned template at the time, with one participant usually taking on the role of groom, and the other the role of bride.

For women in same-sex relationships, a queer subculture was less tangible. Although many same-sex marriages took place between women across the eighteenth and nineteenth centuries,[21] only the most private of ceremonies was possible. An unknown number of women, like Anne Lister and Ann Walker, held secret ceremonies to mark a formal transition in their relationships. When they married in York in 1834, it was through taking communion together: 'Miss W and I stayed the sacrament ... The first time I ever joined Miss W in my prayers. I had prayed that our union might be happy.'[22] The couple marked their solemn, shared communion as the moment of their wedding, the moment that began their marriage.

Two decades later, when American actress Charlotte Cushman

began an affair with a young lover, Emma Crow, she warned her that marriage was not an option – not because of legal barriers but because she already considered herself to be married to her long-term partner, artist Emma Stebbins: 'Do you not know that I am already married and wear the badge upon the third finger of my left hand?'[23] The wearing of a wedding ring, like Anne Lister and Ann Walker, reflected a moment of commitment that had taken place – perhaps more private than the placing of a ring on a bride's finger in a formal ceremony, but with no less intention. With ceremonies solemnizing same-sex relationships pushed underground, the scale of the history, and the customs created, are difficult to grasp today.

While same-sex and trans ceremonies were repressed or persecuted by authorities in Britain, they flourished for centuries across continents around the world. The wedding feasts of husbands and their nkhonsthana, or 'boy-wives', were recorded by Swiss Presbyterian missionary Henri Junod in 1912, in modern day Mozambique.[24] Bride prices were paid and Junod recorded a dance in which the nkhonsthana donned wooden or cloth breasts. In modern-day south Sudan, within the Nuer community, anthropologist Edward Evans-Pritchard observed weddings 'in which a woman married another woman' in the 1930s. He found that 'the woman-husband married her wife in exactly the same way as a man marries a woman'.[25]

European colonialism systematically shut down same-sex and trans wedding traditions across the globe between the sixteenth and twentieth centuries. Not only queer customs but a broad diversity of wedding traditions were lost to European imperialism. Matriarchal structures and ceremonies, like those found in the Haudenosaunee, a confederacy of six Native American nations, were opposed and repressed by white colonisers. The Haudenosaunee continue to follow a matrilineal structure in which leadership, status and inheritance pass down the female line – at the end of a wedding, it was traditionally the husband who moved into the wife's family home.

While spreading their Christianized, patriarchal and heteronor-mative marriage practices to more people around the world, British authorities explicitly excluded others. In British territories in the Caribbean and North America, and within the young United States, in the nineteenth century, enslaved Black people were forbidden from accessing marriage. Couples looking to solemnize and celebrate their commitment to each other performed broomstick ceremonies. Accounts of plantation weddings survive from the 1800s, shared by a younger generation of former enslaved people. A wedding in Virginia was recalled as having been led by a community elder, a woman. Friends and family formed 'a ring' around the bride and groom. The officiant, 'Ant Lucy', read from the Bible and laid a broomstick down on the ground. The young couple locked arms together and jumped over it.[26] Today, some African Americans choose to end their wedding ceremony by jumping over a broomstick, building on the tradition founded by enslaved Africans, centuries ago.

In nineteenth-century Britain, 'Broomstick wedding' was shorthand for the private weddings associated with the poorest and most marginalized of the working classes. In the 1860s, Dickens' *Great Expectations* told the story of Jaggers' housekeeper, Molly, revealed to be Estella's mother. Molly had her young daughter taken away years before, after being accused of jealously murdering a woman. We are told that she and her husband 'had been married very young, over the broomstick (as we say)'.[27]

As late as 1960, a London newspaper reported 'anger' that 'broomstick weddings' held in Roma and Traveller communities were not recognized in English law.[28] The article claimed that 'four out of every five' members of some Traveller communities married in a service in which the bride jumped a broomstick at the groom's door.[29] It lamented that English law did not recognize the 'centuries-old ceremony', which some people within the community claimed was 'more binding to them than any church or register office marriage'.[30]

The rules that govern wedding ceremonies held in England and Wales today were consciously built to serve a white, Anglican, largely upper-class and middle-class community and centred on the priorities of men. In a quirk of law, Hardwicke's Act created an exception for Jewish and Quaker couples who were free to officially marry within their faiths.[31] People of other faiths had one legal option: to marry in the Church of England. Nonconformists, Muslims, Catholics and Hindus were put in a difficult position. Women from these communities who held weddings within their faiths, consummated their marriages and lived with husbands for years, had no legal standing as wives. They had no recourse following abandonment, no protection of their rights and the legitimacy of their children could be called into question.

These challenges have not gone away. Unregistered weddings have been on the rise in the UK in recent decades. Lawyer Aina Khan founded the organization Register Our Marriage in 2014 to raise awareness of the lack of legal protection 'in rapidly rising unregistered religious marriages'[32] and to lobby for legal change. Working particularly in Birmingham, Bradford and Leicester, the national campaign found that the practice of unregistered marriages is particularly common among young Muslims but also rising in some African churches and among Hasidic Jews, Sikh and Chinese communities.[33] A 2017 survey found that over 60 per cent of Muslim women in the UK who had married in a nikah had not gone through a separate civil ceremony.[34] A wedding had taken place, but their marriages were not legally recognized. Khan's research suggests an increasing trend, and that over 90 per cent of mosques in the UK are not registered to perform weddings on site.[35]

If these marriages break down, couples are unable to access UK family courts and the processes designed to create a fair division of assets. Women can find themselves either suddenly divorced through relatively quick religious processes or, conversely, be refused separation. On the incapacitation or death of their spouse, they can struggle to access next of kin rights or pensions.

The messy legal inheritance of the 1700s and 1800s means that, in England and Wales today, there is a requirement for Anglican, Jewish and Quaker leaders to officially register their religious ceremonies. However, all other faiths can volunteer to register a ceremony as legally binding or not. It is clear that, even today, where ambiguity exists in the legality of wedding practices, with a patriarchal legacy it is invariably women who suffer most.

An 1836 Act allowed secular ceremonies to be held in registry offices for the first time since Thomas Cromwell, providing an alternative to strictly defined religious practice. The state began to take over on a massive scale. By 1900, religious ceremonies had dropped to 85 per cent of all weddings in the UK.[36] In 2017, only 23 per cent of weddings between opposite-sex couples were religious ceremonies, 0.6 per cent of marriages between same-sex couples.[37] Most major religions continue to refuse to host same-sex wedding ceremonies.

It is a trend seen across most of Europe and the West. In Ireland, religious ceremonies have dropped dramatically in the last few decades. In 1990, Catholic marriages accounted for 93 per cent of all weddings in the Republic. By 2019, just 43.6 per cent of weddings took the form of a Catholic service, compared with 41 per cent civil or humanist ceremonies.[38] In Australia, in 2018, weddings performed by civil celebrants accounted for 80 per cent of all marriages.[39]

Today, some countries, like Croatia, recognize civil ceremonies as the only valid form of wedding service. In France, the only legally recognized weddings are civil ceremonies that take place in council offices or a town hall. Couples who would like a religious, humanist or other form of wedding tend to marry legally in the town hall and then hold their preferred wedding shortly after, free from state intervention.

In many countries it is the person performing the ceremony who must be registered with the state, rather than the location. In Scotland, most of North America, Australia and New Zealand there are no restrictions to where a wedding can take place, with relatively straightforward rules as to who can perform a service.[40]

Civil ceremonies in England and Wales are restrictive and can be difficult to personalize. They are led by a Registrar, who the couple may not have met until the service, and they can only take place in a licensed location. Any religious reference within the ceremony is prohibited and they follow a predetermined template. The sharp distinction between religious and civil ceremonies leaves interfaith couples with the choice of a wedding within one faith, or a wedding that reflects neither. Humanist ceremonies are not recognized in English law at all.

In the year my wife and I married, we attended two humanist weddings. The couples had each already legally married in a small private ceremony in a registry office before sharing a larger event with their guests, choosing unrestricted, personalized music, readings and celebrants. The ceremonies within these celebrations were similar to a civil ceremony in many ways but free from regulations around location, officiant and language.

People are forced to get around antiquated restrictions to enjoy personal and meaningful ceremonies in all sorts of ways. It emerged, in 2021, that Meghan Markle and Prince Harry exchanged personal vows privately in their garden, three days before their official Church of England wedding in Windsor Chapel. Other than the presence of the Archbishop of Canterbury, it does not sound so different from Britain's forgotten tradition of informal weddings. It became legal to marry in specific, registered outdoor locations in England for the first time in 2021, in a rather late reaction to the Covid-19 pandemic.

Nations and communities around the world were forced to review their wedding practices as the Covid-19 pandemic struck. In April 2020, the United Arab Emirates launched an online wedding service in which couples could be married online by a religious leader before receiving their wedding certificates via text message. Later that month, New York Governor Andrew Cuomo signed an order to allow weddings to take place, with photo IDs, through video conferencing platforms. Zoom weddings were born.

In India, the wedding industry, thought to be worth around $50 billion a year, struggled as typically large celebrations became impossible.[41] Chaitali Puri and Nitin Arora's plans for a 450-guest wedding in New Delhi, in May 2020, were prevented by lockdown. In the end, they chose a small ceremony of only 16 people, including the priest, with the rest of the guests joining via Zoom: 'My living room became the wedding venue, I wore my mum's magenta sari and my grandmother's jewellery, the photographs were taken by Nitin's brother, and we had a potluck lunch.'[42]

In the UK, the pandemic shed new light on the 'confusing maze of rules' surrounding English weddings as couples faced cancellations and found themselves struggling to navigate legal restrictions.[43] In September 2020, the UK government began a consultation programme in recognition that couples and communities face different rules and limitations, with some given more freedom to have a ceremony that is meaningful to them than others.[44] Put more simply: 'the law is an ancient and complex hodgepodge of different rules.'[45] It may be that, in the coming decades, the definition of wedding ceremonies in England and beyond can recentre the couple undergoing the transformation to newlyweds; can move back, closer to the personal, spoken agreement to be married, of two eligible people.

Around the world, the rules and choices around our weddings are changing. As they always have done. Some state and religious authorities are slower than others to relinquish the powers and preferences inherited from an often-problematic past. The people making the rules around these transformative ceremonies have rarely empowered women navigating their journey into marriage, or desired or prioritized gender equality. For centuries, couples around the world found various loopholes in their efforts to circumvent the restrictions that both spiritual and state leaders sought to impose. For couples looking to formalize their relationships, it is easy to feel stuck with the template and traditions inherited, sanctioned and expected by figures of authority. However, even where restrictions are tightest, there has always been more than one way to tie the knot.

PUTTING ON A SHOW

To church in the morning, and there saw a wedding
... strange to see what delight we married people have
to see these poor fools decoyed into our condition, every
man and woman gazing and smiling at them.[1]

– SAMUEL PEPYS, WRITER AND DIARIST

In 2021, my wife bought afternoon tea at a stately home in Northumberland for my birthday. A wedding reception was underway on the terrace just outside from where we were sitting. It was lovely. Festive. It gave a sense of special occasion to our meal, and people-watching at a wedding is a fun activity. Imagining relationships; judging outfits; enjoying the setting.

My wife said, 'We couldn't have got married here anyway. I saw on the poster on the way in that they have a "one bride policy".' I am pretty sure they meant one wedding at a time – the idea of two brides still feels synonymous with two weddings for a lot of people. We reminisced about and compared past celebrations we had been to. The restrictions of the Covid-19 pandemic forced couples to challenge and rethink the more performative elements of their wedding celebrations; to question the added extras. Though superfluous to requirements, it is hard to resist the more theatrical elements. Even in the most modest of weddings, there has usually been a performative element to nuptial celebrations: standing up and saying your lines, often in a carefully chosen costume and in a set-dressed venue, before witnesses and usually some kind of congregation or audience.

The scale of these productions has varied wildly. For generations of couples in poorer communities, wedding performances beyond the ceremony would have been relatively small – though choices around dress, guests and celebrations would rarely be casually made. For those with means to put on a show, extravagant nuptial performances have been amplified to large audiences. The weddings of the rich and powerful have long been consciously curated to make a statement, the smallest choices and details speaking loudly.

Today, a certain level of broader theatre is expected in wedding celebrations across the world, almost irrespective of class and wealth. Theatrics of dress and set design, careful choices of venue and flourishes of sentiment are usually present. Where technology is accessible, the intended audience reaches beyond the guests invited into the room. The production is increasingly enjoyed on the small screen, opened up through the distribution channel of social media and into the future of the couple and their families through potentially thousands of images and hours of video. Historians of the early twenty-first century will not have to wonder what the weddings of our time were like. Ceremonies and celebrations today are documented and shared on a level unthinkable even a generation ago.

In the West, twenty-first century weddings can be relatively individualistic affairs. The big white wedding centres the preferences and personalities of the couple in a way that would have been unrecognizable for much of our past. People planning their weddings are encouraged to make a personal statement in their choices, in the ceremony, themes, colours, venue, food and decorations. There is pressure to find distinctiveness, self-expression and innovation. To transcend the 'cookie cutter' wedding, the homogenizing wedding magazines and websites tell us.

In the last 30 years, hundreds of novels, plays and movies, and hours of TV have been built around the details of a couple's big day. Bollywood has produced thousands of weddings of explosive colour, music and dance. In the US and UK, Golden Age movies like the popular *The Philadelphia Story* (1940), later reimagined as the musical *High Society* (1956), which romanticized and satirized marriage, with Hollywood stars such as Cary Grant and Grace Kelly, set the foundation for 1990s' romcoms like the UK *Four Weddings and a Funeral* (1994) and US *My Best Friend's Wedding* (1997). A constantly renewing wedding genre was born.

The first decades of the twenty-first century saw a Hollywood obsession with the minutiae of wedding celebrations, with box-office successes like *Wedding Planner* (2001), *My Big Fat Greek Wedding* (2002), *27 Dresses* (2008), *Bridesmaids* (2011) and *Crazy Rich Asians* (2018). And then there was *Bride Wars* (2009), a film seeing Kate Hudson and Anne Hathaway as two committed, loving, childhood best friends who violently fall out and sabotage each other over their competition to hold the perfect, rigidly defined, dream wedding. A movie written and directed by men. More recently, reality TV programmes have given us access to other people's weddings to enjoy, gawk at – and judge.

Ambitious movie and television productions set and redefine the fairytale standard for weddings around the world. Production budgets grow as couples take their chance to escape the realities of life into a Cinderella-style fantasy. Princesses until the clock strikes midnight. In a lavish celebration, people getting married can live like celebrities for a day.

Months or years of planning, large budgets or hours of labour are not simply the route to fantasy. They are a statement of your commitment to this new union. Memory-making for future bumps in the marital road. They are a hunt for self-expression, recognition and validation.[2] My wife and I designed and made themed decorations for our wedding venue, embracing the creative opportunity.

Today, large-scale wedding productions are accessible to more people than ever before. Choices historically reserved for the elite few have been opened up to the many in the twenty-first century through capitalist mechanisms and consumerist pressures. The wedding receptions and celebrations expected and enjoyed by many today would have been beyond the reach of almost all newlyweds in the past. The festivities that followed a wedding ceremony would correspond with the means of the couple and their communities. For centuries, though the largest household expenditure for many working families would be on food, a wedding would be marked with some kind of meal.

In Islam, secret weddings are forbidden and the publicity, the sharing with a community, has often been achieved through a walimah, or marriage feast, following the ceremony. A wedding feast has long been an integral part of Jewish and Hindu weddings. By the time that Hardwicke began to set the boundaries of wedding ceremonies in England and Wales in the middle of the 1700s, some kind of meal or 'wedding breakfast' was also common. In November 1810, a Reverend William Holland recorded the wedding of two of his servants in his diary: 'I went to church and married my servants Robert Dyer and Phebe, and I trust they will be happy in each other.' He 'gave them and their friends a dinner on the occasion' and reflected that 'they are to continue with me as servants till Lady [day] next'.[3]

The trend was for modest celebration – as Jane Austen's niece, Caroline, recollected of her sister's wedding, in 1814:

> No one was in the church but ourselves, and no one was asked to the breakfast, to which we sat down as soon as we got back ... The breakfast was such as best breakfasts then were. Some variety of bread, hot rolls, buttered toast, tongue, ham and eggs. The addition of chocolate at one end of the table and the wedding-cake in the

middle marked the speciality of the day ... soon after the breakfast the bride and bridegroom departed. They had a long day's journey before them to Hendon ... In the evening the servants had cake and wine.[4]

As in all things, fashions changed. Rowdier medieval customs were replaced by a dignified meal for those who could afford it. The sister of the bride reflected: 'Weddings were then usually very quiet. The old fashion of festivity and publicity had quite gone by, and was universally condemned as showing the bad taste of all former generations.'[5]

Although wedding fashions were 'in the extreme of quietness' at the time of Anna Lefroy's nuptials in the early nineteenth century, public celebrations, publicity and festivities were about to be revived by generations of Victorians looking to their trendsetting new monarch for inspiration. As Queen Victoria's big day approached, in 1840, the *Satirist Journal* published a lament that:

We are all going stark, staring mad. Nothing is heard or thought of but doves and cupids, triumphal arches and whit favours, and last but not least, variegated lamps and general illuminations.[6]

Some weddings caught the public imagination and shaped perceptions more than others. Victoria's wedding to Albert was to become one of the most influential in defining a 'traditional' wedding in the West in the centuries that followed. It was a public event, planned carefully with Lord Melbourne, the British Prime Minister. Designed to allow the couple to be seen, thousands of people stood in London's damp smog on a cold, wet February morning to glimpse the bridal procession drive past on its way to St James's Palace, in London.[7] The day was choreographed to increase the popularity of the new Queen, to shore up the monarchy and reinforce the imperialistic and elitist ideologies of the time. In many ways, the wedding of Victoria to Albert was Britain's first celebrity wedding. It was an event promoted though a newspaper and print industry that was exploding in scale and beginning to reach around much of the world.

The monarch's wedding, though particularly iconic at the time, was not alone in using the growing nineteenth-century press to project the carefully curated political messages of the elite. Just over 20 years later, when the Queen's favoured protégée, Sarah Forbes Bonetta, walked down the aisle, it was another consciously choreographed performance. One that captured the public's imagination.

On 14 August 1862, the 19-year-old bride and her new husband left the parish church of St Nicholas, in Brighton, on the south coast, to a ringing of its bells and cheers from thousands of spectators. Born in West Africa, in what is now southwest Nigeria, Sarah had been enslaved as a child and, at seven, was given by King Gezo of Dahomey (Benin) to Captain Frederick Forbes as a gift for the queen.

On the wet Thursday afternoon of her wedding, the spectators' interest was sparked by both the royal connection and by the imperialistic symbolism of the wedding. The *Brighton Herald* celebrated 'the spectacle of the natives of a distant Continent [Sarah's husband was a Sierra Leone-born merchant], separated from us by strong natural barriers, assembled under the wing of the Church of England, partaking of its rites'.[8]

For the burgeoning newspaper industry, weddings were fuel to promote political values and moralist judgements. Some celebrations provided sentimental or aspirational narratives; others provided stories of scandalous gossip. There is a long trend of public feelings of entitlement to other people's weddings. The flipside of being a celebrity for a day.

The wedding party, including Sarah's 16 bridesmaids, entered the church two by two, 'an English gentleman and an African lady; then an African gentleman and an English lady ... and so on'.[9] The wedding projected the evangelical values that were used to reinforce British colonialism across Victoria's reign. Uncomfortable reading today, in 1862, the *Herald* claimed the wedding procession to be 'a triumph' of an enlightened age.[10]

Sarah's wedding produced a statement, hopeful and imperialistic. And one strongly supported by Queen Victoria. It was not Sarah's choice to marry. At the age of 19, having received the proposal from her husband-to-be, James Davies, she wrote:

> *Others would say 'He is a good man & though you don't care about him now, will soon learn to love him.' That, I believe, I never could do. I know that the generality of people would say he is rich & your marrying him would at once make you independent, and I say 'Am I to barter my peace of mind for money?' No – never!*[11]

However, Queen Victoria approved of the match.

On her wedding certificate Sarah recorded her name as 'Ina' Sarah Forbes Bonetta. It is possible that Ina was connected to her Yoruba name, erased by her English guardians but reclaimed by her through the legal record of her wedding day.[12]

The Victorian era defined the big white wedding, built on white Christian tradition. While this model was exported across much of the globe, British colonialism in the nineteenth and early twentieth centuries opened up more diverse practices at home, and an influx of people from different places and of different ethnicities.

South Shields, a coastal town in northeast England, saw a flow of Yemini migrants, following the British invasion of Arden, in 1839. The pressures created in Yemin led hundreds of men to take harsh jobs as seamen on British ships and later settle in the town. By the early twentieth century, marriages between Yemini seamen and local women were common, with couples often integrating wedding traditions to celebrate the union. When Rosetta Sultman married Mohammed Muckble, one of the first Yemini seamen to settle in South Shields, they celebrated twice: 'my mother married my father in a mosque and my father married my mother in a church.'[13] The community grew to build the first purpose-built mosque in the region, the same mosque in which the wedding of heavyweight boxer Mohammed Ali and Veronica Porsche was blessed in 1977.

The realities of colonialism have shaped the choices of couples celebrating their weddings across classes in Britain, and around the world, for centuries. Many have navigated differences in religion in curating their wedding choices. Prativa Devi, a princess of Cooch Behar in India, married Anglican Englishman Lionel (Miles) Mander in 1912. Prativa's education had largely taken place in the United Kingdom; her mother described her as 'just like an English girl, although at home she lived as an Indian Princess'.[14] The couple chose to celebrate their wedding in the residence of the Maharajah of Cooch Behar, both dressed in Indian costume, and married in the Brahmo Samaj Hindu rites. Two years later, Prativa's younger sister, Sudhira, fell in love with Lionel's brother, Alan, and the couple married in a similar, though relatively low-profile wedding in Kolkata (former Calcutta) in 1914, before both serving in the First World War.

Colonial practices have ensured that nearly two centuries after Queen Victoria's big white wedding, the formula is still holding strong and is instantly recognizable across much of the globe. Details of Queen Victoria's celebrations were quickly imitated across Britain and the formula was picked up and amplified in the United States. The diamond ring, extravagant cake, professions of romantic companionship and virginal dress, joined Thomas Cranmer's sixteenth-century ceremony and together laid the foundation of today's 'traditional' Western wedding. The white wedding became internationally popular and continues to perpetuate specific ideas relating to gender, class, race and sexuality around the world.[15]

In 2011, when the British royal family came to plan another significant wedding, the formula was there – a carefully choreographed blend of accessibility and unobtainable fairytale. In a period of economic 'austerity' and severe government cuts to public services, the British people enjoyed an extra bank holiday – a free day off work – for the nation to virtually attend and celebrate the £20 million wedding of Prince William and Kate Middleton.[16] Like Victoria's, William and Kate's wedding utilized an emerging communications infrastructure and was pitched as a global celebration. The Palace press team described the day as nothing less than 'every girl's dream come true' and around two billion people were said to have tuned in across the globe.[17] When an ancient Roman poet observed the power of mollifying the masses with a combination of 'bread and circuses', he could not have imagined a more affective circus than a public wedding. The bells of Westminster Abbey pealed for more than three hours in public celebration.

Our weddings continue to be shaped by the choices of history's wealthiest people, as well as the most privileged today. From colour palettes to spiritual choices, decoration schemes to clothing, it is difficult to resist reinforcing other people's messages. For most of us, the statements we make through our weddings will not shore up powerbases or affect the politics of the day; they will not be reported on through international press. However, the choices we make continue to make a statement, to reflect values, to reinforce or disrupt expectations and to be interpreted by others.

For women curating the day described as 'their big' one, there is a delicate balance of expectations to juggle in the choices they make: between traditional and contemporary, community and individualism, self-expression and silence. However archaic, brides around the world are still expected to express themselves at their weddings through aesthetics, while barely speaking at all.

In the celebrations that follow wedding ceremonies, toasts and speeches often ring out to wish the newlyweds well, to express thanks to the people who have supported them, and to take a moment to look back together to the past and forward to a new shared future. In British wedding breakfasts, toasts tend to follow a formal running order, led by the father of the bride, the ostensible host of the day. The groom picks up the baton to speak second, before speeches close with light relief provided by the best man.

Women are expected to remain silent in the formal celebration of most UK weddings. The bride routinely flattered, spoken for and passive. Saying it best when she says nothing at all. American running orders more frequently include the maid of honour, though not necessarily the new bride. In European-tradition, women increasingly participate as the speeches unfold on their big day but hearing the bride's voice at the wedding meal is still unusual. A deviation. I have very rarely heard a bride speak at the many weddings I have attended. Ten minutes before delivering a speech at my wedding, I could not help but wonder: 'What the hell am I thinking?!' I understood why so many of my female friends and relatives took the get-out-of-jail-free card and let themselves relax over their meal. Pressure off once the ceremony has concluded. The patriarchy has to have a silver lining somewhere. Right?!

When I married my wife there was no groom to take the default role of thanking guests, the wedding party and the people who had helped us. No expectation that the fathers of the brides should represent us or speak on our behalf. My wife and I invited our mams to lead a toast together, before we spoke. Then our 12-year-old best man, my wife's nephew. Having women and children deliver your speeches is a good choice if you want to move your guests to tears.

Although opportunities to use their voices might be limited for brides in some 'traditional' wedding formula, women are still very much expected to make a statement on their big day: just usually non-verbal. Choices around venue, decoration, food and drink, the labour poured into the minutiae of wedding planning, can all be interpreted in multiple ways. The very outfits we wear can be packed full of meaning. No choice is more open to judgment than when we reach into the, generally overpriced, closet to find expression for the day. Bridal clothes around the world are loaded with tradition; influenced, dictated and weighed down by brides who have long since departed.

For centuries, people getting married have been keen to look their best on their big day. For those with money to spend, a bridal trousseau was an opportunity to confer status, to show off. In Austen's *Pride and Prejudice*, Mrs Bennet hears that the man who ran away with her daughter, Lydia, has been bribed to marry her. Her anxiety is all for the dress: 'But the clothes, the wedding clothes! I will write to my sister Gardiner about them directly. Lizzy, my dear, run down to your father, and ask him how much he will give her.' In *Northanger Abbey*, the wealth of a family is judged by the cost of their daughter's £500 bridal trousseau: the same value as the yearly income of Mrs Dashwood's newly impoverished family in *Sense and Sensibility*.

Costume has long been an important element of a wedding performance, but choices were likely to have been less extravagant for most, and generally more diverse for history's weddings. Not all trends would catch on.

In September 1775, a Derby newspaper reported the wedding of a bricklayer 100 miles to the south. Mr Richard Elock wed Mrs Judith Redding,

> *Who, to exempt her future husband from the payment of any debts she might have contracted, went into one of the pews in the church, and stript herself of all her cloaths except her shift, in which only she went to the altar, and was married, much to the astonishment of the parsons, clerk, &c.*[18]

In eighteenth-century England, some local custom suggested that if a bride married without clothes, she was understood to have brought no property to the union – her husband-to-be could not be held accountable for any debts she might have. It was a practice particularly popular among widowed women looking to shake off any arrears left by their late husbands. In December 1797, Birmingham Cathedral was reported to have hosted the wedding of a surely uncomfortably cold bride 'in the exact state of Eve in Paradise'.[19]

As the 1800s dawned, the quirks of local customs were already dying out. As the century progressed, nationally popular fabrics and fashions were beginning to become more accessible through colonial trade, and the clothing choices of English brides were starting to grow more aspirational. One of the most iconic legacies of Victoria's 1840 wedding in London was her choice of gown. Although many royal women chose to wear white in the centuries before Victoria, it was not particularly common. Furthermore, when white was chosen, it was more to do with demonstrating wealth through the costliness and impracticality of the fabric than any particular virtue or value – the cleaning requirements of clothing were a serious business before mass-produced soaps and the invention of the electric washing machine.

Like those before her, Victoria's choice was influenced by practical considerations, white being easier to see through the crowds encouraged to attend. However, with purity so central a middle-class value in the 1800s, the virginal white dress went viral, and the Victorians used their romantic ideals to rewrite the history of the white dress from a statement of wealth to a statement of purity. The trend began to slowly trickle down through the aristocracy and wealthy, and proved a usefully high-contrast colour for the emerging new trend of photography to capture.

Victoria's choice, the new 'tradition', of a white gown, with tiny waist and full, long skirt, defines the bridal look for millions of women still in the twenty-first century – yet it was only very partially adopted in the 1800s and 1900s and a small minority of history's women, both in European tradition and around the world, have worn white to tie the knot. Among the working classes, a wedding outfit involved little more than sprucing up your Sunday best for most Western brides, whatever colour or style it happened to be. Until recent decades, women about to get married would forgo an expensive gown for something more practical. For those with a small budget for something new, it would make sense to choose materials in coloured or patterned fabrics. Creating dresses that would last through many future wears, perhaps accessorized by something borrowed or passed down.

The big white wedding is a very new tradition in the working classes. In 1958, one of my grans wore a practical skirt suit to marry my grandad, in his military uniform. Wedding dresses were just too impractically expensive. When worn by her friends and peers they were generally hired. The following year, my maternal gran wore a calf-length white dress to her wedding. Her mother, my great-grandmother, then cut it up and sewed it into a First Holy Communion dress for my mam. What could be reworked or reused would not be bought to be hoarded at the back of a wardrobe or wasted by working women. Even Queen Victoria's wedding dress and veil were repurposed to be worn again.

Many of the most iconic dresses of the twentieth century defy the Victorian bridal silhouette. For the wealthy, straighter lines dominated the early decades, with Grecian shapes like author Vita Sackville-West's sleek 'golden' dress for her 1913 wedding at her family home, Knole, in Kent. The bridal silhouette was shortened in the middle of the century before the Swinging Sixties. The year 1969 saw both style icons Yoko Ono and Audrey Hepburn push hemlines further, keeping the minidress alive, in their marriages to John Lennon and Andrea Dotti, respectively. Others still wore suits – like my gran long before Bianca Pérez-Mora Macías's iconic bridal suit for her marriage to Rolling Stones front man Mick Jagger, in 1971.

Despite its rejection by women across the twentieth century, the bridal silhouette and virginal white palette popularized by Queen Victoria's wedding had become ubiquitous with Western weddings by the dawn of the twenty-first century.[20] A new wedding industry had emerged as prosperity grew in the US and began to power and homogenize expectations on an unprecedented scale. The machine of wedding marketing spread consumerist wedding standards across huge chunks of the globe. I attended the wedding of a friend in 2016 who wore a beautiful dark green evening dress down the aisle, because she preferred the style and colour. It was a big deal: a quite shocking deviation. And beautiful and fitting. I crumbled under the pressure of trying not to spend too much money on a wedding dress and panic-bought an overpriced ex-display model.

In 2014, feminist author and activist Laura Bates debated in the UK paper *The Guardian* what to wear to marry her fiancé: 'should it be white?'

> *I get that the historic, one-sided virginal connotations are stupidly sexist. But I also feel quite confident that those associations have largely fallen away – nobody at our wedding will be under any illusions, knowing that we've lived together for five years ... I'm reclaiming the right to wear a white dress.*[21]

Exploring the complications and frustrations of trying to plan a feminist, opposite-sex wedding in the twentieth century, Bates concluded, 'surely at least a small part of being a feminist means forging new paths through old traditions?'[22]

White remains the choice of millions of brides today. Through a combination of British and American imperialism, an essentially Victorian white gown endures around the world. In East Asia, many Chinese women choose to wear two or three dresses at their weddings, including a white gown. Research with contemporary Vietnamese brides found women juggling pressure to create a harmonious balance between European tradition and local influences in the decision to wear a white gown or traditional áo dài. One bride in the 2013 study, Nga, expressed pressure from her future mother-in-law to wear a Western gown. 'I want to please her [so that] it will be easier for me when we live in the same house. I do not lose anything, right? I wore áo dài to greet guests; then I changed to the gown ... a wedding gown would make his mother happy.'[23]

In Japan, a white kimono in a Shinto wedding brings different symbolic meaning, representing the bride's willingness to be coloured by her new family, their values and customs. A blank canvas for the husband to write on. A traditional Japanese wedding might see the bride have several costume changes through the day. Shinto-style weddings dominated Japanese choices in the early twentieth century but are on the decline today, with European-influenced weddings making up two-thirds of ceremonies.

With the potential for diverse symbolism, tradition and choice, it seems a shame that it is Queen Victoria's tiny waist and emphasis on sexual purity that dominates the bridal industry in the UK and large chunks of the world today. Now an elaborate costume tradition, it was, ironically, a celebration of simplicity for the royal bride at the time.

In China, India and much of Asia, red is the bridal colour of choice, signifying life and luck, with white more traditionally worn at death. Red bridal clothing also has deep roots in Europe. Ancient Athenian brides, in Greece, wore reddish robes, cinched at the waist by a girdle that the groom loosened as a symbol of her impending sexual experience. Ancient Roman brides wore long, flame-coloured veils, transforming them into symbolic torches, bringing light and life to their new home and family. The procession of a heavily veiled bride was a definitive feature of a Roman wedding.[24] Around the world, very little bridal symbolism has been about empowering the bride's choices; more often reflecting the bride's sexual and procreative status and potential.

Bridal head coverings are an inherited costume tradition that cuts across religion, ethnicity, geography and class. From a Spanish mantilla to a bridal hijab, an Indian ghoonghat to a Japanese wataboshi hood. From fabrics designed to conceal the bride's face, to a sweep of material complementing an elaborate hairdo, it is easy to draw a line between today's bridal veils and ideas of women as protected, valuable, modest or sexually inexperienced beings. Most crucially of all, preserved for their new husbands. In European tradition, they are often connected to the moment where one man (the celebrant) gives another man (the groom) the permission to kiss the bride. It can be difficult to reconcile with feminist values.

However, veils are also beautiful. An opportunity for intricate, interesting and elaborate fabrics. Sometimes decadent and distinctive. I could not resist having a long tulle veil reach the ground behind me at my wedding. My wife was not tempted at all. She was far more keen on white Dr. Martens boots as her statement accessory. Decisions around wedding clothes can be empowering at a time when we are redefining what it means to be a person getting married. Old traditions can be understood in new ways, challenged, given new meaning and subverted.

Anjum Mouj, activist and board member of Queer Britain, the UK's first national LGBTQIA+ museum, has talked about the importance of adopting traditional practices and dress in her 2006 civil partnership ceremony with her wife. Speaking in 2020, she recounted her mum calling her on her engagement: 'I'm your mum and it's my job to buy your partner's wedding outfit' and transferring money into her account.[25] For Anjum, it was an important and moving moment, 'my mum doing something that she would do for all of her children'.

Anjum, and her wife, Dipti, travelled to India to shop for their wedding clothes. Both consciously chose to incorporate traditional bridal colours for their same-sex union – 'both brides in our beautiful bride way'.[26] Dipti chose a gold-and-ivory two piece with a classically Indian short top and gold and ivory scarf. Anjum chose a pink-and-red sari: 'it glittered and it sparkled and it was all the things that is me ... It was so fun to wear red and pink on my wedding day.'[27]

Just like me and my very-soon-to-be wife, Anjum and Dipti walked down the aisle together with their nieces and nephews. They chose Labi Siffre's protest anthem, 'So Strong', to play them into the room where the 250 guests awaited them. Civil partnerships had been available to same-sex couples in England for less than a year at that time. Same-sex marriage was still illegal.

> As we walked in, and the first note of that song went on, people stood up, stood on chairs, and started applauding and screaming ... There wasn't a dry eye in the house.[28]

Anjum, 'an Asian, Muslim lesbian', found 'peace and tranquillity' in Siffre's inspiring, political and resolute lyrics, 'as well as absolute rage ... rage to speak up and speak out ... It still sends shivers down my spine.'[29]

Anjum and Dipti consciously chose to curate their wedding 'with that component that *this is our right*' – a right previously denied to them, and others in the LGBTQIA+ community.

> At that point of our civil partnership in 2006 we were critically aware that there were many people, like us, that didn't have that privilege to be able to come out about their relationship, to come out and to share the joy of their love. So we absolutely went for a big Indian wedding, a big Asian wedding.[30]

These choices are rarely accidental.

Despite a long history of same-sex and trans weddings on every populated continent, there are 72 countries around the world where queer relationships are criminalized today. Where same-sex and trans weddings are allowed to take place, they remain a powerful statement of equality and love. There was not a dry eye at my wedding. Particularly mine. I cried my way through a ceremony that would have been unthinkable in my childhood, struggling without a tissue until one of the guests handed me one across the front row. Weddings are a joyous celebration of how far we have come. Looking back on her moving ceremony, Anjum also recalls, 'it was a real blast'.[31]

It is not easy to plan these powerful and romantic events, to make celebratory, fun and value-led choices outside of the pressures of the consumerist wedding industry – an industry increasingly looking to, sometimes clumsily, embrace new commercial opportunities. Wedding desirables continue to be transformed into essentials as budgets balloon. Some people actively resist and manage the material trappings of a wedding. A nikah is a relatively simple ceremony and celebration in many Muslim communities. Small ceremonies in registry offices provide an alternative for some to the paraphernalia and costs of a larger service and celebration. For feminist and activist Germaine Greer, writing in England at the dawn of the 1970s, 'The wedding is the chief ceremony of the middle-class mythology, and it functions as the official entrée of the spouses to their middle-class status. This is the real meaning of saving up to get married.'[32]

In the West, definitions of what a wedding is, and should be, have grown beyond the reasonable affordability of a large proportion of the population. And the planet. From plastic decorations, accessorises, ribbons and confetti, to long-distance travel to wedding venues and honeymoon destinations, lavish weddings leave a footprint. The clothes of the wedding party are often worn only once and then stored or discarded. Even guests feel pressure to change outfit from one occasion, one set of social media pictures, to another. It is a bubble that has to burst.

In 2022, I attended the Lancashire wedding of a friend whose guests had travelled a total distance of 39,544 miles to attend. Instead of traditional favours they donated to offset the carbon of our travel. In 2021, Indian actress Dia Mirza chose to raise the profile of environmental impact in the planning of her wedding to Vaibhav Rekhi. From local flowers and carefully planned food to wedding outfits that would be reworn and hired décor that could be used elsewhere, the avoidance of waste was prioritized in the relatively simple, high-profile celebrations.[33] So called 'green weddings' are the newest wedding trend around much of the world. From ethically sourced stones in engagement rings to eco-friendly paper for invitations, charity donations in lieu of gifts to sustainable decorations, people are beginning to become more conscious of the multiple costs – aside from financial – of the choices they make for their big day.

Despite the fact that only a handful of people in the past participated, it is the extravagant and performative choices of the wealthy and powerful that disproportionately define 'traditional' customs for many of us today. Class, race and religion have shaped the choices available to couples looking to celebrate their transition to newlyweds. The fashions of the elite went in and out and trickled down to the general public at variable speeds, for people to adapt, roll out, tweak and spread, according to their means. It is only very recently that these choices have been accessible on any scale. In planning our contemporary weddings, celebrations can speak to tradition, to religious faith and inheritance, to family, to values, personality and preference and to politics. Conscious statements can be curated and projected in the smallest of decisions. However, questions remain. Can more of us take control of the templates and messages that we have inherited when we share, mark and celebrate our weddings? Can we embrace the creative freedom newly accessible to us, while looking beyond both the problematic statements of the past and profit-driven pressures of today?

A CONSUMMATION TO BE DEVOUTLY WISHED?

Lie back and think of England.

**– APOCRYPHAL ADVICE FROM A MOTHER TO
A YOUNG BRIDE**

In whatever way your ceremony has been officiated, and by whom, whatever choices you have made for the celebrations afterwards, you are not done yet. Your wedding does not end there. The climax of the wedding, the consummation of the new marriage, lies ahead.

Across centuries and around the world, couples have known that their wedding would fail to transmute the relationship, to create a marriage, without this important end to their day. A variety of nuptial customs have hinted at this essential event, the beginning of a married life. Weddings have provided the one and only gateway to permitted sexual practices for communities around the world and sex has been required to define a marriage in many. Lack of consummation remains one of the few grounds for annulment to be recognized by spiritual and secular authorities around the world. For centuries, if you wanted to ensure that your wedding was valid, some energy would need to be saved for the finale.

The history of marriage is indivisible from the history of sex. Marriage has been a means for community leaders to restrict, control and sanction women's sexual practices throughout its long and diverse history. In Britain, medieval priests preached that women had insatiable sexual appetites that needed to be constrained. As the centuries unfolded, Georgian philanthropists found themselves supporting thousands of destitute babies, children lacking in a safety net after the abandonment of their mothers by their fathers. Victorian leaders, in the context of rapid and dramatic social change, decided that it was best for angelic women to have no sex drive at all. However, women's sexual experiences could not be shut down entirely – if nothing else, where would the next generation come from? The social and moral structures created by marriage allowed exclusively male authorities to enshrine the cognitive dissonance they experienced towards women's sexual desirability and power.

It was within this context that a major function of weddings in the West became the transformation of erotic experience from shameful taboo to celebrated act. Choices reprehensible one minute became required of you the next, and the conception of any children was no longer understood as a degenerate thing but a blessing, a celebrated and legitimized creation thereafter. The importance of this subtle, elusive transformation needed to be reflected on the big day.

From the ceremony itself to celebrations that followed, the fact of sanctioning a new sexual relationship has been present in wedding traditions for millennia. Emphasis on a bride's fertility were common. Ancient Romans threw fruit and nuts, symbols of fruitfulness, as confetti and the custom endured in Europe for centuries. In 1487, over 260 pounds, more than 18 stone, of dried fruit and honeyed nuts were said to be thrown and consumed at the wedding of Lucrezia Borgia.[1] Rice is thrown as a symbol of fertility at weddings around the world today.

In England, from the Tudor era, wealthy couples began to cut a cake together with a superstition that it might help the marriage to be sexually productive. For those who could not afford the symbolic ingredients of fruits and nuts, alternative recipes might be used. The earliest nuptial recipe recorded in Britain is that for a Bride's Pye in 1685. It includes, among other things, lamb's testicles.[2] A less charming fertility charm for poorer newlyweds.

Once the eating and drinking was done, it was time to turn more explicitly to the climax. For millennia, one of the most significant, communal elements of a wedding was the escort provided to newlyweds en route to their new sexual life together. The journey to the marital bed was simply too important to leave to the new spouses themselves. Until its fall in fashion in the eighteenth century, formal bedding was one of the most enduring European wedding traditions.

Two-and-a-half thousand years ago, countless Athenian potters sculpted vases with depictions of wedding processions: brides being led by torchlight to their new homes. So many were made between the sixth and fourth centuries BCE that many survive millennia later to provide glimpses into these young women's journeys. On arrival, the Athenian bride would be ceremonially separated from her mother and welcomed into the house with the same ritual of incorporation through which slaves were welcomed into a household.[3] Brides began to be physically, passively carried over the threshold by their new husband in a symbolic act of protection or ownership – the two often conflated in marriage. The newlyweds would then be taken into a bedchamber by family and friends. Guests of Athenian and Roman brides might stay late, after the procession, and sing and play music outside of the room.[4] The bedding ritual was widely adopted and adapted across Europe, alongside the rise of Christianity, in the millennia that followed.

Expectations regarding privacy were very different before the twentieth century and the marital bed was simply not a private space. The consummation of a marriage, and procreation of children, were public concerns. In a particularly invasive ritual, the bedsheet might be inspected, and sometimes displayed, the morning after a wedding night, so that blood from the bride's hymen might be seen. This humiliating 'virginity test' is a ritual that continues to be practised, despite its unreliability, following wedding celebrations in some communities today.

Numerous detailed records survive of the bedding ceremonies of the wealthiest couples in medieval and early modern Europe. A range of customs, habits and rituals fell in and out of fashion as generations of newlyweds were publicly put to bed. On arrival in the medieval or Tudor bedchamber, the groom might remove a garter worn by the bride and toss it for unmarried men to claim. It was known for the men to fight to remove the garter, or stockings, from the bride themselves. For centuries, guests threw the bride's warm stockings across the marital bed to determine who might marry next. The idea of men fighting to remove a woman's underwear is fairly repellent in the twenty-first century and, with the invention of nylon, garters have largely lost their original purpose. However, with their sexy symbolism, they remain an important wedding accessory for many brides today. In sixteenth-century Germany, the couple were put to bed with the sound of pipers, drums and 'obscene' noises. The music would continue long after the bedding, ostensibly drowning out any noise from within.

A bedding ceremony might be a light, relatively informal, part of the day for guests at many weddings but the ritual remained a crucial step on the road to creating a marriage. Something taken seriously. The participation of spiritual, family and community leaders asserted the authority of these moral guardians to authorize sex for the couple. When Catherine of Aragon was finally married to Arthur Tudor (then heir to Henry VII) after years of haggling, the fifteen-year-old bride was escorted from the feast by her ladies; she undressed and climbed into bed. Courtiers, musicians and the fifteen-year-old groom, wearing only his shirt, joined the semi-naked bride in the bedroom for the public celebration of the impending consummation. The most powerful bishops in the Church joined the revellers to perform a solemn blessing of the act.[5]

Following Arthur's death in 1502, Catherine later married his brother, Henry VIII, with papal dispensation, in 1509. Catherine's sister-in-law, Mary Tudor, was forced to endure a similar formal bedding ceremony in 1514, in order to marry the King of France, reluctantly; he was more than 30 years her elder. Mary lay on a bed in front of her brother, Henry, and his courtiers, semi-dressed. The Ambassador to France, acting as proxy for the French king, took off his scarlet stockings and lay beside her so that their bare legs touched.[6] The marriage to Louis XII was considered official and celebrated through the Court. There was no way back from there.

Public bedding ceremonies were not just for the aristocracy. In Scotland, where rules around weddings were less stringent than elsewhere in Britain, bedding ceremonies might be used as the legal foundation of marriage across class and wealth divides. In 1778, Margaret Ferguson and David McKie were put to bed in lieu of any other ceremony. A friend of the groom stood next to the bed and asked:

> *'You David McKie, take this woman to be your married wife.' To which McKie replied, 'I do before God and these Witnesses,' and then put the same question to [Margaret] To which she, from the confusion arising from her situation before strangers, answered 'Yes'. Whereupon Blair addressing himself to the Company, said, 'Friends, you hear and see this.'*[7]

The witnesses were largely David's friends and Margaret claimed that she did not realize that the ceremony was valid. When the case came to court, poor Margaret's bed-based wedding was found to be legally binding.

Bedding ceremonies must have been a humiliating prospect for generation after generation of women, gawked at by spectators in this intimate space, at this intimate moment. And terrifying. It was far too usual for women to be deliberately raised not just in ignorance of their own bodies, but that of the bodies of their potential sexual partners, across eras and nations – and the practice continues today. Historically, many women, particularly in the poorer classes, would have approached their wedding night with well-informed confidence, if not anticipation – perhaps drawn from previous sexual experience. For the fortunate ones, weddings could open the door to relatively safe, healthy and hopefully enjoyable sexual expression, but the reality was that this was not the norm for many.

By the eighteenth and nineteenth centuries, public bedding traditions had died out across much of the West, often replaced by some kind of ritual 'sending off'. The wealthiest Georgian brides would expect a new carriage for the occasion. However, like too many of their ancestors, countless brides continued to find themselves en route to their wedding night entirely ignorant of what was to come, unequipped to participate in what was about to happen to them. As Dr Charles A. Hoff, author of *Highways and Byways to Health,* reflected:

> *What wonder that some brides have come to their mothers and female friends after marriage, to whom they had a right to look for advice and warning concerning these things, and, with passionate tears of shame and indignation, have reproached them bitterly, saying: 'Oh, why didn't you tell me!'*[8]

In the 1920s, a small study of more than 2,000 married American women found that a quarter had been 'repelled' by their first sexual experience. The few women who expressed pleasure within their marital sex life reported feelings of shame at their own passion or enjoyment.[9]

Greater access to knowledge about their own bodies, and those of their sexual partners, was gained by swathes of women across the West as the century unfolded. The value of sex education remains contested by networks like the US Christian Right, however, as well as other often religious organizations, which campaign against educating young people about sexual practices before they experience them. Ignorance has rarely been bliss for girls and women, more commonly breeding vulnerability, fear, exploitation and pain.

With such poor education, the idea of consent has had little meaning in women's marital beds throughout swathes of our shared history. Women and girls prevented from accessing information around their own bodies had very little ability to consent to what happened to them. If information is power, a power imbalance was consciously created in diverse societies around the world for this very vulnerable moment. And, on first marriage, many were very young. This first sexual experience as man and wife was not for pleasure or for the gratification of either party. Among the wealthier classes, there was no question of not being in the mood and the pressure on boys and men was not insignificant. Consummation was a duty for both, and a public one.

Tragically, for many a bride, her wedding night might have been the last opportunity for her to exercise sexual consent at all. For centuries, in European tradition, having expressed their willingness at the altar and followed through with consummation, brides sacrificed their right to withdraw it. For many, the man they shared a sexual experience with on their wedding night had unrestricted sexual access to them for the rest of their life. A husband had the right, under law, to have sex with his wife – consent irrelevant: it was not until 1991 that women in England had legal protection from rape committed by their spouses.

With cohabiting before marriage now the norm, in the twenty-first century, for huge numbers of people across much of the West, the wedding night holds fewer surprises today. My wife and I travelled to our wedding from our flat in London together and stayed in the same hotel room the night before and the night after the big day. Nothing felt more natural than continuing the routine intimacy. However, it is still far more usual for even cohabiting couples to spend the night before their wedding apart. The pull of tradition is irresistible, it seems, and superstitions abound – it is thought by some to be bad luck for a bride and groom to see each other the morning of their wedding.

Customs relating to the marital bed survive around the world. In traditional Chinese weddings, the An Chuang ceremony takes place in preparation for the big day. A chosen group of people, usually relatives, decorate the bed with symbolic gifts to bring blessings of happiness and children to the new couple. A child may be allowed to jump on the bed to bring good luck to the fertility of the newlyweds. Similarly, babies are placed on wedding beds in the Czech Republic and symbolic items like money and rice may be strewn across beds in parts of Europe and Asia.

For couples already living together, relatively little changes immediately after a wedding. For brides of the past, a wedding might bring with it a relocation, a new house and household, sometimes some distance away from their former familial homes. It signalled the beginning of new relationships, a new family, a new routine to their daily lives. It was the start of expanded or restricted opportunities. The conclusion of one chapter and the start of a new one. As the sun set and the Big Day drew to a close, many women found that everything in their lives had changed.

—

It has always been at moments of transition, as we move sometimes subtly, from one life stage to another, that we are most drawn back to the past, to tradition, to the customs passed down to us. When we feel most compelled to walk in the footsteps of those who have gone before us. It can be a powerful and moving experience to access that privilege. However, we should be cautious of walking blindly. It is not difficult to draw a line between the choices available to couples planning their weddings today and systems that embedded inequalities around sex, gender, sexuality, class, race and religion. Many of the traditions that we inherit and continue to pass down in our weddings today are tainted by the injustices of the past.

From expectations of who wears what to symbolic gestures throughout the day; from who may speak, in what order and when, to the continued exclusion of marginalized groups, we find it difficult to deviate from the default assumptions within our communities. Slow to change, customs and traditions can feel at odds with contemporary value systems and the lives of couples themselves.

People in authority have long fought over control of the ceremony that would transform a woman into a wife – dictating who was eligible to participate, how and where – tweaking and adapting for their own ends along the way. It is a battle that continues to be fought vigorously today in resistance to marriage equality, and one in which women were long excluded from participating. In Britain and the West, generations of male authorities found weddings to be a useful tool in forcing women to prioritize the role of subordinate partner and mother across their lives. Generation after generation of women were forced to solemnly promise to obey a man. Keen to prioritize the paternity of children in their inheritance structures, male leaders heavily regulated women's sexual practices through the promises made at their weddings. Until relatively recently, the rules, taboos and laws around weddings and marriage were routinely tightened, restricted and homogenized by state leaders within Britain and through its colonial expansion across the globe. In recent decades, private companies, who together form a multibillion-dollar industry, have found themselves increasingly invested in the choices made by couples as they say 'I do' – another set of stakeholders who bring their own agenda to your big day.

The diversity of history's wedding practices has become obscured, hidden, sometimes lost. For millennia, people have taken the leap to formally commit to each other in marriage, creating moments understood to mark the transition. Communities have come together, stepped outside of the everyday and celebrated a new bond. They have often looked back to the past at this moment of stepping forward into their future together. The vows made to define the new relationship, the style and scale of ceremony and celebrations chosen, the happiness and anxieties experienced by participants on the day would each hint at what was to come next. How we marry can cast a long shadow through a marriage. Sometimes joyous sanctuary, a place to return to, to renew and energize the relationship through time; and sometimes full of sorrow. History shows us that inequalities on display at a wedding risk playing out in the marriage.

WHAT COMES NEXT?

WHAT'S IN A NAME?

I'd be very content if I could take a story of two perfectly normal newlyweds, bursting with good health and sexual energy, and make a good story out of it.

– PATRICIA HIGHSMITH, WRITER, DIARY ENTRY,
7 AUGUST 1942[1]

Good stories are rarely made of the comfortable, happy marriages of 'normal' people. In history, so many of the quiet, everyday relationships of the past have been hidden or lost. Narratives of turmoil, conflict and upheaval have been more often recorded and survive to tell a tale today. In reflecting on the lived experiences of history's marriages, stark inequalities deeply entrenched in culture and in law provide an often-challenging picture. These inequalities and oppressions have been fiercely protected by generations of people in positions of privilege and power. Yet often fought and overcome by the resistance, fearless campaigning and activism of women forced to endure injustice in their own lives, inside their homes and within their most intimate of relationships.

For women around the world, weddings have opened doors. Generation after generation of women found that marriage created opportunities that would have been otherwise inaccessible to them – changed prospects in work and status, a new home, family and community, a loving partnership, the chance of parenthood and the opportunity for sexual development. For millennia, brides have understood that, following their weddings, a new set of rules would apply to them. Expectations around everyday routines would shift and bring practical changes to their lives. As wives, the laws imposed by distant authorities now would or would not apply to them; legal rights and responsibilities were often altered. For many women entering into marriage, their identity, their expression as a person of independent body and mind, underwent great transformation.

—

In 1855, the death of a Charlotte Nicholls, profession 'wife of curate', was recorded in West Yorkshire. She had made the short walk to her wedding, from parsonage to church, just nine months earlier and is better known to many globally by her maiden name, Brontë. By the time she married, Charlotte, along with her sisters Emily and Anne, had already written some of the most iconic novels in the English language, published under the names of Currer, Ellis and Acton Bell to preserve their identities as women. They had worked not only as writers but as teachers and governesses, locally and abroad.

On marrying her father's curate, Charlotte Brontë relinquished not only her name, but her public, legal voice. The right to sue or be sued or enter into contracts as well as the rights to her property and income. From her wedding day, her novels belonged to her husband. She relinquished legal ownership of her physical person, her body and anything it produced: intellectual or manual labour, sex and children.

For centuries in the West, a wedding expanded the rights of men and contracted the rights of women. Within Brontë's most famous novel, *Jane Eyre*, the eponymous heroine's interest, Mr Rochester, imprisons his first wife. He has transported the woman known as Bertha Mason more than 4,000 miles from her home, from her family, friends, climate, continent, everything and everyone she has known. He denies her existence and locks her up in a cold, lonely wing of his Yorkshire house. She becomes the proverbial madwoman in the attic. And he can do that: Rochester's a wealthy, powerful man and he has broken no law or cultural taboo. His power and authority are not questioned until Jane discovers Bertha's existence on the day she herself is meant to marry Rochester, and leaves. Rochester was about to commit bigamy and make Jane complicit. Yet, he is still the happy ending for Jane at the end of the book.

European laws were based on an early medieval inheritance. In the Bible, Eve was a secondary creation drawn from Adam's rib. They were one and, in marriage, man and woman became one entity again – an entity defined by the husband. In Britain, for centuries, a woman's existence as an autonomous person was relinquished at her wedding in a 'civil death'.[2] In the 1760s, Sir William Blackstone, a judge and Tory politician, articulated the long-standing position of married women in English law:

> *By marriage, the husband and wife are one person in law: that is, the very being or legal existence of the woman is suspended during the marriage, or at least is incorporated and consolidated into that of the husband: under whose wing, protection, and cover, she performs everything ... her condition during marriage is called her coverture.*[3]

The idea of coverture is built on Anglo-Saxon and Norman foundations. In early medieval cities, some women had managed to circumvent restrictions in France and England as *feme sole* [sic] (in Norman French 'single woman', although this also applied to divorcées and widows). They successfully petitioned authorities to allow them to conduct their own businesses despite their marital status and to act independently of their husbands. However, by the eighteenth-century, Blackstone's definition had taken deep root and germinated across England. Throughout the country, the very existence of a woman in law was automatically and routinely lost, 'suspended', following her wedding.

As European authorities spread their colonial mission across the globe, coverture became a major export. Blackstone's definition oppressed the rights of women in territories colonized by British rule sometimes long after colonial oppression had ended. In North America, as the Revolutionary War began, Abigail Adams, a leading and early advocate of women's rights, saw an opportunity to shake off the marital yoke of the past. Writing to her husband, John Adams, the second US president, in March 1776, she encouraged him to abandon the medieval English laws still practised across the Atlantic: to abolish coverture. She requested that:

> *In the new Code of Laws which I suppose it will be necessary for you to make I desire you would Remember the Ladies, and be more generous and favorable to them than your ancestors. Do not put such unlimited power into the hands of the Husbands. Remember all Men would be tyrants if they could.*[4]

John replied to Abigail's challenge by writing 'I cannot but laugh.' He argued that the struggle for independence had caused children to be more disobedient, Native Americans to 'slight their guardians' and the Black population to grow 'insolent to their masters'. In the face of so much dissent, he stated, 'depend upon it, we know better than to repeal our masculine systems'.[5] In other words, eighteenth-century freedoms were for white men.

Throughout the West, laws were written by these white men with the intention – expressed explicitly by John Adams and other Founders – of keeping the social and economic lid pressed down very firmly on everyone else. The subjection of women by the men they married shored up male power at every level of society. Power dynamics are unique to every marriage and, of course, not all husbands would exercise the tyrannical power they gained at their wedding. Recognizing and acknowledging the 'full force' of coverture and 'masculine systems' over women, Adams went on to tell his wife not to worry – that 'we dare not exert our power in its full latitude'.[6] Very reassuring.

However, power corrupts. And absolute power corrupts absolutely. The reality for women entering marriage in British tradition, for centuries, was that the law would provide them with no protection from the men they married and would give them no independent, social, political or economic voice. This was not new. In ancient Rome, a wife held the equivalent legal status as that of her husband's child[7] and for centuries, in England and in territories under its colonial rule, children had more legal power, more legal standing, than married women.

Across class divides, husbands could spend resources taken from their wives as they pleased. They might squander money, spend it on drinking, gambling or sex; throw it away to nothing; or prevent their wives accessing their own money to meet their most basic needs or to exercise choice and pursue their own pleasure. None of these circumstances would provide women with any recourse to support, appeal or escape. Only the very wealthiest of women, able to access a settlement to be held in trust by the courts, could access security through independent property. Most women had no alternative but to hand over any income to the man they married.

A century after Abigail Adam's appeal to her husband, in the middle of the 1800s, women began to campaign for reform across huge swathes of the world. In London, leading suffragist Millicent Garrett Fawcett had her purse stolen and proclaimed when the thief was charged with stealing the property of her husband: 'I felt as if I had been charged with theft myself.' Both the resources women brought to their marriages and the earnings they generated within them belonged to their spouse. Some marriages were supported almost entirely by a wife's inheritance or income. In a political speech, Fawcett recalled the absurdity that, when her husband made his will, he was required to bequeath her the copyright to her own book.

In 1855, Fawcett, alongside other frustrated and angry women, formed the Married Women's Property Committee (MWPC). Some 26,000 signatures were collected to petition Parliament for reform. The petition stated:

> *It is time that legal protection be thrown over the produce of [women's] labour, and that in entering the state of marriage, they no longer pass from freedom into the condition of a slave, all whose earnings belong to his master and not to himself.*[8]

In the middle of the nineteenth century, suffragists in the United States fought for their rights to be recognized as independent people and citizens.

In the same year as the MWPC petitioned Parliament in London, across the Atlantic in Massachusetts, suffragist Lucy Stone walked down the aisle to marry fellow abolitionist Henry B. Blackwell. They did not enter the institution lightly. Stone and her husband-to-be prepared a long statement to be read out within their service that explicitly protested the presence of coverture in American laws:

> *We believe that personal independence and equal human rights can never be forfeited, except for crime; that marriage should be an equal and permanent partnership, and so recognized by law.*[9]

Stone amended her marriage vows and insisted on retaining her name. Fellow suffragist Susan B. Anthony described Stone as 'the first woman in the nation to protest against the marriage laws at the altar, and to manifest sufficient self-respect to keep her own name, to represent her individual existence through life'.

Laws, customs and practices change at varying speeds. Over the last 150 years, legal reforms have been made, slowly, incrementally, to shake off coverture in laws around the world, but its cultural legacy has not died. More than a century and a half since Lucy Stone resisted pressure to relinquish her family name on marriage, the identities of millions of brides are still routinely absorbed into a new husband's.

In 2016, a survey found that 70 per cent of married women in America had begun their married life by conforming to an expectation that they change their name.[10] In Britain, research in the same year found it to be nearly 90 per cent.[11] In opposite-sex marriages, the new family name, it is still expected for many, will automatically be the groom's. In Japan, the law does not recognize the marriage of a husband and wife who have different surnames: in 2021, 96 per cent of wives took the last name of the man they married.[12] And at the time of writing, same-sex marriage has yet to be legalized in Japan.

I have the same surname as my sisters-in-law, who married into the family, but not my sister, who ostensibly married out. In the UK, women in opposite-sex relationships can change their surname simply with their wedding certificates. However, any other name change, including a man taking his wife's surname, requires a deed poll, a more complicated legal process.

In 2019, research into women's motivations for changing their name on marriage highlighted the pressure of expectation. In one interview, a participant felt that it was 'traditional and conventional'.[13] For another: 'I think if you've kept your name it's kind of like saying I'm not really that committed to you.'[14] Another respondent went further: 'I actually didn't want to change my name but ... he said if that hadn't changed there would have been no point getting married

... he said the wedding would mean nothing.'[15]

I have heard men I grew up with say that they would be angry if their fiancée did not want to take their name – meaning give up their own. I think they meant embarrassed. In a culture of toxic masculinity, anger feels like the more socially acceptable expression of hurt. The pressure of tradition and convention can feel very heavy.

In countries and communities around the world, billions of women marry without expectation that they relinquish their family names. In much of East Asia, including China, Korea and Taiwan, women do not routinely give up the name they received from their parents at birth when they commit to a partner. A new spouse has not traditionally trumped a filial relationship. The same is true in much of the Islamic world. From Iceland to Spain, and in many Spanish-speaking countries, it simply has not been the custom. In the 1970s and 1980s, in an effort to combat gender inequality within the wide-reaching feminist wave of the time, laws were passed in Greece, Italy and Quebec, Canada, prohibiting women from giving up their surname following a marriage. The bans instantly rewrote the custom within those territories and, even today, have proven to be uncontroversial.

There is a long history throughout the UK of women holding on to their family names when they could. In England, women were not routinely expected to give up their names on marriage before the Norman Conquest. It was relatively unusual for Scottish women before the twentieth century. In 1777, when Mary Eleanor Bowes, Countess of Strathmore and Kinghorne, married Andrew Robinson Stoney, in Piccadilly, London, the latter took her name. With her enormous wealth and status, and his lack of either, Stoney was very happy to become a Bowes. Similarly, when writer Vita Sackville-West married diplomat Harold Nicolson in 1913 there was little doubt that she would keep her illustrious moniker. There are numerous other examples, yet still, in the twenty-first century, many women assume that the man's name is the default, the best or the easiest option on marriage. There has always been more than one way to make a 'traditional' choice.

In same-sex, trans and nonbinary marriages, we are generally more free from the pressure of expectation and idealized tradition. I did not change my name. My wife and I discussed it and considered double barrelling but did not follow through in the end. We were happy with our names as they were. And changing your name is about more than symbolic identity – it has practical consequences. Consequences only rarely faced by men. In many careers, in the creative industries, academia, family businesses and jobs that require active networking and reputation building, women suffer for the loss of their professional 'brand'.

With more than a third of marriages in the UK ending in divorce, thousands of women are left in an uncomfortable position, and faced with a difficult choice, every year. Do they change their names back? And incur social confusion? I have worked with a number of women who have changed their surname. Watching them correct their colleagues to their new name, be congratulated on getting married and having to correct them again after they have just got divorced is not great. Or should they keep their ex-husband's name? While they may be unable to fully escape the shadow of what is often a painful time, their ex-husbands roam free with one less thing to worry about.

And then there is the question of children. What do you do? If you keep your own name in an opposite-sex marriage, might you then have a different name to your children who, by default have the last name of their male parent? And surely that would be confusing at parents' evenings? Or passport control?

The choice for brides does not have to be between giving up their name or having a different name to their children – there are other options to explore – but the right of fathers to have their children bear their last names is still rarely questioned in the United Kingdom and, indeed, much of the world. Even women who are not married and intend to be the primary carer of their baby can feel compelled to give it the last name of the father over their own. I have watched friends pressured into that decision in young relationships and regret it when the relationships broke down. Close-knit family groups of siblings, with different fathers, who live their whole lives together with their mother can end up with different names from each other and their primary carer. It is not the obvious choice.

Brides, in the United Kingdom, and much of the English-speaking world today, continue to not only be conferred a new name at the commencement of their marriage but a new title – as they forgo the 'Miss' of their childhood and graduate to 'Mrs'. In the 1970s, as the Women's Liberation Movement swept through the West, the alternative 'Ms' began to take off, catapulted by the success of *Ms* magazine in the United States.

Half a century later, the commercialization of wedding practices puts new and increasing emphasis on becoming a 'Mrs' on your big day though. 'Future Mrs Smith' veils and T-shirts are sold to brides-to-be and 'Mr and Mrs' is a recurring motif on the wedding cards, mementos and gifts sold through a wedding industry keen to celebrate the dramatic change in social status for a bride. Yet nothing new for a groom. The archaic practice of sticking 'Mrs' in front of a man's last name to create his wife's formal address is still practised. I remember, as a child, the first time I saw my mam's name expressed in that way on an envelope, I assumed it was some kind of error. What a silly mistake to make! It just made no sense.

I am routinely asked whether I am 'a Miss or a Mrs' in the most absurd situations. I have always been grateful to have the choice of opting out and introducing myself as 'Ms'. Why does the salesperson selling me a car need to know whether I am married? The National Trust volunteer signing me up for membership? The cashier at the bank? They would not be finding out my brothers' marital status in the same situation.

These inequalities and intrusions are expected and accepted and do not seem to come at much of a cost, but they are a symbolic and a practical legacy of the very recent past. Why does the salesperson selling me a car need to know whether or not I'm married? Because, barely more than a generation ago, married women were prevented from applying for financial credit without their husband's permission. It was the 1960s and 1970s before married women in the UK and the US could open up a bank account, access a mortgage or make a non-routine purchase without proof, written permission, that their husband had authorized the choice.

In Margaret Atwood's seminal novel, *The Handmaid's Tale*, when these measures are reintroduced into a fictionalized North America, protagonist Offred realizes that her husband 'doesn't mind this [...] We're not each other's anymore. Instead, I am his.'[16] When she later finds her identity suspended under a man's 'wing' once more she reflects of her new name:

> *My name isn't Offred, I have another name, which nobody uses now because it's forbidden. I tell myself it doesn't matter, your name is like your telephone number, useful only to others; but what I tell myself is wrong, it does matter.*[17]

When the *Ms* periodical was launched in 1972 by Gloria Steinem, Patricia Carbine and a team of activists, it challenged the marital labels that followed women throughout their lives. It is difficult for me to imagine entering into the institution of marriage that existed in the generations before the Liberation Movement of the 1970s and the LGBTQIA+ activists since. We owe them a huge debt. For the privileged few, it is now possible to imagine and to live a married life as a partnership of two autonomous equals.

LOVE, FAIR LOOKS AND TRUE OBEDIENCE

Don't forget that it is every married woman's duty to come down in the morning with a smile.

– DOS AND DON'TS FOR WIVES, 1936

I am not full of smiles for my wife before my morning coffee. In fairness, she is pretty bright first thing, but the obligation to smile is a grim one. Give us a smile, love.

The *Good Wife* guides of the nineteenth and early twentieth centuries defined the role of a wife very clearly. A wife should sacrifice, she should smile for her husband, dress herself and their home for his pleasure, bear and raise his children, repress any unhappiness and, daily, negotiate his mood to ensure that she could anticipate and meet his every whim. However, be warned: 'Don't be one of those wives who demand their husbands to do this or that for them.'[1]

A woman could not expect the sacrifices made for her husband to be reciprocated though. In British tradition, the wedding set the tone. A woman's rights and responsibilities as a wife were well reflected in the solemn promises she made at her wedding: to love, honour and obey her husband. To submit, unconditionally, mind and body, and to be happy about it.

A promise of obedience to the groom standing next to them was made by brides for centuries in British tradition. Although most of the world's major religions and cultures do not require specific vows to be made from one partner to another on their wedding days, a similar emphasis on wifely submission has long been reflected in patriarchal customs, laws and expectations around the world. In much of the West, the Anglican promises penned and propagated by Thomas Cranmer in the 1500s provided a cornerstone of 'traditional' marriage until relatively recently, as we have seen.

It is difficult to imagine how the promise to obey a partner throughout a marriage could ever have been imagined reasonable. Or realistic. Or desirable. However, from the medieval period to the twentieth century, promises of obedience reflected the expectation that a wife should submit to a husband. It was a promise that risked being enforced. Legally disabled, married women faced moral, social and cultural pressure to dedicate their lives to their husband's decisions and desires. It is difficult to overstate the power of these layers of pressure and expectation.

Nowhere is the submission of a woman, the obedience of a wife, more clearly celebrated than in Shakespeare's *Taming of the Shrew*. Said shrew Katherine is forced to marry a man who wants her for her money: 'I must forsooth be forced / To give my hand opposed against my heart.'[2] Her new husband humiliates her at the wedding and openly aims to subjugate Katherine's will. Not only is her property now his, *she* is: 'She is my goods, my chattels. She is my house, / My household-stuff, my field, my barn, / My horse, my ox, my ass, my anything.'[3] He drags her away from the wedding and isolates her in his country home where he tortures her, gaslights her and prevents her from eating or sleeping until she submits to his tyranny.

I have wanted so strongly to boo the stage when Katherine admits, at her husband's insistence, that the moon is in fact the sun – 'Then God be blessed, it is the blessed sun, / But sun it is not when you say it is not'[4] – knowing herself to be right and him to be wrong and that he is deliberately toying with her. Subjugating your reason for the comfort of a, perhaps less capable, man brings a cost. Being told that it is your moral duty to be less than you are, is a lose-lose situation. It is not enough that Katherine submits her wealth, her body, her health and pride to her husband, he wants her intellect and her will. And he is entitled to it.

The play ends with a competition between the three new husbands as to whose wife will obey them first when summoned. Katherine responds first, and quickly, to her husband's call and gives surely the most difficult speech of Shakespeare's canon for an actor to deliver today.

> *Thy husband is thy lord, thy life, thy keeper,*
> *Thy head, thy sovereign, one that cares for thee,*
> *And for thy maintenance commits his body*
> *To painful labour ...*
> *And craves no other tribute at thy hands*
> *But love, fair looks, and true obedience,*
> *Too little payment for so great a debt.*[5]

The shrew has learnt to let go of her temper and wit. To no longer 'bandy ... frown for frown'[6] but happily kneel and place her hand under her husband's foot. Should it please him to trample her. Directors, theatre companies and filmmakers still struggle today to find ways to interpret the taming of Katherine Minola for new generations.

The *Taming of the Shrew* is not an anomaly. Two hundred years before Shakespeare penned his play, William Langland lamented, in a narrative poem, the three things that might drive a man from his home. A leaking roof, a smoky fire and, most surely of all, 'a shrewish wife who will not be chastised; her mate flees for fear of her tongue ... ' *Vision of Piers Plowman*. In Shakespeare's England, a rhyming proverb casually joked: 'A spaniel, a woman and a walnut tree, the more they're beaten the better they be.'[7] It reflected the dark reality that, as the *Taming of the Shrew* was being written, it was illegal in London for a husband to beat his wife after 9 p.m. in case the noise disturbed his neighbours' sleep.[8] The submission of women through love and marriage is a theme that runs across centuries of literature and culture. Women are chastised and corrected by their romantic partners from Austen's novels in the eighteenth century to romcom movies in the twenty-first.

The moral and social pressure on wives to happily obey has a long history around much of the globe. In China, in the sixth century BCE, Confucius defined a wife as someone who acquiesces to another. 'While at home she obeys her father. After marriage she obeys her husband. After he dies, she obeys her son.'[9] In the third century BCE, the Chinese philosopher Xunzi, declared 'women shall not disobey her husband and son, she shall be mild with obedience and listen to the orders'.[10] Confucianism was built into Chinese law and still influences women's rights in parts of East Asia today. In most of the world's major religions and philosophies, centuries of interpretation and practices developed by men built the submission of women into the very definition of marriage.

In much of the West, the subjugation of wives was justified by biblical means well into the nineteenth century. A marriage guide published in Boston in the 1840s claimed of wives that:

> *Something of submission is certainly due. There was a time, in the history of our world, when woman did not exist. Man was not only alone – without a companion – but destitute of a 'help-meet' – an assistant. In these circumstances, almighty Power called forth … the name of woman and presented her to man. She was to be man's assistant.*[11]

The hierarchy was clear – and divinely ordained. Victorians took the idealization of female submission to a new level. Society embraced the idea of man and wife becoming one, witnessed by God, under the leadership of the man. Coventry Patmore's iconic narrative poem, 'The Angel in the House', first published in 1854, epitomized the ideal of a married woman as docile and domestic. She was self-effacing, self-sacrificing and, above all, devoted to pleasing her husband. She held no ambitions independent from him and happily obeyed the man of the house.

The romantic ideal of the angel-wife was reinforced in poetry, novels and popular periodicals. A nineteenth-century American publication, *The Ladies' Garland*, tells of Hester, a beautiful young woman who is thrilled to marry a good husband but then lets herself go.[12] Once 'her fortune made', she dresses well only when going out. Her husband is, of course, repulsed by her slovenly look when she relaxes at home. Hester finds herself chastised by her sister when the young wife is discovered 'dressed in her dirty, though fashionable frock, her hair partially papered' on an unannounced visit.[13] Her sister warns her against taking her responsibilities as a married woman too lightly: 'Believe me, a wife's assiduous endeavours to please her husband is [sic] the only way to secure an interest in his affections. What can yield such a rich reward for our labors as a husband's approving smile?'[14]

Hester does not heed the advice. Embarrassed by his wife's lack of effort in her appearance, the husband begins to meet friends at the local tavern rather than at home. 'From that day his flourishing business and his handsome wife become more and more neglected.'[15] He descends into alcoholism and bankruptcy and they lose everything. A cautionary tale for wives everywhere. Something for us all to think about the next time we reach for jogging bottoms and a scrunchie.

Most wives from across social divides, as actual human beings, failed to live up to the vision of the 'Angel in the House'. So what was a man to do if his wife's looks faded? Or she relentlessly nagged? Asked for too much money? If she enjoyed the company of other men? Or held, and even shared, strong opinions? What if she got angry when he was unfaithful, wasted their money or made harmful choices? What if the clothes her husband dumped on the floor last night were still there the next day?

Women became the responsibility of their husbands on marriage. Politically and economically, they were entirely hidden behind them and socially their responsibility. Husbands were not only entitled but obliged to correct their wives, should they see fit. Married men were empowered to exercise all kinds of coercive control, manipulation and psychological and physical abuses. Of course, not all husbands exercised the power they were given by society and the state – some lived supportive roles as loving and respectful partners – but many did.

For the romantic Victorians, actively creating a new ideal of domestic wedded bliss, the celebration of a submissive wife was accompanied by a growing distaste with the means by which a husband might achieve obedience. As the nineteenth century progressed, awareness of the problem of 'wife torture' grew. Novelists returned to the theme of intimate partner violence again and again. Works by Anne and Emily Brontë, George Eliot, Anthony Trollope and Arthur Conan Doyle all depict women suffering physical and emotional abuse at the hands of their husbands. Some fictionalized creations, like Dickens' Nancy in *Oliver Twist*, epitomized impoverished, uneducated and sympathetic young victims, vulnerable to the abuse of rough, villainous men. Many narratives, particularly in the writings of women, reflected the reality that abusive husbands were not confined to the crowded homes and slums of the poor.

Newspaper owners, editors and journalists, reluctant to peek too closely behind the closed doors of friends and peers, focused on the problems of the working poor. They reported extreme cases of abuse to the outrage of the literate public. The Industrial Revolution had created brutal working practices in booming industries, piling thousands of families into cramped and impoverished living conditions. In 1853, a London paper stated that 'wife and woman-beating' had 'become a custom'.[16] Furthermore, 'public opinion, which is the great regulator of social intercourse, does not declare itself against wife-beating amongst these classes'.[17] Another newspaper reported that 'this crime, deepened now and then with the darker of murder' seems to be on the increase.[18]

Public attention was stirred. In 1853, the Criminal Procedure Act, also known as the Act for the Better Prevention and Punishment of Aggravated Assaults upon Women and Children, was passed by the UK Parliament. The Act was the first major effort by the authorities to dictate that not all violent chastisement of a woman by her husband was acceptable. However, this legal landmark represented little real change in people's homes. Victims rarely had means of escape and victim blaming was the norm.

Centuries of court records show the relatively rare cases where women were empowered to try to find recourse. In 1858, Charlotte Bostock, the wife of a relatively wealthy London druggist, went to court after 30 years of violence, to secure her freedom and safety. Her husband attempted to justify his behaviour towards her in the court by citing her extravagance and her neglect 'of her household duties'. She recounted being forced to lock herself in the children's bedroom to escape his violent sexual advances and taking the children away to stay with relatives. Escapes that usually resulted in further conflict.[19]

When women sought justice, they were regularly encouraged by authorities to seek safety in submission. Sacrifice more. Bend. Make the best of it. Some nineteenth-century magistrates provided homilies on the sovereignty of husbands and the responsibilities of wives to submit and be docile. Sir William Scott reminded a Mrs Waring that if she provoked 'danger to her person' from her husband the law had no interest in intervening:

If the conduct of a wife is inconsistent with the duties of that character, and provokes the just indignation of the husband, and causes danger to her person, she must seek the remedy for that evil, so provoked, in the change of her own manners.[20]

In the eyes of the law, the violence she was victim to was a natural punishment for her choices.

Reformers, political writers, lawyers and activists took up the pen to express their concern. In 1869, British philosopher and economist John Stuart Mill published *The Subjection of Women* and observed, like the American Abigail Adams before him, that the tyrannical power granted to husbands in the law made abusers of them. He wrote that husbands were given 'a notion that the law has delivered [wives] to them as their thing, to be used at their pleasure', further reflecting the tragedy of marriage was that they are not expected to practise the consideration towards her, which is required from them towards everybody else.[21]

In 1877, lawyer Alexander Pulling called for new legislation, pointing particularly to England's fast-growing, young industrial towns:

Nowhere is the ill-usage of woman so systematic and so little hindered by the supposed strong arm of the law; making the lot of a married woman whose locality is the 'kicking district' of Liverpool simply a duration of suffering and subjection to injury and savage treatment.[22]

These northern women were already fighting to survive poverty, disease, low pay, long working hours and harsh conditions to support their families. The 'supposed strong arm of the law' continued to be designed, enforced and prosecuted exclusively by privileged men, and, largely, for them.

However, the 'first wave' of feminism was beginning to build. In

1878, Frances Power Cobbe published an article titled 'Wife Torture in England'. Born in Dublin in 1822, Cobbe was an animal-rights campaigner, suffragist, writer and lesbian. Within her lifetime, she wrote over 20 books on Victorian women, medicine and religion, and published innumerable articles and pamphlets.[23] 'Wife Torture in England' drew attention to both the physical and the mental torture endured by women unable to escape their marriages. Cobbe stated that, for working women, 'the whole relation between the sexes ... is very little better than one of master and slave'. Evoking Britain's recent history with slavery, she called on the support of evangelical abolitionists and presented the moral and spiritual imperative for reform.

Cobbe was successful in shifting public opinion. In 1878, the Matrimonial Causes Act enabled some wives to access some freedom from violent and abusive husbands. In her autobiography, Cobbe reflected:

> *The part of my work for women ... to which I look back with most*
> *satisfaction was that in which I laboured to obtain protection for*
> *unhappy wives, beaten, mangled, mutilated or trampled on by*
> *brutal husbands.*[24]

Suffragists like Cobbe, organized into local, national and international networks in their fight for the right to vote, campaigned against injustices faced by women in all areas of their lives. Decade after decade, they began to rewrite the role of women within society. They challenged women's obedience to the men they married and fought against the idea that women should dedicate their lives to becoming domestic angels.

Three years after women achieved the vote on the same terms as men in the United Kingdom, in 1931 Virginia Woolf wrote that 'Killing the Angel in the House was part of the occupation of a woman writer'.[25] After falling briefly out of fashion at the start of the twentieth century,

Patmore's spectre still haunted women across the West as conservative forces worked hard to keep her alive. The 1930s to 1950s saw a resurgence in the idea of a 'traditional' wife. Popular 'good wife guides' encouraged brides to embrace obedience to their partners:

> *Don't sneer at the word 'obey' in the marriage service and call it old fashioned. There is a great deal of truth in Tennyson's words that an obedient wife commands her husband.*[26]

Despite an attempt to remove the vow of obedience from the Anglican wedding service in the 1920s, generations of women continued to find themselves promising submission to the groom on their wedding days. In 1947, when Princess Elizabeth (the future Elizabeth II) married Prince Philip, she promised to 'obey' him. After the liberation of women from the domestic sphere in the Second World War, authorities were quick to push them back in again. The American magazine *House Beautiful* reminded wives in the years immediately following the end of the war that 'He's Head man again.' 'Your part ... is to fit his home to him, understanding why he wants it this way, forgetting your own preferences.'[27] Patmore's Angel found itself at the height of fashion once more, repackaged for a new market.

The burgeoning advertising machine growing across the West tapped into conservative feeling and celebrated the subservience, the submission and the domination of women by their husbands. A Chase & Sanborn coffee advert of the early 1950s showed a woman thrown across a man's knee as he raises his hand to spank her. The caption above threatens: 'If your husband ever finds out you're not "store-testing" for fresher coffee ... '[28] Newspapers published articles and opinion pieces debating the extent to which husbands should still physically assault their wives. In the 1950s, the New York *Daily Mirror* asked, 'If a woman needs it, should she be spanked?' One responder was published as saying: 'You bet. It teaches them who's boss.'

The cultural legacy of a violent past endured, and little had changed for many women behind closed doors. In London, a century after Charlotte Bostock tried to escape her husband, midwife Jennifer Lee, the writer of the books on which the BBC's popular *Call the Midwife* are based, witnessed the lack of real progress for many of the city's working-class wives. In her memoirs, she recounts antenatal visits to a 19-year-old mother, Molly, pregnant with her third child and living with her husband and children in one of the East End's many overcrowded slums.

Lee recalled interrupting a violent argument between Molly and her husband. When she examined Molly, she discovered a 'great black bruise on her chest' from a previous confrontation. When asked how it had happened: ''Im,' she said, and spat on the floor.'[29] The midwife later noticed Molly's other children, two small boys of two or three years old, hiding behind a chair. 'Their silence was unnatural. They had big eyes, full of fear, and they took a step or two forward, then clung to each other as though for mutual protection and retreated behind the chair again.'[30]

In the UK, the mid-twentieth century saw the creation of a massive welfare state, an expansive public sector that provided a practical network of support for women beyond their husbands, giving them, and vulnerable people, a safety net should they need it. Nurses like Jenny Lee were on the frontline of this change. The help that she was able to provide to Molly and her children was frustratingly limited, but reflected a small step forward for future generations, hinting at the work of support services to come.

For reformers who sought to reach into people's homes, to affect behaviours within their most intimate of relationships, change was slow. In the 1960s and 1970s, the Liberation Movement began to tackle the social, economic and cultural pressures on women to submit to their spouse. Some 'first wave' feminists, like Elizabeth Garrett Anderson in the UK and Lucy Stone in the US, had refused to include the vow of obedience in their weddings more than a century earlier. However, it was in the second half of the twentieth century that the 'second wave' shifted expectations from the inclusion of the promise to its omission.

In the UK, the work to help keep women safe within their relationships and marriages continues. In 1989, a woman was raped by her husband in northwest England, six weeks after securing a family protection order against him. The following year, Judge Fawcus decreed that the fact that the wife had sought and secured an order that he should not use violence against her did not mean that she had withdrawn her consent to sex.[31] The consent provided at her wedding. It was 1991 before rape within marriage was made illegal in England and Wales, although in 2019 a UK judge stated: 'I cannot think of any more obviously fundamental human right than the right of a man to have sex with his wife.'[32] Certainly not her right to refuse him.

The cultural inheritance of the past remains present. We still consume and celebrate novels, plays, films and TV that sentimentalize female devotion and submission and glorify male dominance. Is it not romantic? The irresistible urge to romanticize the past can feed insecurities and unequal entitlement between men and women in their relationships. Binaries remain. Resistance to progress manifests again in a resurgence in toxic masculinity. Trans people face increasing abuse, inequality and persecution in parts of the West, in press and in politics, as 'traditional' gender lines are politicized and promoted. 'Trad wife' movements are on the rise in the UK and North America as conservatives seek to return to a vision of marriage promoted and sold in the 1950s. To make marriage Stepford again.

Every couple navigates their own way with this inheritance. For some it feels irrelevant. For others, legacies surrounding the entitlement of husbands, the supposedly desirable submission of wives and the hesitation of authorities to intervene behind the closed doors of marriage, are inescapable. Between April 2019 and March 2020, 2.3 million people, 5.5 per cent of adults in England and Wales experienced intimate partner violence. More than a quarter of trans people have faced violence from a partner and many trans women then find themselves excluded from support for victims. Across the UK, a woman is killed by a man every three days, and the majority of those murders are committed by the woman's current or former partner. In recent years, a third of the women had reported previous violence and abuse to the police ahead of their deaths – they still died.

In the United States, one million people have been shot at by an intimate partner. Nearly 20 people are physically assaulted by a partner every minute. Legal protection for victims is hampered by discourse that centres 'family values'. Defenders of the 'traditional family' continue to attest that marriage is sacrosanct and not to be interfered in by the state. The same argument leaves people with almost no protection from intimate partner violence elsewhere in the world. In India, a 2018 survey found that 31 per cent of women, who were or had been married, had experienced physical, sexual or emotional violence from their husbands.

British colonial-era laws continue to legalize marital rape, with reform to the 1860 legislation resisted. In 2017, Vladimir Putin passed a law in Russia to decriminalize some forms of violence perpetrated against women by their husbands, despite the fact that it was estimated that a woman was being murdered in Russia every 40 minutes in an act of intimate-partner violence. In these conservative, politically motivated choices, the recent history of what it means to be a wife continues to have a direct impact on women today, as the inherited cultural rights of male partners continue to be prioritized.

Legal, social and cultural systems worldwide continue to unpick the legacy of a difficult past. In 2021 Hillary Clinton reported that, 'In 1995, domestic violence was a crime in just 13 countries. Today it is illegal in more than 100.'[33] In 2016, coercive control was recognized as a crime in the UK. Patterns of threatening behaviour, humiliation and intimidation that had previously been invisible to the law have now been recognized. A 2021 Domestic Abuse Act seeks to improve the justice system for victims in England and Wales. From the most personal, individual choices to the most political, we work to reset the power balance of our intimate relationships. Women continue to find power in a collective voice. To defy, to challenge, to champion – and to disobey.

FORSAKING ALL OTHERS

*The couples were triangles and everyone
lived in squares.*

**– ATTRIBUTED TO DOROTHY PARKER, DESCRIPTION
OF THE BLOOMSBURY GROUP**

Marriage has defined the sexual rules and taboos imposed on newlyweds throughout its long and diverse history. Beginning on the wedding night, the pressure to practise sex with a new spouse has often been combined with the expectation to, thereafter, abstain from other sexual partners. Though not always. For millennia, across the globe, newlyweds entered into marriages involving multiple spouses. For communities in which marriage has been designed to take place between two people, vows to be faithful have rarely prevented sexual activity from spilling out of marital unions – formal and informal routes to infidelity have always thrived. Today, we continue to aspire to monogamy on a huge scale within our marriages. Whatever the histories of the individuals involved, we continue to define our sexual practices and make a serious, public, sexual commitment on our wedding days. For many, the very survival of a marriage depends on the maintenance of this vow.

Although monogamy dominates marriage around much of the world today, polygamous marriages, co-spousal arrangements and polyamorous relationships have a deep and broad history across religious and cultural practices around the world. For millennia, across every populated continent, relatively powerful men married multiple women. Acquiring new, additional wives might increase their chances of leaving behind an heir, provide a means to fulfil sexual desire or build alliances with several families.

Women marrying into polygynous marriages (relationships between one husband and multiple wives) would often find themselves placed into a hierarchy of primary wives and wives of lower status. As mothers of half-siblings it was not uncommon to experience conflict between the rights of children competing for inheritance. In pre-Colombian Mexico, the sister of the powerful Aztec emperor Axayacatl married the ruler of the city-state of Tlatelolco. Chroniclers recorded that she was neglected by her new husband in favour of others: 'He took all the presents that her brother Axayacatl sent her and gave them to his secondary wives … And King Moquiuixtli would not sleep with her: he spent his nights only with his concubines.'[1] In 1473, her brother 'grew furious'.[2] In retaliation for the insult, he invaded and destroyed the kingdom.

Women leading their married lives alongside the other wives of a shared husband would not always find threat or familial confrontation in these family structures. Relationships with your husband's wives might be varied and complex. In ancient China, a bride might bring her sisters to her new husband's home as backup wives.[3] In the nineteenth century, at least 40 Native American cultures were said to practise sororal polygyny, with eldest sisters typically marrying first before being joined by younger ones when they came of age. In Botswana, there is a strong tradition of allyship between wives of the same husband – it is said that 'without cowives, a woman's work is never done'.[4]

Throughout the world, women have married multiple husbands. In parts of Tibet, India, Kashmir and Nepal women might expect to be married to, and share sexual practices with, multiple brothers.[5] Anthropologist Kathrine Starkweather has identified over 50 cultures, from the Arctic to the tropics, where women have routinely married more than one spouse.[6] The Bari people in Venezuela recognize multiple fathers of a single child.[7] All male sexual partners of a pregnant woman are granted paternity, whatever the stage of pregnancy at which sexual encounters took place. Children understood to have two fathers are significantly more likely to survive longer.[8] Research suggests that polyandry (relationships between one wife and multiple husbands) has been more commonly practised and for longer than previously thought. Starkweather has remarked that perceptions about its rarity date back to the mid-twentieth century, when anthropology was a field dominated by men: 'there seemed to be a fairly pervasive belief that polyandry didn't make any sense from a male's perspective.'[9]

All of the world's major religions have sanctioned polygamy at some point in their evolution and many have branches somewhere in the world that continue to practise polygamous marriages today. In Europe, polygamous marriages were common through the early medieval period until the Christian Church officially banned them around a millennia ago.[10] Between the seventeenth and twentieth centuries, colonial practices spread a monopoly on monogamous marriage across swathes of the globe. For millions of women, the commitment to have sex only with your, one, husband became a defining commitment of marriage – transgression from this rule was understood as a threat to marriage itself.

Taboos relating to sex outside of marriage have varied hugely across time, place, religion, class and gender. Restrictions and freedoms were rarely experienced equally by both husbands and wives. In England, Anne Boleyn was notionally executed for the supposed crime of adultery by a husband who had had several mistresses, had likely fathered children with her own sister and who had already lined up his next wife. In the seventeenth century, Puritans introduced new punishments for extra-marital sex. Men were subject to imprisonment. Women to execution. It took 158 years for Britain's colonial-era laws criminalizing infidelity to be repealed in India, in 2018.

Countries governed by Islamic law today, including Saudi Arabia and Pakistan, enact punishments for sex outside of marriage that include imprisonment, flogging and death. Women are overwhelmingly targeted and can be accused and convicted even when they are the victim of rape. Until very recently in the UK and across the West, an affair could cost a married woman her children, ther social standing, her money, home and the security brought by marriage. Men rarely faced similar consequences, the cost of opposite-sex infidelities more regularly falling on an implicated third party.

In European tradition, centuries of women found themselves in unfulfilling marriages – often in relationships that had never been designed around romantic or sexual needs. They found themselves stuck, unable to aspire to sexual pleasure. Some women escaped this fate by carving out a life beyond the strict rules of marital monogamy. Elite and royal women, like Russia's Catherine the Great, used their extreme power to share the privileges enjoyed by their husbands, brothers and peers, and took lovers. Among the uber wealthy, having a lover was not unthinkable for privileged women before the nineteenth century. At the other end of the social spectrum, in the poorer classes, rules might be much more flexible in some communities than others. However, for many married women, until the twentieth century, seeking sexual satisfaction from someone other than the man you had married would have been unimaginably impractical.

Husbands rarely suffered the same restrictions. Across classes and around the world, men more often enjoyed a range of acceptable options for sexual fulfilment beyond the marital bed. Among elite classes in much of East Asia, formal concubinage was practised until the twentieth century. Concubines might hold official positions; they could amass significant personal power through their role and their children could inherit huge wealth. European monarchs have a long history of openly seducing, supporting and rewarding whole series of mistresses. In the

1660s, in Britain, Barbara Villiers was known as the 'uncrowned queen' to Charles II's king. In 1745, Madame de Pompadour took on the position as chief mistress to the King of France, Louis XV. This prestigious job allowed her to secure titles, land and wealth for herself and her family; it came with its own dedicated workplace accommodation, and it gave her the influence and resources to patronize the artists and philosophers of the European Enlightenment.

Throughout the history of the institution, many people found themselves drawn into other people's marriages, taking on relatively formal roles as mistresses and concubines, or informal ones as sexual partners, lovers and sex workers. If you were going to be a mistress, a royal mistress was the one to be. Even then, the rules could be slippery and your position precarious. Alice Keppel was the established mistress to the British king Edward VII for over 20 years, and a central figure at the British court until his death in 1910, when she was excluded. At the end of the twentieth century, her great-granddaughter Camilla Parker Bowles, later redeemed as Queen Consort, was portrayed as the great villain of the Prince of Wales' affair with her, during his marriage to Diana. For centuries, sexual proclivity and deviance was almost universally blamed on the other woman involved. The stigma and the consequences fell almost entirely on her. Of course, a husband's affairs did not always involve a woman at all. When sex took place between two men, both could face execution in England between 1563 and 1861, and prosecution up to 1967.

For people in the poorer classes, forming temporary sexual relationships with married men has brought higher risks than for their elite counterparts. In Britain, the taboo attached to extramarital sex in the eighteenth and nineteenth centuries particularly, created a large underclass of women and men, girls and boys, to serve the desires and bear the shame of husbands who could not keep it in their pants. Female sex workers were often girls and women who had been abandoned by a lover or who had suffered abuse at home or work. Once the victim of sex outside of marriage, women were judged as the perpetrator – and harshly. Often rejected by their support networks, they were excluded from safe employment and housing options and left with no other means of supporting themselves, and any children they may have conceived. People who expressed gender diversity and same-sex attraction also routinely found themselves disproportionately excluded from safer means of survival. Trans women today, particularly women of colour, continue to face vulnerability to sexual exploitation, with homelessness, family rejection and high levels of workplace discrimination all contributing factors.[11]

Throughout history, some people found relative freedom in an underworld on the edges of marriage. In his banned 1894 play, *Mrs Warren's Profession*, George Bernard Shaw presented prostitution as not only equivalent to marriage but often preferable to the life of a married woman within the working classes. At times, it was possible for women in sex work to achieve greater independence than the wives with whom they shared their sexual partners. However, sex workers and mistresses were unthinkably vulnerable – to disease, violence, poverty, abandonment, to losing their children, and to young deaths. In the 1730s, William Hogarth created a series of paintings and engravings charting the life of a young girl recently arrived in London from the country. *A Harlot's Progress* reveals her to be supporting herself as a mistress and a prostitute, before being imprisoned, robbed and dying of syphilis at the age of 23. In the Victorian era, as chastity was being celebrated, and the 'Angel in the House' revered at the centre of marriage, prostitution and pornography grew exponentially at the edges. The greater the stigma on sexuality, the more deeply sex was pushed underground, and the worse the lives of those who fell outside of the celebrated 'norm'.

For wives with few outlets for sexual expression, watching their husbands enjoy extramarital pursuits could result in more than frustration and a sense of injustice. Wandering husbands have regularly passed sexually transmitted infections on to their often unknowing wives. In the early seventeenth century, a ballad designed to caution unmarried women against 'hastie Marriage, by the example of other Married women', lamented:

> *A woman that to a whore-monger is wed*
> *is in a most desperate case:*
> *She scarce dares performe her duty in bed,*
> *with one of condition so base:*
> *For sometimes hee's bitten with Turnbull-street Fleas,*
> *The Pox, or some other infectious disease;*
> *And yet, to her perill, his mind she must please.*[12]

Married women might not even be informed of their diagnosis when symptoms started to show. A 1904 treatise by American dermatologist Prince Albert Morrow debated the virtue of doctors informing women of the diseases they were experiencing, when the infections were brought home by their husbands.

> *It is a question whether it is better in the interest of the wife as well*
> *as of the husband that she not know or even suspect the nature of her*
> *disease, if it can be possibly concealed from her, and thus spare her*
> *the mental anguish, the sense of injury, shame, and humiliation*
> *which would come from the revelation.*[13]

Somebody, please, think of *his* best interests.

Throughout Christian tradition, married women might find themselves blamed for the infidelity of their spouse. A 1930s marriage guide instructed young brides: 'it is a wife's duty to look her best. If you don't tidy yourself up, when you have done the bulk of the day's work, don't be surprised if your husband begins to compare you unfavourably with the typist at the office.'[14]

In 1964, the Grammy award-winning song 'Wives and Lovers' similarly warned women to actively maintain their attractiveness to their husbands – or they might not see them again.

For centuries, across much of the West, a man's adultery was accepted and even expected, while a woman's was deplorable. This grating double-standard was deeply ingrained in culture and law well into the twentieth century.

—

Throughout the history of these hypocrisies, rules and repressions, networks, groups and communities within the UK opted out of these binary norms, rejected Christianized laws and traditions and defined the rules of their own relationships. At the end of the eighteenth century, Mary Wollstonecraft had an active sex life before her marriage to William Godwin. She consistently derided loveless marriages in her writings. The couple's colleague, William Blake, similarly advocated for sexual freedoms for women in his poetry:

> *Till she who burns with youth and knows no fixed lot; is bound*
> *In spells of law to one she loathes: and must she drag the chain*
> *Of life, in weary lust!*[15]

The next generation was to continue the tradition. Wollstonecraft and Godwin's daughter joined Percy Bysshe Shelley and Lord Byron's circle of sexually uninhibited creatives at the age of 16 – though Mary Wollstonecraft Shelley, and her sister, were to struggle to escape the higher costs of sexual freedoms paid by women within their society. Experiences of monogamy and non-monogamy have usually been defined by the relative power of the participants and by the presence, or absence, of consent around choices made.

Although history's women often found the balance of power to be against them, many continued to defy the limitations placed on them by monogamous definitions of marriage.

In the 1850s, as Victorian family values were becoming increasingly ingrained, Mary Ann Evans, known in her literary works as George Eliot, began a relationship with philosopher George Henry Lewes, despite the fact that Lewes was already married to Agnes Jervis. Evans and Lewes travelled to Germany together in 1854 and considered themselves married following their shared honeymoon. For the duration of their relationship, Evans referred to Lewes as her husband and, following his death, changed her name to Mary Ann Evans Lewes. The marriage between Lewes and his wife, Jervis, was an open one: in addition to her three children with her husband, Jervis had four children with journalist Thornton Hunt, son of Leigh Hunt, a friend and ardent supporter of Mary Wollstonecraft Shelley.

The propensity for generations of creative networks to imagine other sexually liberated ways to live their marriages continued as the Victorian era fell away. In the early 1900s, the Bloomsbury Group and their wider circle laid a foundation for self-expression and sexual and gender non-confirming that continues to be built on today. Virginia Woolf and her sister artist, Vanessa Bell, both openly enjoyed sexual and romantic relationships alongside their marriages to their husbands. In the 1920s, Virginia began a passionate affair with aristocrat and writer Vita Sackville-West, who wrote to her: 'I am reduced to a thing that wants Virginia. I composed a beautiful letter to you in the sleepless nightmare hours of the night, and it has all gone: I just miss you, in a quite simple desperate human way.'[16]

Vita enjoyed romantic and sexual relationships with many women – as did her husband, Harold Nicolson, with men. Their 'liaisons' were a long-term feature of their married life together. Vita managed even to have affairs with both of the women who had been bridesmaids at her wedding. Although the arrangement seemed to work fairly well for Vita and Harold, it could be challenging for those on the edges of their marriage. Violet Trefusis and Rosamund Grosvenor, two of Vita's first girlfriends, struggled with jealousy and their uncertain position, and ultimately had their hearts broken by Vita on multiple occasions.

Marriages within the Bloomsbury circles provided more options and choices to the people within them. When Virginia Woolf reflected on what women required to be creative and productive in *A Room of One's Own*, she considered physical space, money, solitude, time and also freedom. Vita and Virginia managed to find that kind of opportunity and inspiration within, and alongside, their unconventional marriages.

The group, like creative networks before and since, formed their own social structures. They built their marriages and their families unrestricted by the idea of a nuclear grouping of one man, one woman and their children. Sometimes these chosen families would host lifelong relationships. Sometimes they would be more transient. They enjoyed relationships that are still revolutionary today when monogamous heteronormative marriage remains the dominant and expected model.

The term 'open marriage' was popularized a few decades after the pioneering Bloomsbury group and the idea of non-monogamy continues to provoke polarized opinions. One 2016 survey of American adults found that 56 per cent of respondents expressed the belief that open relationships were morally wrong.[17] In 2020, another survey of just over 1,300 American adults found that 32 per cent said that their ideal relationship was non-monogamous in some way, with 43 per cent of millennials particularly likely to desire non-monogamy within their romantic and sexual relationships.[18]

Across much of the West, ethical non-monogamy is on the rise, with increasing numbers of people in romantic relationships involving more than two consenting adults. In recent decades, Labi Siffre forged his own model of marriage with two men, Peter Lloyd and Ruud van Baardwijk, in south Wales. 'For nearly 16 years the three of us lived together in a ménage à trois. And I realised I'd made the family that I'd been trying to make for the whole of my life.'[19] The three enjoyed their 'perfect life' together until the deaths of Lloyd and van Baardwijk in the 2010s. In 2016, research suggested that one in five adults in the US had previously been in a consensually non-monogamous relationship. A 2017 Canadian survey suggested a similar picture north of the border.[20] Legislation in North America is beginning to recognize polyamory. In Newfoundland, Canada, in 2018, two men and a woman were all recognized as the legal parents of a child. Two years later, a Massachusetts city council voted to recognize polyamorous domestic partnerships.

Marriage has sought to define sexual behaviour across the globe for millennia. In most of the world's major religions, sexual practices have been strictly restricted to the institution. Expectations that, from your wedding day to your death, your sex life be confined to one person are still high. Through marriage, we continue to choose sexual fidelity on an enormous scale.

For women, the decision to enter into a marriage has both expanded options and contracted them. Across every continent, unequal power structures continue to grant greater sexual freedoms to men and many people continue to find their marital commitment to monogamy harshly enforced. Punishment for choices that deviate from the institution remain obscenely high for far too many. Efforts to dictate the romantic and sexual choices of other people through marriage structures continue today, though the power of religious and state authorities to determine sexual freedoms has been greatly diminished in much of the West. As we move towards a more equal balance of power within our relationships, we can more confidently govern our own sexual choices through open consent. The belief that, throughout a lifetime, sexual choices need always be connected to marital status continues to be challenged in new ways.

A FRUITFUL UNION

Being a mom has made me so tired.
And so happy.

– TINA FEY, ACTRESS, WRITER AND COMEDIAN

Generation after generation of newlyweds found their wedding to be a precursor to parenthood. Marriage set young wives on a path to pregnancy – whether they desired children or not. However eager or reluctant for this aspect of their new relationship, excited or terrified for the reality of motherhood, for many, there was an expectation that their wedding would aim to quickly bring children into the new marital home. In the West, sex was an expected duty within marriage and birth control taboo. For centuries, the most reliable form of pregnancy prevention was not to say 'I do'. As joyous and hopeful as the creation of new life can be, it was consistently extremely risky for history's women – as it continues to be for so many today. Pregnancy posed numerous dangers to health. Childbirth was often fatal and infant mortality was an unavoidable element of life in many communities. If you survived the procreation gauntlet to become the healthy mother of a healthy child, you might find yourself with no rights to them. For centuries in the West, marriage both enabled the choice of parenthood for women and entirely disabled women's ability to exercise choice about that element of their life at all.

In recent decades, greater numbers have enjoyed more control than ever before about when and whether to become parents, regardless of marital status. Today, people increasingly choose to start a family and step into parenthood single, with support from donors or coparents – the right time to have children does not always coincide with the right relationship. For people struggling with barriers to conception, many in the world's wealthiest nations find that science continues to offer new options. Fertility treatments provide a route to parenthood for relationships like mine. The choice to be child-free no longer means limiting sexual practices and relationships for millions. In England and Wales in 1941 just 17.9 per cent of women under 30 years old were child-free. In 2022, for the first time, more than half (50.1 per cent) of women turned 30 without having had a child.[1]

Although it is a choice directly under attack in the United States, millions of people can now decide whether or when to have children for social, financial, health, personal and professional reasons. In recent centuries, many women found that their wedding day provided the last chance to exercise choice or control over their own bodies and their families.

For much of its history, the institution of marriage was built to be indivisible from systems that governed procreation. Across the globe, marriage was set up in large part to provide the structures in which children were conceived and raised. In Europe, the rise of Christianity established one clear set of norms across much of the continent; rules that were later spread across much of the globe.

Until recently in the West, marriage was the means used to prioritize the paternity of children and the rights of their fathers; to essentially remove women's powers of procreation and parenthood and give them to men. Taboos limiting women's sexual practices outside of marriage helped to assure the paternity of a child. Within marriage, women were actively prevented from knowledge that would help them to choose how and when they might conceive their husband's children. Once born, a child inherited their name, rights, status and inheritance through their father, as discussed in earlier chapters. It was the responsibility of married fathers to support them and, until well into the twentieth century, women had very few rights to the children they bore within a marriage. Only children born to a woman with a husband were considered 'legitimate'.

However, this has never been the only way. In matrilineal societies, like the Khasi in northeast India, and many Native American tribes, including the Haudenosaunee, children have primarily belonged with their mothers and inherited through them. On marriage, husbands tend to move in with their wives. Children take their mother's name, and, for the Khasi, it is the youngest daughter who inherits the bulk of any ancestral property. Within the Mosuo in China's Himalayas, women enjoy sexual freedom through 'walking marriages', literally translated as 'back and forth'.[2] Men are invited to a woman's private bedroom only at night, before walking back to their own home. Any children are solely the responsibility of their mother and mother's family. However long the relationship, fathers continue to reside in their own mother's homes and, though potentially embarrassing, no stigma is attached if a woman might not know who the father of a child might be. The child's place is clear.

On the other hand, across many of the world's major religions, including Islam, Christianity, Judaism and Hinduism, marriage has been used to establish patriarchal and patrilineal norms. Societies that have grown in line with these traditions have long promoted parenthood as the duty and moral obligation of married people. Religious authorities authorized sexual practices through marriage and that permission was often combined with the pressure to reproduce.

In Europe, by the medieval and early modern eras, procreation was widely acknowledged as the primary responsibility, the main purpose, of a wife. Aristocratic women were married as baby breeding machines.

Breastfeeding was taboo. New mothers were expected to menstruate quickly and be back in their husband's bed, conceiving the next child, as soon as possible. Ideally, a male one. A healthy daughter achieved a silver medal at best for royal wives – the role of married royal women was essentially to be the vessels through which princes could make more princes.

Some of these elite wives found power in fulfilling the purpose of their marriage through procreation. Eleanor of Aquitaine was able to fight wars with her husband through their sons. Margaret Beaufort ran the English Court and fashioned herself 'My Lady the King's Mother', after her son's successful seizure of the crown. Wives might step back and carve out their own preferred role once their primary responsibility to bear children had been met. The pressure was off, they could enjoy their privilege. When Henry VIII's son eventually arrived, the Seymour family rode high for a generation, although Jane did not survive to enjoy the legacy.

For many women, marriage provided an exciting, joyous and hopeful opportunity to become a mother. I have always known that I wanted to be a parent, to raise a family. For people who felt the same, for centuries, marriage opened the door. It created the structures in which your children could be conceived in relative safety and raised with comparative security.

However, even for the most powerful of women, pregnancy and childbirth were a life-threatening experience. History provides an unrelentingly grim picture of maternal mortality around much of the globe. The experiences of history's most powerful women remain the most visible today but represent only a tiny fraction of the wider picture. The medieval death rate for mothers has been guessed at around one in every 50 pregnancies and a married woman might very commonly have had 10 or more pregnancies in her lifetime.[3] It was fashionable for wealthy Stuart women to have a portrait painted of themselves before labour. Something to remember them by.

Other than controlling the sexual expectations of their husbands, married women had little means of regulating how many pregnancies they experienced or children they were to raise. In 1671, a French aristocrat advised her 22-year-old daughter, already the mother of three children: 'I beg you, my love, do not trust to two beds; it is a subject of temptation. Have someone sleep in your room.' She later reminded her daughter that her husband had 'already killed two wives under him'.[4] When women have lacked the means to control the number of pregnancies their bodies went through, and the number of dependants that they created, the consequences were always tough. Often tragic.

In the early 1700s, in Britain, Queen Anne became pregnant at least 17 times. None of the children survived. With high rates of infant mortality, it has been estimated that Georgian families had, on average, around 2.5 children – but estimates and averages can be misleading. In February 1798, the *Derby Mercury* reported: 'Mrs Banning, of Little Rissington, near Stow-in-the Wold, Gloucestershire, was safely delivered of a daughter, being the thirty-second child by the same husband.'[5]

Within working families, children could sink a family into poverty. Women had to run the gauntlet of potential conception, pregnancy and labour – and having another mouth to feed and bum to keep clean – with every sexual encounter. And providing for children in poor conditions could prove an overwhelming and impossible task. In the eighteenth century, the poet Phillis Wheatley overcame abduction, from her home in West Africa, and enslavement in North America, to become the first published African American poet, achieving international fame. Having married a free Black grocer in 1778, she had three children and fell into a battle with poverty to support them. Two of her babies died. Her husband was imprisoned for debt in 1784 and, with another baby to provide for, she was forced to take gruelling work in squalid conditions as a scullery maid at a boarding house. She died shortly after, in her early thirties. Until well into the twentieth century, there was little social safety net for people struggling with the responsibilities their marriages brought.

For centuries in European tradition, for all that women endured as they brought children into the world, they were left entirely unsupported and unrecognized as parents by the governance structures of marriage. Children belonged to their fathers. Of all the rights that secular and religious authorities automatically stripped from a bride at her wedding to give to the groom, the rights over any future children feel like the cruellest.

Women who separated marriage and procreation did not fare better – and were usually harshly punished. Unmarried women generally retained legal rights over their children but also full responsibility, and, through moral pressure and lack of practical support, many would be forced to give up their children until the middle of the twentieth century – their status as mothers denigrated by that naked finger on their left hand. The treatment of women and children, from laundries and institutions in Ireland to forced adoptions in Australia, reflected attitudes and persecution endured for centuries around the world.

The harsh judgment of illegitimacy was widely exported through European colonialism and built into the trafficking and enslavement of African people. In the seventeenth century, the colony of Virginia passed a law declaring that, regardless of the status of their father, the children of enslaved women were born into slavery. Through marriage structures, men held full authority over the children and heirs that they desired and relatively little responsibility for children they chose to reject. There was no doubt as to who was making the law – and for whose benefit. In 2013, Pulitzer Prize and Nobel Prize-winning author Toni Morrison reflected on reproductive justice for Black women: 'I never felt more free in my life until I had children ... for Black women, enslaved, to have a child that you were responsible for that was really yours, that was really freedom ... To be a mother was the unbelievable freedom.'[6]

For centuries in European and Western law, a married father could remove his wife's children from their mother's care, from the moment of birth, without justification. He automatically held custody in the event of a separation. If he was abusive, adulterous, cruel or neglectful, his wife had no recourse to appeal. Their complete absence of power left women vulnerable to all kinds of manipulation, exploitation and abuse in their marriages. Forcing them to stay, to continue to access and protect their children.

A young Mary Wollstonecraft became an aunt in 1783, when her sister, Eliza, gave birth to a healthy daughter. A few months later, Wollstonecraft travelled to visit her new niece and found her sister without 'the least tincture of reason'.[7] It seems likely that Eliza was suffering from a form of postpartum depression, a condition without a name in the eighteenth century. However, as she improved with her sister's care, it became clear that something else was going on. Wollstonecraft noticed her sister flinch and shudder when her husband was nearby. She had been 'ill-used'.[8]

Mary Wollstonecraft wrote to their sister, Everina, that 'those who would save Bess must act'.[9] On a cold January day, Mary waited for her brother-in-law to leave home before escaping with her sister to a lodging house around five miles out of London. They were forced to leave the baby behind. They had no right to take her with them. The furious father forbade his wife from seeing their daughter and cut her off financially. Just eight months later they heard that the baby had died, shortly before her first birthday. Wollstonecraft suspected that the little girl had been intentionally neglected by her father in revenge on his wife. Eliza's freedom from his abuse had been punished with her child's death.[10] It was a cautionary tale for other women, wives and mothers, suffering at their husband's hands. Wollstonecraft later reflected:

Considering the care and anxiety a woman must have about a child before it comes into the world, it seems to me, by a natural right, to belong to her ... but it is sufficient for a man to condescend to get a child, in order to claim it. – A man is a tyrant![11]

Wollstonecraft's experience as a sister and an aunt undoubtedly coloured her later work advocating on behalf of women's rights. In her *Vindication of the Rights of Woman*, first published in 1792, she was at the vanguard of marriage reform when she declared: 'The DIVINE RIGHT of husbands, like the divine right of kings, may, it is hoped, in this enlightened age, be contested without danger.'[12]

The divine right of husbands had long been embedded into custom and law in the West. At the end of the eighteenth century, writers like Wollstonecraft began to unpick the assumptions on which this entrenched inequality was based. They laid the foundation for the activists of the century to come. In the following generations, women began to successfully campaign to have their rights as independent people, and as parents, regardless of marital status, recognized in law.

Thirty years after Wollstonecraft's death, the wedding of Caroline Sheridan took place in London. Caroline, a friend of Wollstonecraft's daughter, Mary, was to be one of the first women in the country to transform her lived experience as a woman, and as a wife, into legislative action. In 1835, she found herself without access to her children. Her jealous, violent husband, George Norton, had accused her of 'criminal conversation' with Lord Melbourne, the Prime Minister. As there was no evidence of an adultery that likely did not take place, his claim was thrown out of court and divorce was unobtainable for either party.

Caroline was stuck. Her abusive husband removed her three sons, who were just seven, five and three years old, and refused her access to them. He continued to own all her property, including the novels she had written, as well as her family inheritance. Caroline wrote to Mary

Wollstonecraft Shelley that 'a woman is made a helpless wretch by these laws of men'.[13] Without access to her own money, she ran up bills to support herself and told her creditors to sue her husband.

Norton held full control over their children throughout their separation and unashamedly used them to torture his wife, allowing her to see them only briefly and rarely. He repeatedly offered visits, only to withdraw access at the last moments. In an impossible position, she began to campaign for legal reform, writing pamphlets and treatise and exploiting her personal networks.

> *The law has no power to order that a woman shall have even occasional access to her children, though she could prove that she was driven by violence from her husband's house and that he had deserted her for a mistress ... The father's right is absolute and paramount, and can no more be affected by the mother's claim than if she had no existence.*[14]

She revolted at the reality that husbands were both 'accuser and judge' in marriage separation and reflected that, when estranged from their wife, a man was often left 'certainly angry, probably mortified and in nine cases out of ten is eager to avenge his real or fancied injuries'. She continued, 'To this angry man, to this mortified man, the law awards that which can rarely be trusted to any human being, even in the calmest hours of life, namely, DESPOTIC POWER!'[15]

Norton's activism, and her personal plight, stirred public sympathy and reached Parliament in the form of the Custody of Infants Bill in 1839. Despite opposition in the House of Lords, the Bill passed and some women were granted some legal rights to see their children after the breakdown of their marriages. The women must not have been convicted of adultery and could only achieve access to, and not custody of, children over seven years old. The law did not apply to Scotland, where Caroline's children were taken by their father.

It was a limited victory, but Caroline's success laid a strong foundation for future reform: the divine right of husbands within the law began to be unravelled. Her campaigning continued. She challenged the rights of husbands over the property of their wives and sought escape for victims of intimate partner violence from their persecutors. She denied 'radical' tendencies, claiming to simply seek redress to some of the wrongs married women found themselves subject to. Through her campaigns, she was to have a significant impact on the choices available to married women in the UK, and on the feminists to follow, well into the next century.

Change was relatively slow. Many of these subsequent generations of activists were to make significant sacrifices for seeking to enable women's choices – few rights of husbands were as fiercely protected as their right to control the procreation potential of their wives and any children they produced. In 1877, the year of Caroline Norton's death, Annie Besant, radical activist, socialist and feminist, found her daughter removed from her custody for the crime of providing married women with access to information about contraception. She was judged unfit to raise her.

Besant described her husband, Frank, in her autobiography as having 'very high ideas of a husband's authority and a wife's submission holding strongly to the "master-in-my-own-house theory"'. Depicting herself as 'accustomed to freedom, indifferent to home details, impulsive, hot-tempered, and proud as Lucifer', she reflected that they were 'an ill-matched pair'.[16] Three years after their separation, Besant and her colleague, Charles Bradlaugh, published a birth control tract that argued for the rights of married women to 'check' conception and provided practical advice on how to limit numbers of pregnancies for working-class families struggling in poverty.

Fruits of Philosophy had originally been printed in the United States in the 1830s by Charles Knowlton, who had been sentenced to three months' hard labour in Massachusetts for obscenity. Forty years later, Besant and Bradlaugh were prosecuted in London for the same crime. Although legally acquitted, Besant was punished by the man she had married with the loss of her child. Mabel was torn from her mother 'nearly frantic with fear and passionate resistance' and Besant was left with grief and loneliness, 'like an evil dream'.[17]

Annie Besant is thought to be the first woman in Britain to publicly advocate for birth control for married women. Although crude methods of contraception and abortion had been documented across the ancient world and practised for centuries, within Christian tradition the subject became taboo and knowledge limited. However, efforts persisted. There is evidence of the withdrawal method being widely practised within marriages in some communities. Crudely put: 'to make a coffee house of a woman's privates, to go in and out and spend nothing'.[18]

Even this simple, unreliable, effort to prevent a pregnancy was still considered deeply immoral by spiritual and secular leaders in the West as the nineteenth century progressed. American pseudoscientist, Orson Squire Fowler declared to husbands and wives that 'PREVENTATIVE CONTRACEPTION OUTRAGES EVERY SEXUAL LAW'. He continued:

> *Think you, after God has created you men and women, and ordained all this creative machinery solely to secure reproduction, you can thwart and cheat Him without incurring His retribution commensurate with His highest law you break? Prepare to meet your god, ye who persist.*[19]

Condoms had existed to thwart our creative machinery since at least medieval times.[20] Long associated with prostitution, sheaths made from animal-intestines were used up to the mid-1800s when rubber condoms appeared – and were quickly banned in America. The Comstock Act of 1873, named after conservative evangelical Anthony Comstock, made it illegal to send 'immoral goods', including basic information about pregnancy prevention, through the mail. Abortions were widely practised but illegal and unsafe, often damaging the woman's health or resulting in death.

Pregnancy and childbearing remained a dangerous consequence of marriage. In the 1800s, childbirth was the most common cause of death for women. Florence Nightingale reflected of midwifery that, 'though everybody must be born, there is probably no knowledge more neglected than this, nor more important for the great mass of women'.[21] Pregnant today, and approaching an inevitable labour, it is hard to not feel relieved to live in the twenty-first century. In 1850, maternal mortality in the United Kingdom was thought to be around 548 per 100,000 live births.[22] In the United States, 50 years later, it has been estimated that 850 of every 100,000 births resulted in the death of the mother.[23] Within the working classes, it is likely that the number was much higher. In the mid-twentieth century, nurse Jenny Lee looked back to the challenges for sexually active women, unable to control their pregnancies in the 1800s, and claimed that 'maternal mortality among the poorest classes stood at around 35–40 per cent, and infant mortality was around 60 per cent'.

At the vanguard of the early NHS, Nurse Lee represented a significant shift towards greater safety and opportunities for married women, but, early in her career, in the 1950s, she found that little had changed for London's poorest wives. Like their Victorian mothers and grandmothers, many experienced the reality of married life as a sequence of relatively dangerous, unmanageable numbers of pregnancies and the endless responsibilities that motherhood brought. Condoms had been declared legal in the US in the 1930s – because of their more socially acceptable use as a disease preventative. Although relatively accessible in parts of the West, they were still heavily stigmatized – and required men to make the choice to wear them. Centuries after their introduction, condoms would have remained an alien, inaccessible option for most women looking to prevent a pregnancy within their marriages.

Lee found the women of London's East End to live 'an endless life of child-rearing, cleaning, washing, shopping and cooking'[24] and was shocked to attend to the pregnancy of a woman with 23 other children. The hard, unrelenting and physical labour of child-rearing made paid employment difficult for many. The social and financial costs of unprotected marital sex were endured alongside the physical, which could commonly range from back pain to a prolapsed uterus.

In her memoirs, Nurse Lee recorded the life of Brenda, a woman who grew up with rickets in the early twentieth century and suffered a contracted pelvis.[25] She had no chance of giving birth naturally. Having married and conceived in the 1930s she underwent a long, obstructed labour and the baby died. With a sexually active marriage and no access to contraception or abortion, the same thing happened again. And again. And again. Until her husband was killed in the Second World War. When Lee met Brenda, she had remarried two decades later and, through the introduction of socialized medicine, was able to access a caesarean section and become a mother to a healthy baby girl: named Grace Miracle.[26]

Access to life-saving knowledge around birth control was widely repressed well into the twentieth century. Despite the risks of pregnancy to your health and family and whatever your motivation to avoid a pregnancy, secular and religious leaders fought successfully against your right to make that choice for centuries. Religious networks, like the Christian Right today, preached abstinence from sex as the only moral way of preventing a pregnancy, but where did that leave married women? As a wife you were told that it was your obligation to have sex with your husband. It was a Catch-22. You had no right to control the consequences of his rights to your body.

The introduction of the pill in the early 1960s gave women control over their sexual choices like never before.

Within five years of the FDA (Food and Drug Administration) approving the contraceptive pill in the United States, more than six million people were taking it. By 1970, it is thought that 60 per cent of all American women were using the pill or another, similar form of contraceptive.[27] When Country singer Loretta Lynn released her song 'The Pill' in the middle of the decade, she spoke for countless married women, looking back at a reality of having been stuck at home, pregnant with a new baby, year after year, now liberated by the revolutionary contraceptive. Lynn herself had six children with her husband, four of whom were born before she was twenty.

In the UK, in 1967, the Abortion Act became law, legalizing abortion in certain circumstances. Six years later, in 1973, the US Supreme Court struck down widespread laws that had criminalized women for accessing induced abortion. The 2022 decision of the Court to overturn *Roe v Wade* has brought back to life a familiar history in the United States of women losing their lives from desperate and unsafe attempts to end a pregnancy; an increase in women, particularly poor women, disabled women and women of colour dying from poor access to reproductive healthcare; of women in prison for refusing to endure a forced pregnancy; more families living in poverty, unable to support their children; more girls and women carrying the babies of abusers and rapists and millions of women facing suspicion and criminal investigation as they suffer a miscarriage, the result of one in four pregnancies.

Reforms of the 1960s and 1970s increasingly liberated women's reproductive choices from the controls of marital structures in much of the West. The reforms were all actively resisted and the desire to go backwards has not died. Conservative forces find a louder voice in this territory once again. The ruling of the Supreme Court, a deliberate backwards step, sets a dangerous precedent. In response to the decision across the Atlantic, Conservative MP Danny Kruger proclaimed in the UK Parliament that women do not have 'an absolute right to bodily autonomy', arguing that the reproductive nature of women's bodies makes them 'a proper topic for political debate'.[28]

In 1963, in her classic book, *Feminine Mystique*, Betty Friedan launched the fight against the rights of husbands, fathers and political leaders to determine women's reproductive choices:

> *Chosen motherhood is the real liberation. The choice to have a child makes the whole experience of motherhood different, and the choice to be generative in other ways can at last be made, and is being made by many women now, without guilt.*[29]

The ability to choose parenthood has made the lives of married women longer and safer. It has empowered them with greater choices and allowed their experiences to expand beyond the unrelentingly domestic.

Activists from Wollstonecraft to Norton, Besant to Friedan, fought for the rights of women to exercise control over their bodies and their children. To choose parenthood and to separate that choice from marriage. Over the last 50 years, LGBTQIA+ activists have opened the door for families like mine. In 1988, Section 28 was passed in the UK by Margaret Thatcher's Conservative government, labelling LGBTQIA+ families as 'pretend' – as opposed to 'real' – and prohibiting the 'promotion of homosexuality'.[30] By the end of the year, the Lesbian and Gay Foster and Adoptive Parents Network (LAGFAPN) was created in London to battle legal and social discrimination.

The 1970s and 1980s saw activist and support groups pop up across the West to defend the rights of LGBTQIA+ parents. Despite pleas from the frontline of overwhelmed public services, political and religious leaders fought to prevent (inevitably unmarried) couples within the LGBTQIA+ community from fostering and adopting children in care. In the 1970s, New York became the first American state to not automatically reject adoption applications on the grounds of 'homosexuality'. Florida overturned their ban on LGBTQIA+ adoption in 2010.[31]

It has been a long, hard battle to reach recognition of same-sex partner families and parenthood has been politicized alongside marriage for centuries. Marriage requirements prevented thousands of couples across the United States from starting a family until same-sex marriage was legalized and protected by the Supreme Court in 2015. In 2016, the ban on adoption by same-sex couples was finally struck down by a federal judge in Mississippi. In Texas today, around 25 per cent of foster care providers are faith-based, and still refuse to work with same-sex and gender-diverse families.[32] It is clear that the rights of same-sex couples to family life are at risk in the United States under today's Supreme Court.

The 1970s and 1980s saw the birth of new routes to parenthood through medical advances, particularly for single women, lesbians and bisexual women. Artificial inseminations took place at home before fertility clinics began to spring up and serve this market, wrapping more formal medical and legal protection around treatments and introducing a huge cost. My wife and I cut back our wedding and the deposit for our home to afford pregnancy and parenthood. We were lucky. Many people simply cannot afford access to safe clinics. Legal processes complicate the route to parenthood for trans and nonbinary parents, who can find themselves misgendered and unsupported as they grow their families.

Although marriage is no longer socially required as a step on the route to parenthood today, many people continue to choose to marry, to make a formal commitment to each other, before becoming co-parents. The institution can protect the rights of fathers if something were to go wrong and non-pregnant mothers are more clearly recognized as the parents of children carried by their wives. Although marriage and parenthood have been legally uncoupled in much of the West, we continue to walk this well-trodden path in large numbers. People continue to experience their marriages as a parental team.

Across much of the West, in most cases women's careers suffer as a consequence of parenthood, while the careers of fathers benefit.[33] Poor access to paternity and parental leave continues to reinforce gender inequalities based on marital stereotypes from the past. However, for people who choose to become parents today, their experiences no longer need to be determined by the strict roles and responsibilities built into recent definitions of wife and husband, mother and father. The joys and responsibilities of raising children need not be divided out on the basis of sex and more and more people choose to opt out of inherited templates. In 2018, when New Zealand PM Jacinda Ardern became the second elected leader of national government to give birth in office (following Pakistan's Benazir Bhutto in 1990), her partner, Clarke Gayford, became a 'stay at home dad' to support his wife at this pinnacle of her career. Three months after the birth, Ardern became the first world leader to bring her baby to the United Nations general assembly, delivering a speech with her daughter on Gayford's knee, close enough to be nursed when needed.

Ardern builds on the legacy of thousands of mothers whose relationships and marriages have enabled their parenthood to fulfil but not wholly and exclusively define them. When Ida B. Wells, the mother of the civil rights movement and anti-lynching crusader, had her first child, she toured the United States with her six-month-old baby at the turn of the twentieth century. The venues she visited hired a nanny to enable her to be heard. She later reflected, 'I have often referred to it in my meeting with the pioneer suffragists as I honestly believe I am the only woman in the United States who ever travelled throughout the country with a nursing baby to make political speeches.'[34] Her marriage to attorney and activist Ferdinand L. Barnett enabled them to support each other's work as they raised their six children.

In recent decades, politicians from Iceland to Australia, Spain to Argentina, have continued to fulfil their responsibilities as elected representatives while breastfeeding their babies in their national chambers. Perhaps one day, British MPs like Stella Creasy, banned from Parliament in 2021 for nursing her three-month-old baby, will be able to follow suit.

The idea of one legitimate path to create and raise legitimate children is now behind us in much of the West. Regardless of their marital status, people now have the potential to choose whether to become a parent or not, when the right time to try might be and to stop having children when their family is the right size for it to thrive. If only politicians could get out of the way. It has never been more important to recognize the horrors of the forced pregnancies that populate our history, to celebrate how far we have come and to resist complacency about the risks of going backwards. Over the last century, countless lives have been both saved and created through scientific and social advances in the fields of healthcare, medicine, midwifery and fertility. Millions of people have become able to separate procreation and marriage on a scale not experienced before. And to enjoy the challenges, delights and joys of both sexual relationships and of parenthood, with fewer of the sacrifices and fewer of the risks.

HAVING IT ALL – DOMESTIC, SOCIAL AND PAID LABOUR

*Women are, by their numbers and labour, an unpaid
continent, who give their labour away for free because
... we just always have. There has never been a point
where our work has been re-evaluated for the role
it plays in holding up every country's economy and,
frankly, soul.*

**– CAITLIN MORAN, FEMINIST, WRITER AND
BROADCASTER[1]**

The unpaid work of women globally has been valued at more than
$10 trillion a year.[2] Women are an invisible, unremunerated economic
force rivalled only by the economies of the US, China and the EU. We
have long been expected to provide care to children, parents, family,
in-laws, neighbours and friends. For free. To fill in the gaps in our
communities and to hold them together. Women have borne this array
of unremunerated burdens while also working in paid employment.
They have commuted to fields and factories, shops and offices, schools
and hospitals, laboured in other people's houses, cared for other people's
families and pioneered new professional opportunities. Having it all
is not a recent challenge. Women have accepted, fought and struggled
with this balance for centuries. Marriage has opened the door to some

forms of work for women and closed it on others. For centuries, the labour undertaken by women was expected to be determined by their marital status. As men and women have openly debated how they should best define a woman's work, the labour of married women has been particularly heavily politicized.

In European tradition, medieval and early modern women often joined their husband's work on marriage – whether labouring in trades and businesses in the towns and cities or undertaking agricultural work in the country. In addition to generating income, newly married women were usually expected to take over a household and lead the physical, social and mental labour that went with running a home. In 1557, Thomas Tusser wrote in his *Fiue Hundred Pointes of Good Husbandrie*:

> *Some respit to husbands the weather may send,*
> *But huswiues affaires haue neuer an end.*[3]

The task of keeping themselves and their families sheltered, safe and healthy was no mean feat. Domestic labour was transformed by the technological advances of the last century. Until the 1900s, in order to cook or bake, wash or iron, people had first to source fuel and to clear out, build and maintain a fire, however hot the day. For centuries, in order to clean, women had not only to find and carry clean water but to make the soap. To fashion their clothes, they would first make the fabric.

A fifteenth-century poem, the *Ballad of a Tyrannical Husband*, tells the comedy of a husband who thinks he works harder than his wife. Hilarious. He works at the plough and moans and chides her for not having his dinner ready on time. We are told she has no servant and 'Many smale chyldern to kepe besyd hyrselfe alone'. Swearing at him, she remonstrates that he'd be weary if he were to do her work for a day:

I have mor to doo then I doo may;
And ye shuld folowe me foly on day,
Ye wold be wery of your part, my hede dar I lay.'[4]

Having been awake all night with the youngest baby, 'Whyn I lye in my bede, my slepe is butt smalle', she gets up, without rest, before her husband to milk the cows and take them out to pasture. In addition to feeding the children, she feeds the chickens, ducks and geese. She teases, cards and spins wool and makes the family's clothes, to save money on buying them. She makes butter and cheese, bakes and brews; she provides food for her husband without a kind word from him: 'And met for owrselfe agen het be none /Yet I have not a feyr word whan that I have done.' In the face of her skilled, physical, and emotionally draining drudgery, I cannot help but feel hugely grateful for sleepily struggling through my first maternity leave with one baby, a washing machine, an electric oven and a choice of handy supermarkets.

The labour expected of women on marriage remained largely unchanged for centuries. As the eighteenth century came to an end, the Industrial Revolution was beginning to transform the working lives of millions of people across Britain. As some women continued to work in older trades, more and more went out to work in harsh jobs in the new industries, from the mills in Lancashire to potteries in Shropshire, the mines in Wales to London's laundries. They provided a significant proportion of the cheap labour that fuelled the technical, social and cultural innovations taking place.

The middle classes debated the ethics and practicalities, of wives and mothers spending long hours, sometimes 60 hours over six days a week, in factories and mills.[5] The welfare of the industrial classes became a public concern, taken up by politicians and human rights advocates alike. Decade after decade, inspections were undertaken, reports were written. Malnourished married women working long hours in dangerous and dirty working conditions were a common sight. The Victorian ideal of a female homemaker, managing a well-ordered household financed by a male breadwinner, was nowhere to be seen among these working families.[6]

Many women were forced to work to survive. Marriage, and often inevitable parenthood, would only increase pressures and limit any choices further. Women had no rights and few options. Reform was slow. By the end of the nineteenth century, a law was passed to prevent women from returning to long days of monotonous, physical labour in factories for four weeks after giving birth. No maternity pay or right to return to work was offered and the law was, inevitably, widely evaded. Women worked through pregnancy, recovery from childbirth and breastfeeding afterwards, to support their families.

Outside of the factories, married women took on casual work to support themselves, their husbands and their children. In London, Fanny Eaton, having immigrated to the UK as a child from Jamaica, worked as a Pre-Raphaelite model. She became the iconic face of characters like the Mother of Moses, Morgan le Fey, the Mother of Sisera, and unnamed exoticized women in paintings by the most famous artists of the age. Her marriage brought 10 children and she worked as a domestic servant, a charwoman, a seamstress and a domestic cook, as well as a model, to support them. Meanwhile, concerned liberal elites and organized working men wanted to see men paid more so that married women could stay at home.

The poorest women, forced to work to feed their children, were generally viewed as virtuous, though the situation was seen as unfortunate. Married women who actually enjoyed their work were judged to be deeply problematic. Many of the women building Britain's industrial wealth chose to work after marriage – to increase their household revenue, to hold a sense of independence and to generate some disposable income. In Lancashire's cotton towns, most women had generated a wage since childhood. Many would have found it restrictive, isolating and unnecessary to move into a small domestic sphere on marriage.[7]

As thousands of women in the industrial classes expected little interruption to their employment following their weddings, in the middle classes things were very different. Relatively privileged working brides, women who would not need to work to support themselves and their families, were strongly encouraged to take up a purely domestic role. The nineteenth century created new employment opportunities and not all of them were physical, gruelling and radically underpaid. The ability of women to access these opportunities became a political question of the day: 'the woman question'. What did it mean to be a woman and a wife in this new modern world?

In the middle of the nineteenth century, the earliest suffragists began to argue that women should not only have the right to participate within public and political life but should enjoy access to better education and the choice to continue their careers after marriage. Agnes (née Heap) Pochin, one of the speakers at England's first public suffrage meeting in Manchester in 1868, published *The Right of Women to Exercise the Elective Franchise*, in 1855, three years after her marriage to Liberal MP Henry Pochin. She observed that: 'Woman's life in the middle classes is, and has been rendered, essentially a dull one.'[8]

By the 1870s, a small number of women were beginning to access university education. Women like suffrage leaders Elizabeth Garrett Anderson and her sisters pioneered new professional roles. Garrett Anderson pursued an active career as Britain's first female doctor, surgeon and mayor, alongside marriage and motherhood. In 1871, on her engagement to James Anderson, she wrote to her sister, Millicent Fawcett:

> *I hope my dear you will not think I have meanly deserted my post*
> *... the woman question will never be solved in any complete way so*

*long as marriage is thought to be incompatible with freedom and
with an independent career.*[9]

During their courtship, Garrett Anderson refused to have a chaperone:
'My position must be an independent one ... it would be injuring all
other professional women a little to allow myself to be treated like a
child.'[10] When they married, the wedding took place 'without millinery
and almost without cookery'.[11] She refused to promise to 'obey' her new
husband and arranged for their shared finances to be managed through
a 'common purse to which each contributed and from which each could
draw'.[12] She aggressively fought the idea that her courtship, engagement,
wedding or marriage should define her work.

Although Garrett Anderson was successful in pioneering a role
for women in her field, women in the late Victorian era were actively
discouraged from pursuing a career after marriage. Decade after decade,
women were told that they should not, and did not, want to work beyond
the home. It was unhealthy. Immoral. They were routinely informed that
they were incapable of undertaking more than the most menial of tasks.
Society worried how a man was to feel as head of his household with a
wife earning independent income. How were other men to provide for
their families if women were allowed to take *their* jobs? Political, social
and religious leaders expressed concern that the idea of a working wife
threatened family harmony and the institution of marriage itself.

Where moral pressure risked failing in persuasion, governments
actively legislated to prevent women from working in influential,
stimulating or well-paid employment after marriage. Across the West,
companies had explicit policies to fire female employees when they
put a ring on that most transformative finger on their left hand. In
the UK, in 1876 a marriage bar was introduced in the General Post
Office, just six years after the first female clerks had been appointed.
As career opportunities began to open to women, steps were taken

to shut them down. By the 1890s, married women were banned from working across central and local government.[13] Teaching and health posts became inaccessible. Relatively middle-class women might be encouraged to work in low-level, poorly paid office posts for a few years, only to be dismissed on marriage. Temporary employees were thought to earn small amounts of 'pin money' while providing flexible, cheap labour. Win-win. For many, the decision to adorn an engagement ring was read as a resignation note to their employers. Working women were consciously and deliberately put in a position to choose between marriage or a professional career for the first time.

Across these class divides, suffragists and suffragettes fought the idea of confinement to wifely work. Their campaigns took them outside of the domestic sphere and into a political one. In 1871, as Elizabeth Garrett married James Anderson, across London, Adelaide Knight was born in the poorer East End. Described as the 'leader' of working women in the suffragette movement, Knight married Donald Adolphus Brown, the son of a naval officer from Guyana, in 1894.[14] Donald took Adelaide's surname on marriage and actively supported her campaigning. Knight had suffered a childhood injury that required her to use crutches for the rest of her life and she experienced repeated poor health and endured regular pain. The couple shared household chores throughout their marriage, from caring for the children to the weekly laundry. Donald's support with the domestic labour at home helped enable her fervent activism.

Described by Annie Kenney as 'extraordinarily clever', Knight worked as secretary of the local WSPU (Women's Social and Political Union).[15] In 1906, when her youngest child was 18 months old, Knight was arrested for taking part in suffrage protest. She faced six weeks in prison unless agreeing to be 'bound over' for a year – committing to give up the campaign. The couple's daughter, Winifred Langton, later recorded that Adelaide asked her husband: 'Can I count on your full support? It will be agonising to be away from you and our children, but with your help I can face this.' Donald is said to have replied: 'We have supported each other for many years we must not fail now that we are to be put to the test.'[16] Knight chose prison: 'I refuse to barter my freedom to act according to my conscience, while my health permits me to fight on.' Langton later looked back to her parents as she reflected on her own lifetime of work as a communist and an activist, and found that she learnt how to fight from her mother and how to care from her father.[17]

Many of the suffragists and suffragettes who campaigned for women's right to vote fought for decades to redefine the work of women regardless of their marital status. They highlighted the hypocrisy of a system that pushed back against women who sought to access education, generate a fair income and contribute to public life, at the same time as exploiting women in the poorer classes. As opportunities to develop stimulating roles, jobs and careers were routinely shut down, the economies of the industrial world continued to rely on the labour of women living in poverty who could routinely be paid less than men. In 1911, despite attempts to define the work of a wife as purely domestic, married women represented 30 per cent of a booming female workforce, working in laundries, textile factories and other industries.[18]

In the working classes, with widespread poverty and little social safety net, married women generally expected to undertake whatever work necessary to support their families. In 1906, as Adelaide Knight was imprisoned for suffrage protest, fellow suffragist Isabella Lawson took a job in domestic service 250 miles from her home in Durham, in northeast England. Recently married, she sold her furniture and valuable possessions and moved to Oxford where her coalminer husband, Jack Lawson, had been given the opportunity to study at Ruskin College.

Both newlyweds had grown up in poverty, within struggling working-class communities, and this rare educational opportunity was extremely expensive for the young family. Bella made the decision to financially support her new spouse. Decades later, Jack Lawson went on to become a UK cabinet minister and Bella pioneered support for children living in poverty decades before the welfare state, establishing and running child welfare centres and supporting a new charity, Save the Children, as well as campaigning as a suffragist, councillor and Labour activist. To thrive, couples and their wider communities would need to provide mutual support and wives might commonly find themselves moving between paid employment, domestic work and unpaid community roles throughout a marriage.

In 1914, the outbreak of war disrupted working norms and expectations. While stalling the activism of suffragettes like Knight and suffragists like Lawson, experiences of the First World War made the entrenched resistance to their campaign untenable. In 1918, Garrett Anderson's sister, Millicent Fawcett, wrote that the idea 'formally very widely entertained that women were incapable of skilled work' had been 'shattered by experience since the outbreak of the war'.[19]

In 1919, the year after some women achieved the vote, the Sex Disqualification (Removal) Act removed barriers that had previously prevented women from entering public, professional roles like teaching, nursing and the law. Although class, social background, race and disability continued to exclude huge numbers of women in practice, the Act began to open the door to new, exciting opportunities for some women, and for women's voices to begin to be heard more clearly in public life. It was an early concession. Marriage bars continued to force women out of their jobs and the 1919 Act failed to remove the exclusion of married women from working within the civil service. Although unmarried women were now, technically, welcome to take on roles, married women were thought to experience too great a conflict between their personal and professional lives: 'Women Civil Servants if married either must deliberately endeavour to remain childless or will be forced to neglect either their children or their duties to the Service or both.'[20] The privileged men who continued to make the rules found it difficult to imagine the juggling of labour that women, and particularly poorer women, had managed for centuries.

The 1920s were to see economic stagnation lead slowly to economic downturn and the Great Depression that would shape the 1930s. The working landscape for married women changed again. Poor wages and rising unemployment made family life extremely difficult among the working classes. In northern England, a large working-class women's movement emerged in the interwar period. Through strikes, lockouts and hardships, married women worked to keep families fed and sheltered and to hold communities together. During the 1926 General Strike, a miner's wife and mother of three from County Durham, Annie Errington, left her children with her husband to join a delegation of the Miner's Federation of Great Britain to the Soviet Union. Having never travelled beyond her home county, she delivered speeches to large crowds in towns and cities from the Donbas region to Vladivostok, in search of international support for the mining community. Two years later, in the year women achieved the right to vote on the same terms as men in the United Kingdom, Errington chaired a workers' rally in Sunderland that attracted 10,000 women from across the mining region.[21] She went on to work as a councillor and Justice of the Peace.

Among the middle classes, the economic hardships and high unemployment of the 1920s and 1930s led to increased resentment towards working women, just as public roles and professions had begun to open to them. Married women in particular faced backlash for being seen to 'double dip' into an already shallow employment pool.[22] Across the Atlantic, the US Economy Act of 1932 banned the federal government from employing two people from the same household. Almost all of the people fired were women. Twenty-six states passed laws restricting the employment of married women in various fields.[23] By 1940, over three-quarters of schools in the US had policies refusing to hire married women as teachers.[24]

In times of economic crisis, the plight of unemployed men was the priority. A 1938 study found that:

> *The woman who is out of work ... is not on the whole left stranded by unemployment as is the unemployed man; she has plenty to do, and looks perhaps as healthy or healthier, as happy or happier than she did when she was working, so that the real problem is to increase the income brought in by her husband's wage sufficiently for it to be possible for her to reject definitely the alternative of going back to work, and settle down instead to make a home.*[25]

The employment of men was always desirable. The employment of women was seen as necessary only when serving others: in dire circumstances, to support family members, contributing to war effort or filling gaps as temporary cheap labour. Better to 'settle down instead'.

In the crisis caused by the Covid-19 pandemic, it was men's jobs that again took precedence around the world and women's careers that were disproportionately sacrificed. Towards the end of 2020, women's global job losses were 1.8 times greater than men's.[26] In the UK, women faced significantly higher rates of redundancy and disproportionately bore the burden and sacrifices of additional unpaid work, including childcare and home schooling.

Just twenty years after the female workforce of the First World War was disbanded, women were called back to employment on a mass scale once more, as conflict ravaged the world again, after war broke out on a global scale in 1939. Not only were single young women conscripted in the new war effort, but wives and mothers were asked to serve. In the US, the numbers of women in employment increased by almost 60 per cent between 1940 and 1945.[27] Three-quarters of the newly working women were married.[28]

In 1943, at least 670,000 wives or widows with children under the age of 14 were employed in the UK.[29] A 37-year-old war worker in Oxford recorded a February morning in her diary:

> *My baby woke me at 6. I got him his bottle & returned to bed & slept till about 7.15. then he wanted to play. I sat him up in his cot, gave him a scarlet penguin ... a wooden mallet & a tin. (I can sleep through bangings but not through howlings.) At quarter to eight I pulled myself out of bed, dressed him & put him on the floor to crawl around while I dressed myself. He enjoyed himself with the hanging brass brandles of the bottom drawer of the chest. I put on an overall over my office clothes & took him down to the kitchen where he sat on my knee and had breakfast (scrambled egg, lease-lend orange juice, and bread & butter). Then I sat him in his chair-and-table, kissed him goodbye & went off to work, leaving him with a girl married to someone in the RAF. She looks after him and her own baby for me in the daytime, & shops & copes with the flat.[30]*

I remember counting the minutes of sleep like this in my baby's first year, before finally pulling myself out of bed. In 1943, this mother's wedding ring, small baby and domestic responsibilities were, quite suddenly, no longer barriers to her employment beyond the home.

As the need for recruits grew, wartime rhetoric stressed how enjoyable employment could be for married women. Propaganda broke down the moral stigma of wives choosing to go into paid work. The *Daily Mirror* reported:

> *These women enjoyed their work ... it gave them two precious gifts – friendship and a sense of being useful to the community. Don't believe that women don't want to get out of their homes for a few hours a day. They do. They like the sense of independence, the*

*absence of loneliness, the extra money they can spend on their home
or children, the sense of usefulness.*[31]

When the war was over, the social, legal and economic structures that
had opened up opportunities for women were quickly shut down again.
Childcare systems that had so recently supported thousands of women
into the workforce were abolished. In 1951, a Medical Officer of Health
from Smethwick in the English Midlands told a conference:

> *Many people would suggest that if the career mother wishes to park
> out her child for a substantial proportion of the day in order to
> devote herself to her career, she should ... not expect the State or the
> municipality to subsidise her.*[32]

As the modern welfare state was being built, it institutionalized the
dependence of married women through both taxes and benefits.[33]
Marriage was incentivized and the desire of women to work outside of
the home repressed. In the United States, single men and all working
women were deliberately overtaxed to support married couples through
new social security policies. The structures that prevented millions of
women from long-term work before the war remained in place. Many
of them are still felt today: low pay, non-existent or expensive childcare,
maternity discrimination and inflexible working hours.

The housewife was elevated once again and celebrated in women's
magazines, popular culture and consumerist marketing. In the US, the
campaign to get women back in the home was a resounding success
and the breadwinner model thrived. By 1950, only 16 per cent of
children in the United States had mothers who earned a wage.[34] In
1955, Adlai Stevenson, a two-time nominee for president, told an all-
women graduating class of Smith College that 'most of you' will go on
to assume 'the humble role of housewife'.[35] For Stevenson, the role of

these bright privileged young women in a world consumed in conflict and crisis was to contribute to their communities, their nation and the wider world through marriage and the maintenance of a harmonious domestic sphere. Behind every great man there had to be a great woman. 'Whether you like the idea or not just now,' later on, 'you'll like it.'[36]

Despite the moral, social and practical barriers put in their way, many of the working women of the Second World War were not for going back into the home. In the UK, the marriage bar had been removed for all teachers, some of the civil service and for the BBC in the 1940s. Employment rates for married women grew through the 1950s reaching 35 per cent in 1961 and 49 per cent at the end of the next decade. In the old mill town of Burnley in Lancashire, where marriage had rarely disrupted a woman's work, 57 per cent of married women were in employment in 1961, although there was often no wage parity with their male counterparts.

The 1960s and 1970s brought with them a social revolution. Sixteen years after Adlai Stevenson addressed Smith College, the commencement speech was delivered by Gloria Steinem. She went on to deliver two others and would remind graduates that their responsibility to contribute to their nation might not necessarily be met through the careful maintenance of a man's home and mood. Steinem, like the first wave of feminists before her, declared that a woman's contribution and voice should not be spoken through a husband's but belonged, independently and equally, in the public sphere.

After years of protest, personal sacrifice and activism, the UK's first Equal Pay Act was passed in 1970. It granted women legal, theoretical protection from unequal pay on the basis of sex. In 1973, the UK Foreign Office lifted the final marriage bar within the civil service, in the same year as the Republic of Ireland lifted their ban on the employment of married women within the public sector. Two years later, the Sex Discrimination Act 'render[ed] unlawful certain kinds of sex discrimination and discrimination on the ground of marriage' within the UK.[37] In 1977, European law finally made it illegal to fire a woman for the act of getting married.

In the century between the 1870s and the 1970s, waves of women had entered new realms of the changing workforce, only to be pushed back out, to find their way back in and be pushed back out again. Attitudes, fashions and challenges came and went, only to reappear again. Throughout this century, marital status, alongside class, social background, race and disability had remained a major factor in the roles available to women looking to earn a wage, to forge a career and to contribute to society beyond family life.

From the beginning of this century, women have made up half of the workforce in the UK. The impact of marriage on the work of women continues to vary across class and cultural lines with women in particularly conservative religious communities continuing to face greater emphasis on their domestic responsibilities on marriage. However, for many women, their marital status now has very little to do with their work, career or employment choices. Within the UK, the employment of married women has been largely transformed from a problem, rooted in economic need, to a norm – a norm that meets a wide range of economic, social, intellectual and health needs both for women and for society.[38]

Yet we are still working in systems designed for, and largely by, men. Women continue to find that their domestic choices have an impact on their income potential and their career prospects. In the UK, a third of employers avoid hiring women of childbearing age.[39] A third think that women are less interested in their career once they become pregnant.[40] Fifty-four thousand women a year are forced out of their jobs for having children.[41] With the second most expensive childcare system in the world (behind New Zealand) and childcare disproportionately falling to women, many simply cannot afford to work full time.[42] Adverts for flexible jobs are rare, forcing women to regularly take roles well below their skill level to meet the responsibilities expected of them at home. On top of this step-down, part-time work is paid at an average rate of £5 less per hour than full-time work.[43] The expectation that women's commitment to work, and their ambitions for their careers, are, and should be, altered by the act of procreation draws heavily from our inherited ideas of what it meant to be a wife.

The characterization of a married woman as someone who devotes herself to the needs of others continues to shape pressures experienced by today's women, regardless of marital status. Deeply entrenched patriarchal and heteronormative models of marriage cast a long shadow across our society. Women still undertake 60% more domestic work than male partners and more than twice as much childcare.[44] A 2022 study found that nearly half of working-age women in the UK provided 45 hours of unpaid care every week, worth £382bn a year. In contrast, 25 per cent of men provided 17 hours.[45] One in five women have reduced their hours in order to care for an adult.[46] The UK's system of parental leave, trailing far behind most of the world's richest nations, assumes a primary carer role for pregnant mothers, setting up women to bear disproportionate responsibility for both raising children and domestic tasks throughout their careers. And, as Betty Friedan reminded the world in 1963, 'No woman gets an orgasm from shining the kitchen floor.'[47]

The Centre for Progressive Policy calls women's unpaid labour 'one of the driving forces of gender-based inequalities in the workplace'.[48] Around the world, women earn on average 68 per cent of what men are paid for the same work.[49] In the UK, by the end of our careers, women's pensions are worth 55 per cent less than men's.[50] Women are still fighting for equal opportunities, fair pay and career security in a world that has yet to shake off the idea that women bear disproportionate responsibilities at home. In a family of two working women, it can feel like these economic inequalities, so deeply connected to the history of the institution of marriage, hit us twice.

However, having a wife is the best. Building a household outside of assumptions and defaults defined by other people is liberating. There is no expectation of how tasks are to be shared. My wife and I split childcare between us. I cut the grass because I enjoy it. My wife does the majority of the cooking because she loves food. I build the flatpack furniture to prevent serious injuries. Neither of us are quite as on top of the bills as we should be because the whole system of household admin is set up to confuse and bore customers into submission and apathy. We share most things. Many of my friends in opposite-sex marriages share responsibilities within their relationships along the lines of strengths and interests, instead of gender. Though, with systems like parental leave working against them, it is not easy to repeatedly, consistently defy both inherited example and contemporary expectation.

People like Elizabeth Garrett Anderson and Adelaide Knight forged models for women to commit fully to a relationship and to the work that they chose for themselves, well over a century ago. Subsequent generations of activists have continued to break down the legal and economic barriers that have prevented women from accessing these opportunities. Cultural and social barriers and pressures remain. Despite the realities around me, I grew up with a general sense that a 'traditional' marriage involved a male breadwinner and female homemaker. Sometimes it feels like the feminists of the twentieth century won, and sometimes it does not.

'Tradwife' movements are on the rise in North America and the UK. They celebrate the idea of one right, one historic and one 'traditional' way to be a woman. They romanticize the happy submission of a dependant wife, supported by a husband and confined to a domestic role. Despite the fact that the Stepford housewife, a reimagining of Patmore's Angel, was created as deeply creepy satirical fiction by Ira

Levin, she has been positively embraced by many and continues to haunt women across the West today.

Responsibilities within the home continue to be disproportionately understood and undertaken as a woman's work. Writer and feminist Caitlin Moran has written about this.

> *If I were magic, and/or had more time, I would form the Women's Union – a union that would lobby to recognise the home as a workplace, throw the doors open wide on the millions of homes across the world and show what really goes on inside: everything that really matters.*[51]

Work undertaken by married women has been questioned, contested and undervalued since the Industrial Revolution. The debate seeped into wider society and shaped perceptions of the responsibilities and opportunities of all women, regardless of marital status. It has not gone away. In 2021, the UK's *Daily Mail* published an article bemoaning the fact that women are retiring later. The headline lamented, 'State picks up £5,600 bill for the caring of elderly relatives that could have been covered by women if they were not still working.'[52] Marriage no longer defines our options as strictly as it did our grandmothers – but a woman's work really is never done.

TILL DEATH DO US PART

A successful marriage requires falling in love many times, always with the same person.

– MIGNON MCLAUGHLIN, AMERICAN WRITER

There are not many decisions that we make that we imagine should last a lifetime. Not a lot that we expect to be or do forever. Our jobs, careers and homes can be as transient as we choose. People often have several relationships in a lifetime. Marriage is set up to be a statement of something different. Around the world today, we continue to make the optimistic choice to commit to another person for the duration of our lives. The success of a marriage is still routinely judged on its endurance.

For centuries, the world's largest cultures and religions have intended marriage to be a lifelong state. Today, the aspiration to be with a partner for life retains its appeal. It is difficult to resist the idea of having someone to share your life with, someone to share yourself with, as you grow and go through life's ups and downs. There is a strong attraction to the dream of having a person in our lives with whom we can trust our most slouchy, slovenly and least performative selves; who will understand us at our least articulate and accept us at our worst; someone who will see the whole picture of our strengths and weakness and continue to have our back. It is always nice to be part of a team. Committing to a person for the rest of your life opens up the confidence to plan for the long term together, to pool your resources and skills and look to the future – to enjoy what George Eliot called 'a solid mutual happiness'.[1] Solidity does not sound very romantic but of course it is. Marriage is an entirely unique commitment that singles out another person as someone life-alteringly special to you and your future.

The romance of 'forever' is seductive. Despite logic and experience, the idea that we are meant to commit to one person, '*the* one', to create our happily ever after continues to pervade the fiction we consume. From eighteenth-century novels to twenty-first-century romcoms, from Disney to Netflix's *Bridgerton*, plots celebrate the central idea that we can find a soulmate and that when we do, the purpose of marriage is to lock in the love of our lives. It is easy to be swept along in the fiction and get carried away. The idea of 'the One' is attractive but flawed. Often bad for our relationships, it encourages people to cling on to the idea of their 'meant to be', whatever the reality, or conversely discourages people from putting in work with partners who do not easily fit the mould.

Our expectations of marriage have never been higher. The idea of putting each other first, of centring and prioritizing one person in every element of our lives for the rest of their duration is relatively new. Through most of the history of the institution, spousal relationships have not featured at the top of social hierarchies – filial and sibling relationships were often expected to take greater precedence.

In Confucian philosophy, the most important and enduring relationships were said to exist between father and son and between brothers – in thirteenth-century China, sons could be beaten as punishment for siding with their wife over their father.[2] In North America, a Kiowa woman told a researcher in the 1930s that 'a woman can always get another husband, but she has only one brother'.[3] Various priorities, gendered norms and social hierarchies have meant that people have rarely been encouraged to consistently prioritize a spouse. However, in Western culture today, we are encouraged to expect nothing less than to be 'completed' by our marriage partners – our 'other half' – to achieve a life-shaping connection and love that can and should endure, year after year, decade after decade. Although it places an enormous pressure on our relationships, we just cannot resist the hope that it might happen for us.

The debate as to whether it is either realistic or desirable to commit to loving a person and living with them for life continues. History, celebrity and fiction proving tantalizing hints at successes, stories of inspiration as we continue to strive for longevity in our intimate relationships. After a 40-year relationship with Gertrude Stein, ending with Stein's death in 1946, Alice B. Toklas reflected on their meeting:

> *It was Gertrude Stein who held my complete attention, as she did for all the many years I knew her until her death, and all these empty ones since them. She was a golden brown presence, burned by the Tuscan sun and with a golden glint in her warm brown hair.* [4]

Decade after decade, Stein and Toklas shared a life at the heart of Paris's intellectual and creative world, supporting each other's work and sharing love letters and erotic poetry about their relationship. When Toklas wrote her autobiography in the 1960s, it ended abruptly at Stein's death.

In *Becoming*, former First Lady Michelle Obama's 2018 Netflix documentary, tour and autobiography, she reflected that 'it's hard blending two lives together'.[5] For Obama: 'Marriage is a choice you make every day. You don't do it because it's easy. You do it because you believe in it. You believe in the other person.'[6] Obama has been very open about her relationship with Barak and their shared vision for the marriage they began in 1992. Sharing their positive experience of marriage counselling, she places teamwork at the heart of a relationship in which two people can thrive both independently and together over time: 'It's important to marry somebody who is your equal, and to marry somebody and to be with somebody who wants you to win as much as you want them to win.'[7]

Although research in the twentieth century seemed to prove an assumption that marriages generally deteriorate over time,[8] recent research and new analysis has challenged that theory, finding that the majority of relationships experience insignificant or minimal changes in satisfaction as they progress.[9] In the early noughties, a three-year study explored hypertension within married couples and found that, in a generally happy marriage, just a few minutes of time spent with a spouse could reduce blood pressure.[10] A 2016 study found that marriage was literally good for your heart – increasing the likelihood of surviving a heart attack by 14 per cent.[11] Multiple studies around the world have suggested that, on average, marriage is good for our physical and mental health.[12]

Of course, that is not the whole story. For people in unhappy marriages, the opposite is true. Not only do unhappy couples not enjoy the benefits of marriage to their health, but they fare far worse than their single peers.[13] The study found that repeated tension with a spouse raised blood pressure and lowered immune functions.[14] In unhappy opposite-sex marriages, by shouldering the weight of domestic and social labour, wives are far worse off than their husbands. Women in unhappy marriages have higher rates of depression, higher cholesterol and higher rates of alcohol abuse than their single female peers. Research at the University of Pittsburgh found that unhappily married women in their forties were more than twice as likely to develop medical conditions that put them at a risk of a heart attack or stroke.

Whatever our intentions, a happy marriage is not always sustainable and we continue to need exit strategies. Marriage may often be judged to be a success or a failure based on length today, but the enormous pressure that that judgment places on our relationships has never been the only way. It can seem that a lifetime commitment has consistently featured in definitions of marriage, but longevity has had little to do with the institution for many of its spouses. At no point in its global history has marriage been intended to last the lifetime of all participating couples. Escape routes were consistently built into an ostensibly lifelong commitment, and, for some, their marriages have been deliberately designed as breakable bonds.

Around the world, marriages have been created as temporary from the outset. Walking marriages, like those practised within the matriarchal Mosuo community in China, are intended to be transient relationships in which women are free to take on multiple husbands. Although participants might choose for these relationships to be monogamous and long term, there is no need for them to aspire to be permanent.

Today, some Middle Eastern societies recognize the pre-Islamic tradition of mut'a, or temporary marriages. Condemned by Sunni Muslims, the practice was accepted by Shi'ites as a means to create a temporary contract between partners.[15] Relatively unusual and often controversial, these marriages have been used for a range of purposes within Islamic communities for centuries and are thought to have originated as a means of discouraging nonmarital sex for men far from home. Strict rules around mut'a have been designed to govern and restrict its practices, often requiring men to ask a woman's guardian for their permission to enter into a temporary marriage and dictating that women wait a period of time before entering into another.

Although the tradition of mut'a has been used by some to legitimize the sexual exploitation of women and girls, mut'a continue to be practised today as a means to allow greater freedoms for young women and men, allowing couples to spend more time together for a set period, before a permanent marriage is undertaken.[16] In the 2010s, Sara, a 30-year-old pharmacist from Birmingham, enjoyed a six-month mut'a before committing to full marriage to her husband: 'It allowed us to meet without breaking the bounds of Sharia [Islamic law]. We both wanted to date, to go out for dinner or go shopping and just get to know each other better before getting married, which we wouldn't have been able to do otherwise.'[17]

Transient marital unions have a deep history across the globe. From the Arctic to Australia, many indigenous communities allowed marriage to be a temporary undertaking before Christianized laws repressed these practices. Generation after generation, Inuit husbands and wives in northern Alaska commonly accessed divorce, remarriage and co-marriages.[18] Among Aboriginal Australians, a marriage might have been ended by simply terminating cohabitation and a wife might have married several husbands in succession. For centuries, European colonizers used the practice of temporary marriage, divorce and polygamy to project ideas of moral superiority and white supremacy over indigenous communities to justify relationships of dominance and oppression.

A person's ability to access a temporary marriage, or to escape an ostensibly permanent one, has depended heavily on the general motivations within their community for marrying in first place. If marriage was primarily created as a regulator of sexual desire, structures might be created around multiple partners – particularly where the legitimacy of children was not defined through a paternal line or same-sex relationships were practised. If marriage was about the formal joining of families and creation of in-laws, there would be more than one relationship to untangle – transient personal preferences and the happiness of individuals, might not be enough to outweigh the practical implications of separation. Where marriage has been understood primarily as a religious sacrament, as in some Hindu and Christian practices, then few have had the power to put asunder. However, if marriage was primarily a contract, perhaps the limits of that contract might be redrawn. Moreover, where marriage has been motivated by the pursuit of happiness, when joy and fulfilment might fail, is recognition of the end not logical?

We place high expectations on ourselves to make our marriages last. Routinely promising the rest of our lives on our wedding days, we strive to keep our vow and hold on to the choice we made. However, separation is a journey couples have taken for millennia. Throughout history, as communities developed ideas, rules and systems of marriage as a long-term commitment, they consistently built in exit strategies.

Several millennia ago, in 1760 BCE, laws governing the end of a marriage were documented on tablets in Babylonia.[19] Largely relating to property, they stipulate clearly how a couple's assets should be divided on divorce. The rights of husband, wife and children are all recognized and, to some extent, protected. An abusive husband would forfeit both his wife and her dowry. A wife had more to lose if found at fault and divorced by her husband and most of the discretion relating to separation lay with the man. A husband could pawn his wife if she had not protected herself on marriage with a special contract, but not for more than three years. The tablets include the painfully practical provision that if a husband was held captive by an enemy, and his wife could not support herself, she could 'enter another man's house' in a temporary union and rejoin her husband on his return – so long as she abandoned any children of this second relationship.[20]

For centuries in Britain, it was relatively common for people desiring the end of a marriage to separate from one another. Marriage was social before it was religious. When marriages broke down, practical solutions would be found. In a divorce between labourers in tenth-century Wales, a king ruled that the man could keep the pigs, which he primarily cared for, and the woman could keep the sheep, because she took them to the higher ground in summer. He got the chickens. She got the milk and cheese-making equipment.[21] It was pragmatic.

Between the sixth and tenth centuries, the Christian Church grew in power. The young Church moved away from a greater openness to separation that had been held in its Jewish roots and began to more strongly forbid divorce. Life-long monogamy was established as fundamental to the definition of the Christian institution. European state laws became slowly, deeply entangled with these values, and ending a marriage could prove challenging for most. But not impossible for all.

European kings were accustomed to putting aside their wives in favour of an alternative for centuries. When Henry VIII first sought a new marriage in the 1520s, it was not an unprecedented or uncommon request – though his married life was certainly unusual in volume of spouses, and in his choice to use the apparatus of the state to make himself a widower in dispensing with his less well-connected wives. History consistently shows that no values, behaviours, traditions, expectations or definitions of marriage could trump the personal preference of men who wielded enough wealth or power – men who usually managed to circumvent the rules to get what they wanted. In 2021, Boris Johnson managed to outdo Henry VIII and have his third wedding take place in the Catholic Church. A Church that routinely turns away once-divorced Catholics. There has often been a loophole to be found.

Outside of Europe's ruling classes, few people could call on powerful allies, forge new churches or face stooping to murder to disentangle themselves from a marriage. For centuries, England remained the only Protestant country in Europe without legal provision for divorce. Having declared his own marriages null and void, Henry VIII refused to join the other Protestant reformers in Europe's Reformation in granting wider access to separation for his subjects.

History clearly demonstrates the cruelty of rigidly forbidding access to the dissolution of a marriage for its participants. It would be another 250 years after Henry VIII formally separated from Spanish Catholic Catherine of Aragon under the new Church of England, that the Church would grant a woman's appeal for access to the same freedom through divorce.

In 1776, Mary Eleanor Bowes was a 27-year-old widow and one of the wealthiest women in Britain; free to enjoy her wealth, liberty and lovers. The following year she found herself at the altar of St James's Church in London, marrying a charming soldier of little wealth or status. Having staged a duel, ostensibly to protect her honour, Andrew Robinson Stoney feigned a fatal injury and requested that Mary Eleanor grant his dying wish – to be married to her. The wedding was a small one, with the groom carried in on a bed and the expectation that he would, shortly after, be carried into church once more. Next time in a coffin.

Mary Eleanor had promised to be Andrew's wife until death parted them – and expected the commitment to be relatively short-term. However, he made a seemingly miraculous recovery. Her husband, now owner of her entire fortune, quickly began to be physically, emotionally and psychologically aggressive to his new wife. He gambled her money, neglected their responsibilities and restricted access to her children. Mary Eleanor recorded that he was often 'out of humour with his mistress or money matters; and always on these occasions came home and beat, pinched, kicked or pulled me by the ears and nose, often thrusting his nails into my ears, which he made stream with blood; spitting also into my face, and telling me that he married me to torment me'.[22] He coerced her to lie about her injuries and imprisoned her in one of their homes.

Eight years into her torture, Mary Eleanor finally escaped on 3 February 1785 with the help of her maid and friend, Mary Morgan, and three other junior women in her household. These four working women, thoroughly disenfranchised in Georgian society, lent Mary Eleanor clothes and money from their tiny wages. Risking violent retribution, they left behind some of their own belongings and their source of future income to help her. Mary Eleanor left behind her children, the youngest just three.

She had limited options and low chances of success in legally detangling herself from her abuser. There was no real precedent to draw on.

Between 1670 and 1857, divorce was possible in England only through an individual, tailored Act of Parliament. This difficult feat required access to influential networks, as well as considerable funds. Across nearly two centuries, only 325 people across the country successfully petitioned for a divorce. Just four of them were women. Divorce proceedings in the ecclesiastical courts had been designed exclusively for men, they were extremely rare and separation, when achieved, was granted only with great reluctance.

Mary Eleanor's husband had her entire family fortune at his disposal to mount a defence against her. She was destitute following her escape, surviving with food parcels from her family's tenants and the work of those hoping to be paid if her case was successful.

> *My Lawyers act most zealously for me ... without Fees, the 4 Maids servants who attended me in my flight, serve me without Wages, & two of them even left behind a great deal of Money which Mr Bowes owes them.*[23]

On 6 May 1786, the first in a series of cases was judged in Mary Eleanor's favour. Her husband immediately appealed. Six months later, he violently abducted her from Oxford Street in London with paid, armed thugs. She was taken out of the city and transported more than 250 miles north. When caught, he was imprisoned, accused of kidnapping, attempted murder and attempted rape. He was ultimately sentenced to three years imprisonment and a heavy fine. However, their divorce was far from over, and, as her legally recognized husband, he retained her entire family fortune, renting himself a grand house adjacent to the prison for his confinement. He remained in control of their two children. In the eyes of the law, Andrew's behaviour had been criminal, but could not override his rights as a husband or the existence of their marriage.

In 1777, the night before her wedding to Stoney, Mary Eleanor had secretly signed and hidden a prenuptial deed. Twelve years later, it was this act that allowed her to regain access to her fortune. With control over the finances, she found herself in the stronger position, and, following multiple legal battles, finally secured custody of her children and the formal separation she desired.[24]

Bowes' case set an important precedent and began to challenge long-established norms, but reforms were slow and divorce continued to remain inaccessible for most. For decades after Bowes' marriage, couples hoping to legally escape their own relationships could look only to have them annulled. Justifications for annulment were extremely limited. Petitioners were required to prove not that their marriage should no longer exist but that the marriage had never existed in the first place.

In the middle of the nineteenth century, Effie Gray sought an annulment from her six-year marriage to writer, art critic and conservationist John Ruskin, on the grounds that it had never been consummated. She was forced to undergo an invasive medical exam by a doctor to prove that her hymen was 'intact'. Effie won her battle, was released from her marriage and embarked on a new, much happier relationship with Pre-Raphaelite painter John Millais the following year. Lack of consummation by penetrative sex remains one of the rare grounds upon which people might seek an annulment around the world today, although this rule generally excludes same-sex couples whose sexual practices are not recognized in law. So important is the idea of penis and vagina penetrative sex to the definition of marriage that we have inherited, that same-sex couples also cannot access divorce on the grounds of adultery in the UK, where same-sex infidelity has taken place.

For centuries, both annulment and divorce remained out of reach for the vast majority of people. In the working classes, informal routes to separation emerged. Like husbands in the most elite circles, working men generally found themselves to have more options than their wives. Thomas Hardy's nineteenth-century novel *The Mayor of Casterbridge* opens with a farm labourer selling his wife to a sailor in a marketplace.

> *For my part I don't see why men who have got wives and don't want 'em, shouldn't get rid of 'em ... Why shouldn't they put 'em up and sell 'em by auction to men who are in need of such articles? Hey? Why, begad, I'd sell mine this minute if anybody would buy her!*[25]

The selling of a woman to a stranger in a public market was a scandalous, but not unknown, end to a British marriage. 'It has been done elsewhere—and why not here?'[26] Wife sales took place from the sixteenth century right up to the twentieth. Although they had no basis in law, the legal system was relatively ambivalent to the marriages of the poor. Keen to keep people out of workhouses, and with only small amounts of money involved, authorities rarely took an interest.

Across the 1800s, newspapers reported widely on 'wife sales' locally and abroad. Some local customs involved women being led around a market with a rope around their neck, in search of the highest bidder. In 1856, the *Dorset County Chronicle* reported:

> *The inhabitants of Retford were somewhat surprised on Friday last, from an announcement by the town crier that a woman of the name of Starkey would be offered for sale in the public market on the following day.*[27]

The husband had marched up to his unwilling wife 'presenting a new halter with which to lead her away'.[28] Violence ensued and the sale was prevented. Having drawn attention to himself, the husband was ultimately arrested as a deserter from the West Riding of Yorkshire militia. It is unclear what happened to his poor wife.

There seem to have been many cases of women, like the wife described in *The Mayor of Casterbridge*, who were willing to actively participate in their sale. Some exchanged money in a 'wife sale' after meeting a new partner. As late as 1907, officials in Canada were 'puzzled to know' how to proceed when faced with the sale of an English woman in Montreal from a man described as a 'drunkard', who she was forced to financially support, to a 'hard-working man' she had chosen to live with.[29] She made 'no complaint' about the transfer of $60 and was keen for the arrangement to be accepted.[30]

The practice of wife selling across hundreds of years reflected people's inability to retract the commitment made on their wedding day. For women seeking a new start, from the most powerful and wealthy wives to those battling poverty to survive, social, economic and legal dependence on their husband made separation impossible for many. As the Victorian era unfolded, the plight of women stuck in abusive marriages gained increasing public attention.

In 1850, British author William Makepeace Thackeray wrote a poem about a woman looking to escape intimate partner torture within her marriage. 'Damages, Two Hundred Pounds', tells the story of a 'wretched' wife, whose husband has 'Beat her, kicked her, caned her, cursed her, left her starving, year by year / Flung her from him, parted from her, wrung her neck, and boxed her ear.'[31]

When Thackeray's victim manages to escape with the help of her lover, the husband sues and is awarded £200 damages for the theft of his property.

If a British wife offends you, Britons, you've a right to whop her.

Though you promised to protect her, though you promised
   to defend her,
You are welcome to neglect her: to the devil you may
   send her:
You may strike her, curse, abuse her; so declares our
   law renowned;
And if after this you lose her,—why, you're paid two
   hundred pound.[32]

By the middle of the nineteenth century, the idea that marriage must be for life, for everyone, under all circumstances, had begun to erode. The Victorian era had so idealized and romanticized the institution that marriage had begun to shift – the belief that love, affection and respect were deeply connected to the success of a marital relationship had taken hold. By 1857, the experiences and campaigning of women like Caroline Norton and Mary Eleanor Bowes had shifted public and political opinion. The Matrimonial Causes Act made divorce part of civil law in England and was rolled out across the world through Britain's colonial legal systems.

The Act made legal separation significantly cheaper and the grounds for divorce were expanded. However, the double standard applied to men and women was retained. Men could sue for separation on the grounds of a wife's adultery. Women could sue for divorce only if their husband's adultery was accompanied by incest, bigamy, sodomy, bestiality, cruelty or desertion. A man's infidelity was an accepted feature of a marriage, a woman's was the end of it. Women were technically empowered to seek a legal escape from their husbands if they could prove that they had been subjected to 'cruelty' in addition to adultery, but almost all forms of physical violence could be judged reasonable. Emotional, psychological, financial and sexual abuse were not recognized at all. Only if repeated violence could be seen to cause long-term, physical damage to a woman's health, could cruelty be claimed.

The new means of ending a marriage offered through the 1857 Act was still beyond the reach of most people but it allowed hundreds of couples a chance to go their separate ways. Little-explored legal records give glimpses into the divorces of classes of people who had not had access to them for a millennium. In 1863, Caroline Avery, an innkeeper, successfully petitioned her husband William on grounds of his infidelity with her sister. Caroline was able to claim the dual sin of adultery and incest – having become one legal entity on their marriage, her sister became his.[33]

Caroline's sister, Emma, married William less than three months after their separation. The couple claimed that William was a widow in order to marry in a Church. They raised William and Caroline's four children as a seemingly stable family, the children referring to their new stepmother, their biological aunt, Emma, as their mother on official records. Caroline remarried seven years later.[34] It is difficult to understand the feelings and experiences of families like the Averys without the letters, diaries and newspaper reports that survive for the wealthy elites. Caroline and William were a relatively average working couple, newly able to access divorce and remarriage and to make a new start in their lives.

By the end of the Victorian era, demand for divorce was on the rise in much of the West. Some women worried that marriage reform and greater access to separation would ultimately harm women, making them more vulnerable to desertion. Emily Acland, anti-suffrage campaigner, wrote of the institution of marriage in 1902: 'Remember that if it comes simply to a physical struggle the men will always have the best of it. It is the Christian religion which has raised women to the position they now occupy. God had protected women by His law of marriage. We do not want to become simply the slave and plaything of men's passions.'[35]

As demand continued to rise, the German American professor Felix Adler blamed the 'evil of divorce' on the 'pernicious' idea that marriage should be about 'comradeship': 'Comradeship is obnoxious and antagonistic to the idea of marriage.'[36] For Adler, companionship, love and affection 'depend[ed] on free choice and free choice can be annulled. There is nothing permanent in the idea of comradeship.'[37]

The idea of comradeship, so central to the definition of marriage today, was deeply radical when placed at the heart of a marriage, just a century ago. In response to a growing emphasis on the compatibility of married partners, as well as rising divorce rates, the controversial idea of trial marriages began to create a direct challenge to the permanent definition of the institution in the US. In 1906, feminist sociologist and anthropologist Elsie Clews Parsons published *The Family*. Parsons had married in 1900 and resisted pressure to resign her university position following either her wedding or the birth of her children. In *The Family*, she mooted the idea that trial marriages, temporary marriages, by offering 'increased tolerance of sexual activity among the young', might help to tackle problems of prostitution:

> *It would therefore seem well from this point of view, to encourage early trial marriage, the relation to be entered into with a view to permanency, but with the privilege of breaking it if it proved unsuccessful and in the absence of offspring without suffering any great degree of public condemnation.*[38]

Although trial marriage formed only a brief section of *The Family,* the publication was quickly condemned for the suggestion in the media and by politicians and religious leaders. A Presbyterian minister in New York, Reverend Charles Parkhurst, preached in response that 'a consecutive harem is no improvement on a simultaneous one'.[39] For Reverend Henry Barber, it was 'utterly abominable, and, coming from the pen of a woman, makes it doubly atrocious'.[40]

The following year, state legislators in South Dakota and Iowa saw bills proposing that a marriage contract might be entered into for the length of five years, after which time the couple would be free to renew the contract or to part ways.[41] In response, just one month later, the Mayor of an Iowan town, Fort Dodge, took it upon himself to defend the institution by passing a city ordinance that required every resident of the town aged between 25 and 40 to be married in the following sixty days or to pay a fine. He himself offered to perform free wedding ceremonies. His efforts were dampened when his young daughter eloped with an older chauffeur keen to escape the fine.

The debate as to whether marriage need always be permanent would continue to play out across the century. In 1920, a high-profile artistic couple in New York, writer Fannie Hurst and pianist Jacques Danielson, announced that they had married five years earlier. Their secret 1915 wedding had marked for them the beginning of a probationary period. Hurst told the *The New York Times* that she had intended never to marry but, on meeting Danielson,

> *I found my youthful determination that marriage was not for me suddenly undermined. But my determination that marriage should never lessen my capacity for creative work or pull me down into a sedentary state of fat-mindedness was not undermined.*[42]

Reflecting that nine out of ten of the marriages around her were 'sordid endurance tests, overgrown with the fungi of familiarity and contempt', Hurst had made the decision to create a temporary marriage – to marry in secret and to try out married life for one year.[43] Although the probation had been a huge success, the couple were determined to prevent their relationship from going stale with longevity by maintaining their own separate residences throughout their marriage:

'We decided that seven breakfasts a week opposite to one another might prove irksome.'[44] Hurst informed the *The New York Times* journalist that their average was two.

Hurst and Danielson suffered outpourings of heavy criticism in the press for their 'experimental marriage'.[45] Columnists openly rejected the idea that this was a marriage at all. Marriage was forever and not something to be tested. Sometimes conflated with cohabitation and sexual experiences before marriage, trial marriage reflected a natural next step in growing emphasis on happiness and compatibility as the defining characteristics of a successful marriage.

As the century progressed, more people began to expect the ability to choose whether to remain married or not. Access to divorce varied hugely. Within America, local state laws, and the laws of neighbouring territories dictated options. With some states holding far more restrictive laws than others, divorce tourism thrived well into the twentieth century. In South Carolina, divorce was unavailable until 1948. For decades, residents could pop over the border to Georgia or head to a 'divorce mill' – regions with relatively easy divorce laws that were set up to host people looking for more than a brief escape.

Divorce mills permitted a long list of grounds for legal separation and had short residency requirements. In the early 1900s 'going to Reno' became almost synonymous with ending a marriage.[46] Travelling might be relatively expensive but, with restrictive laws elsewhere, divorce mills provided a practical offer to meet inevitable demand. And what happened in Nevada did not stay in Nevada. Divorce in one state had to be legally recognized in the others. Between 1929 and 1931, there were 91 divorces per 1,000 married residents in Nevada. The next highest state was Oklahoma, at seven.[47] Conservative fears witnessed in Victorian England resurfaced on a new scale in political life in the United States. Tensions between hotel businesses enjoying the trade, and moralists concerned with defending the institution of marriage, meant that divorce mills came and went.

The menu of acceptable grounds for the breakdown of a marriage evolved dramatically across the twentieth century. In England, women were finally granted the ability to seek divorce on the same terms as men in 1923, just four years after the first woman took her seat as a Member of Parliament in London. Adultery by either partner could now be the sole grounds for legal separation.

It was 1969 before, for the first time, a husband and wife could divorce without one partner being officially to blame in England and Wales. The State of California led the way across the Atlantic in the same year. Divorce became possible because of the 'irretrievable break down' of a marriage. The happiness and fulfilment of both parties was recognized in law as necessary for a successful marriage for the first time. It was a huge step.

The 1960s and 1970s dramatically transformed the options available for married women around much of the world. In the West, the Liberation Movement swept through millions of marriages, creating structures that would allow women the choice to remain married, or not. No-fault divorce, economic independence, maternal custody, equal pay, greater sexual freedoms and a moral challenge to the subservience of women within marriage all empowered women to liberate themselves from the institution.

During the first three-quarters of the 1900s, women were seen to need and desire marriage more than their male peers.[48] Men were generally more likely to complain about the burdens of marriage[49] – to feel tied down by the idea of a wife as a 'ball and chain'. By the end of the century, the reality had reversed, and men were more likely than women to say that marriage was their ideal lifestyle.[50] In 1972, sociologist Jessie Bernard declared that, while men were happier married, women were happier single. Still today, across Europe, Australia and the US, women consistently file for divorce in greater numbers than their husbands and, for a range of social reasons, seem to fare better than men without a spouse.[51]

Between 1966 and 1979, the divorce rate more than doubled in the United States.[52] The death of the institution of marriage was lamented by conservatives. In 1977, sociologist Amitai Etzioni warned that 'not one American family' would be left by the 1990s.[53] The fears of the conservative Right have never been realized. Feminism did not kill marriage in the twentieth century – it made escape from bad marriages possible for some women. It empowered them with more choices than before.

Although access to divorce is undoubtedly an essential component of any feminist society, the intention of marriage remains long term on an overwhelming scale today. Generation after generation, we remain drawn to the aspiration of a committed lifelong partner. And when, for whatever reason, marriages end, people return to the institution again, in love, hope and optimism, to celebrate and to commit to a new relationship. History is full of the love stories of people who did not get it right the first time around – yet leapt again. Country legends June Carter and Johnny Cash shared 40 years of marriage, his second and her third, before dying just four months apart from each other, in 2003. When asked to define paradise in 1981, Cash is said to have replied: 'this morning, with her, having coffee.'[54] Actress Elizabeth Taylor famously married eight times; Zsa Zsa Gabor nine.

Some people choose to remarry their spouse, to renew the vow of lifelong fidelity to their partner. In 2018, *Great British Bake-off* winner, writer and television presenter Nadiya Hussain married her husband in a British civil ceremony, 14 years after her Muslim wedding. Posting on Instagram, she wrote: 'Nothing fancy just love. No frills. Just us. We did it again. I do. I always will. I would do it all over again. #married #secondtime.'[55] Megastars Beyoncé and Jay-Z have renewed their vows at least twice in their 20-year relationship.

For centuries, through memorials, shared graves and headstone inscriptions, people have sought life for their marriages even after death. Although practices vary according to caste, in some Hindu tradition, married women with living husbands have been dressed in red, as brides, after their deaths. Some of history's same-sex couples, their relationships forbidden or formally unrecognized in life, have achieved public unity in shared resting places. When Alice Toklas died aged 89, after decades of struggle to be recognized as Stein's widow, she was buried in Paris beside her partner, her name discreetly carved on the back of Stein's headstone. In New York, Woodlawn Cemetery provides a home to Patricia Cronin's 2002 sculpture *Memorial to a Marriage*. Installed as the future grave marker for herself and her partner at a time in which same-sex marriage was still unachievable, the memorial marks a commitment to something beyond a lifelong partnership.

Marriage remains an optimistic commitment, a decision designed to last a lifetime. The history of modern marriage demonstrates the enduring attraction of a lifelong partner – while teaching us to embrace the end of relationships when they do not work out. It is not difficult to find intense cruelty in the strict, rigid enforcement of a lifelong definition of marriage for all of its participants. And marriage has never been for life for everyone. In having the option to leave, we can make the empowered choice to stay. To return, time and again, to the promise and the ambition to share the years ahead of us with a teammate, partner and spouse. Without the coercion to stay with our partners, we can continue to choose each other, again and again.

KEEPING UP THE FIGHT

You have to believe that change can happen if you are going to be a part of making change. That doesn't mean we don't hurt, that we don't despair, that there isn't grief – there is all of that. But there also must be a belief that we, too, can make the change that we long for.

– ALICIA GARZA, ACTIVIST AND COFOUNDER OF
BLACK LIVES MATTER MOVEMENT[1]

The rights of women, regardless of marital status, have been revolutionized in the West, in the face of powerful resistance, over the last century. The realities of daily life, our relationships and choices, have been transformed. From the 'first wave' of feminist activism in the 1800s, to the 'fourth wave' today, a series of campaigners and leaders have redefined twenty-first century marriage. These separate, sometimes divergent, and not always inclusive movements shared a common understanding that the personal is, and has always been, political.

In Britain, in 1857, a member of the House of Commons defined Parliament as 'a court of men judging women according to their own estimate and for their own purposes'.[2] These were the people who defined marriage for generations and, through the exercise of colonial power, for people around the world. It was these men who legislated against married women's right to hold property or to withdraw consent to sex, who prevented recourse from physical, emotional, psychological and financial abuse and who restricted their powers as parents. In 1866, John Stuart Mill submitted the first petition for women's right to vote to Parliament. It would take more than half a century for women to choose, and to become, lawmakers, but it marked the beginning of a transformation in women's lives within the United Kingdom.

Like each subsequent wave, these early activists faced powerful opposition. In 1897, in Northumberland in northeast England, suffragist Caroline Phillips reflected: 'Monopoly and privilege are naturally the portion of the strong and the powerful, and these privileges always die hard.'[3] Across generations, both men and women passionately fought to prevent the legal equality of the sexes, both inside and outside of marriage. The roles and responsibilities of women were seen as clear – their lives might be defined by politics and politicians, but a woman's place was to be shaped by the institution of marriage and the nuclear family unit.

Octavia Hill, social campaigner and founder of the conservation charity the National Trust, campaigned against women's right to shape the laws that governed their relationships and their lives. She cautioned women that they should confine themselves to 'silent, out-of-sight work'.[4] She urged her sex to concentrate on 'her duties, not on her rights' and to 'fill the place to which by God's appointment she is called'.[5] For fellow campaigner Lady Emily Acland, marriage held greater importance:

> *The stability and happiness of the Empire rests eventually on the stability and happiness of each home in the Empire; and that again rests on one only sure foundation, the inviolability and sanctity of the marriage vow. But the sanctity of marriage is being called in question on all sides today.*[6]

A young Winston Churchill agreed. Writing in 1897, he found the idea of women's participation in political life to be 'contrary to natural law and the practice of civilised states'.[7] He reflected that 'women who discharge their duty to the state viz marrying and giving birth to children are adequately represented by their husbands'.[8] Marital responsibilities and public voice were understood to be incompatible – and, for women, marriage, their 'duty to the state', should of course come first. Concerned, as a Conservative, that newly enfranchised women would vote Liberal, when it came to women's rights to independent political voice, he reflected that 'no necessity is shown'.[9] In 1889, a time in which married women had almost no rights over themselves, their bodies, their finances or their children, an anti-suffrage petition supported by Churchill's American-born mother, Jennie Spencer-Churchill, made the claim that 'during the past half century all the principal injustices of the law towards women have been amended'.[10] Four years later, in 1893, the World Congress of Women more sympathetically proclaimed that 'the legal position of the wife in England is a scandal to civilization'.[11]

In 1918, some women achieved the vote. The next year, the Sex Disqualification (Removal) Act opened up professions to women. A year after that, unemployment benefits were extended to wives. The following year, husbands and married women had the opportunity to inherit property equally for the first time. Parliament welcomed more women members, and the institution began to serve women as constituents for the first time. In 1928, women gained suffrage on the same terms as their husbands, brothers, fathers and sons. One year later, the Age of Marriage Act raised the minimum age for marriage to sixteen years old, from twelve for girls. Suffragists, suffragettes and the first-generation feminists fulfilled Emmeline Pankhurst's wish to become 'law makers', not 'law breakers'. Related movements on every populated continent drove forward some level of reform. Though their progress was often partial, limited by contemporary attitudes to issues of class, race, sexuality, gender and imperialism, they began to redefine the realities of life for many women.

The revolutionizing of the institution of marriage in the twentieth century took time, as the mantle passed from one generation to the next. In the 1960s, feminists looked back to discover that women were still losing their opportunities, their autonomy and their security on marriage. In 1963, Betty Friedan's *The Feminine Mystique* was to light a fire under white middle-class America and women suffering from, what she defined as, 'the problem that has no name'.[12] *The Feminine Mystique* voiced the dissatisfaction, frustration and yearning of many married women who were still being told that 'fulfilment as a woman had only one definition ... after 1949—the housewife-mother'.[13]

As the second wave feminists fought for sexual freedom, reproductive rights and access to divorce, they brought issues of domestic violence and marital rape out from behind closed doors for many and sought economic equality for women. They created a powerful response to the breadwinner-housewife model and myth. In the United States, women of colour began to organize into a political force on a new scale as Shirley Chisholm became the first Black woman to be elected to Congress, in 1968. Around the world, women's activist movements grew to challenge long-established norms. In Japan, sexual liberation became the focus of the movement while in India, burgeoning women's groups and networks exposed challenges to women's lives exacerbated by issues of caste, poverty and exploitation. In Ireland, bans on contraception were heavily protested while in Singapore, concerns around birth rates dominated emerging feminist discourse.

By the 1970s, it was clear to many that the seemingly timeless institution of marriage had become out of step with changing times. It existed as a legal and cultural framework that continued to hold women back. Some in this second wave questioned whether marriage could ever be defined separately from the patriarchal oppression of women.

In the UK, Mary McIntosh, an activist for women's liberation and gay and lesbian rights, founded the Women's Liberation Independence Campaign in the mid-1970s. Its more popular name was 'YBA Wife?'. Drawing attention to the toil, discrimination and abuse women faced within marriage, the campaign asked 'Marriage – what's in it for you?'[14]

Women who questioned and criticized the institution, who rejected it from the outside and challenged it from within, transformed marriage for many of us today. Feminist victories were incomplete, often excluding women of colour and the disenfranchised, missing or misunderstanding the experiences of lesbians, trans and bisexual women and nonbinary people, and deeply ingrained inequalities of class left many women unheard. However, in their disruption, their critiquing and their destruction of assumptions that had endured for centuries, they created a legacy that we can continue to build on today.

Over the last 150 years, wave after wave of questioning what it means to be a wife has led to a redefinition of the role for many. Joining the institution of marriage in the UK, and much of the West today, will not bring the legal and social privileges it once did; your marital status need not dictate your domestic, romantic or sexual life or affect your employment or parenthood prospects. No longer an all-consuming commitment expected to redefine your public identity, determine your economic reality and supersede everything else in your life, becoming a wife or a spouse is an intimate thing – not a role in and of itself at all. For many people, marriage has been transformed into a statement, a symbolic choice. A romantic, profound and serious declaration that we make to our partner and to the wider world – one that echoes the footsteps, templates and language of the past, but need not be defined by them.

Victories and rights achieved by the waves of feminist action that ebbed and flowed across the twentieth century face new threats in the twenty-first. As rights are not only challenged but begin to be rolled back on a new scale, we remember the potent relevance of those battles today. There will always be resistance to change; push back against the questioning of privilege; the argument and perception that, when it comes to equality, we have come close enough.

However, without the chance to enjoy genuine equality in our intimate relationships and family lives, how can we aspire to achieve equal opportunities in wider society? In our careers? In political life? Narrow definitions of what it means to be a wife and a woman continue to demand opposition and resistance. Marriage still needs to make space for trans and nonbinary people and for diverse communities who have previously been unable to access the institution. In 2021, a global survey found that just 54 per cent of people questioned support marriages like mine – 68 per cent of respondents in the United Kingdom support the right of same-sex couples to marry.[15] The fight to protect women's sexual and reproductive freedoms and to ensure that the voices of women are heard more clearly in courts and by criminal justice systems around the world is not over. A cultural change is needed to empower more people to be able to celebrate and to share their intimate relationships free from the pressures of inherited, constructed and limiting gendered roles and expectations.

Recent decades of dramatic reform have proven just how elastic this ancient institution can be. Marriage has routinely transformed, evolved and redefined itself across geography, religion, culture and time. The aspiration towards an institution that serves all of its participants continues to be one worth fighting for.

EPILOGUE

The past is never dead. It's not even past.

– WILLIAM FAULKNER, AMERICAN NOVELIST

History leaves us glimpses of marriage, traces and brief insights into very personal relationships; stories that provide a mirror for us to hold up to our choices today. We have come a long way, but it is not difficult to find the past reflected in the present. In both joyful shared customs and in inherited inequalities, the history of marriage continues to shape our expectations, assumptions and habits today.

Marriage has been declared dead or dying for more than half a century – but it endures. Around the world, at any point in the last fifty years, around two-thirds of women between 15 and 49 years old have been married or in a formal union.[1] In the UK, just over half of the population aged 16 or older are married today.[2] With people marrying later and more people outliving their marriages, single living has seen a dramatic rise in recent decades,[3] but most people continue to make the choice to join the institution at some point in their lives. In the United States, research has shown that the vast majority of Americans continue to aspire to marriage and will join the institution at some point in their lifetimes.[4]

This book emerged as an interrogation of my own decision to marry. Conscious of the institution's long history of repressing and oppressing women, and of excluding same-sex couples, I wondered why I was so very happy to join it. Was it a 'triumph of imagination over intelligence'?[5]

In practice, the decision to marry is rarely about joining an abstract institution. We choose to commit to a specific partner and to our unique relationship. It is an essentially imaginative choice as we make a hopeful leap into an uncertain future together. Research shows that, across socioeconomic groups, people do not simply want to get married, they want to marry someone that they are in love with and then to remain in love, together, for the rest of their lives.[6]

Writing this book reminded me that the institution I joined in 2017 is not the same one that Jane Austen satirized at the turn of the eighteenth and early nineteenth centuries or that Sylvia Pankhurst rejected almost a hundred years later. Decades of legal, social, economic and cultural reforms have created an almost unrecognizable commitment from the one that Mary Eleanor Bowes struggled so hard to escape in the 1770s and 1780s. When Gloria Steinem reflected on her own decision to marry, in 2000, aged sixty-six, she observed: 'I didn't change. Marriage changed ... It is possible to make an equal marriage.'[7]

Women are able to make informed and empowered choices on joining this new and ancient institution on an unprecedented scale. People continue to marry later, with women more often taking opportunities to finish education and establish themselves in work before committing to a relationship.[8] The controversial trial marriages of the early twentieth century are now the norm in much of the West. Sex and cohabiting before marriage are widespread today, and the pressure to marry in order to experience these joys has eased. Where divorce is now accessible, married couples are able to continue to actively choose to be together. Having peaked between the 1970s and 1990s, divorce rates in the West have fallen in recent years.[9] When I chose to marry, I did not face the risks, the pressures, oppressions or exclusions endured by many women in the past. I have been very lucky.

Marriage today can be empowering and romantic; hopeful and

joyful, though largely for the most privileged. There is no injustice or suffering in this book that does not exist in someone's marriage today. No legal inequality that is not still subjugating women and nonbinary people somewhere in the world. Nothing that is not present, or could not return, in the most liberal of democracies.

Women and children continue to be forced into marriages that they do not choose for themselves; bride kidnapping and rape remain the entry route to the institution for too many. As Afghanistan fell to the Taliban again, in August 2021, the routine kidnapping and enslavement of women and girls as brides has been widely perpetrated. Domestic violence, including fatal intimate partner violence, haunts women and girls in every corner of the globe. Pregnancy complications remain a leading cause of death in teenage girls in parts of the world and of women of colour, even in the West.

As the idea of 'traditional' gender binaries continues to be harshly defended, around two in five trans people in the UK fall victim to hate crimes every year.[10] People expressing same-sex attraction and gender diversity have their relationships unrecognized, actively criminalized and suffer persecution in over 70 countries.

Women's sexual and reproductive freedoms continue to be defined by their marital status, and aggressively repressed. So-called 'honour killings' are still performed. The unequal distribution of domestic labour within our families and relationships contributes to a significant gender pay gap and income inequalities. People are coerced to stay in unhappy and unhealthy marriages through combinations of legal, social, moral and economic pressures. The education, freedoms and opportunities of girls and women continue to be deliberately restricted in communities on every populated continent – in order to raise appropriately submissive and dependant wives.

The fight towards greater gender equality, shared empathy and genuine inclusion continues as we strive to let go of the bad habits that we have inherited from previous generations and to find alternative paths. Within the UK, today's institution of marriage was actively forged by generations of activists who persisted in questioning the idea of what it meant to be a husband or a wife. They fought to decouple womanhood from wifehood and to separate a woman's identity from her marital status. Their reforms have created more choices for all genders and enabled more and more of us to determine the roles within our relationships – to reject inherited assumptions and obsolete templates and to shape a commitment that works for us. We can redefine what it means to be a wife or a husband – or reject the labels altogether. In English cockney rhyming slang 'wife' translates to 'trouble and strife'. Thanks to the reformers and activists of the last century, the epithet feels less relevant in the UK today than ever before.

It is important that we recognize progress where it has been achieved – to celebrate how far we have come and to ensure that we do not slip back. Victories are fragile – hard won and easily lost. Questions raised by the Georgian Enlightenment were shut down by Victorian conservatives. Same-sex desire and gender diversity found creative, open expression in Germany in the early twentieth century and the sexual revolution of the 1920s was effectively subdued into 1950s sexual repression. The idea that the #MeToo movement has gone too far pervades mainstream media in much of the West, yet the figures and media reports support that arguably it has not gone far enough. Today's US Supreme Court actively experiments in revoking rights hard won by women and minority groups in the twentieth century. All this shows is that progress is not an inevitable march in one direction.

The idea of what it means to be a wife continues to be under debate and to have political resonance today. 'Tradwife' movements persist in the UK and North America. The middle-class breadwinner and homemaker model of the 1950s has found a voice on social media. Platforms like Facebook, Instagram and Twitter provide a place to share and celebrate the subservience of married women today as the one 'traditional' way of being female and a wife. In the United States particularly, tradwife movements are intimately connected to the alt right and white supremacy.

'Traditional' is often the last defence of the indefensible. The movement romanticizes the good old days, when married women stayed at home, raising children, cooking, cleaning and living lives financially dependent on men whose wages could support a whole household. Women are perpetually well dressed and wearing a smile. This model of being a wife is as traditional as Santa's red coat or a baby girl's pink accessories – traditional because the Western marketing machines of the mid-twentieth century told us so. Santa was more likely to wear a green or tan coat before Coca-Cola dressed him, and the first generation of girls to be adorned with pink, their brothers with blue, were the baby boomers. The ideal of a married woman, later satirized as a Stepford wife, grew from a calculated campaign to encourage women back into the home after their war work in the Second World War. We rarely let history get in the way of a rebrand.

It is easy to sentimentalize past marriages, to foster nostalgia for a vision glimpsed in childhood, through early TV sitcoms or period dramas. It is too easy to forget the experiences of people who fell outside of these narratives. In the romanticized 'traditional', there is no recognition of relationships like mine, of the exclusion and persecution of people expressing same-sex love. The idea of a 'traditional' marriage does not acknowledge the histories of people who lived beyond strict gender binaries. The realities of lives shaped by racism, classism and deep economic inequalities are ignored. The lived experiences of history's people of colour have had no place in the movement. The veneer that the 'tradwife' movement is selling carefully overlooks any definition of 'traditional' beyond a white, Christian, European inheritance. This version of history obscures the trauma and injustices that occurred behind the closed doors of deeply unequal relationships. We should be cautious of letting a partial or idealized history be weaponized to take us backwards. It is our responsibility to keep pulling back the veil on these lives.

Marriage continues and continues to evolve. Each generation navigates their way. Every year, millions of people step outside of the everyday and come together to look to the future – to celebrate love and hope in this most optimistic of commitments. Many Gen Zers make the choice to 'date to marry', aiming for marriage as the ultimate end of their dating experience, while pursuing their relationships with the understanding that not every one needs to end there.[11] People continue to describe their wedding days as the happiest days of their lives. I have friends who enjoyed their proposal so much that, 15 years into their marriage, the husband regularly proposes to his wife when they find themselves in a romantic setting. With marriage still privileged over other relationships, married couples continue to enjoy practical benefits relating to parenthood, taxes, inheritance and international law. Research suggests, time and again, that stable and fulfilling marriages make people happier and healthier and even live longer.[12]

In March 2014, 48 hours after same-sex marriage became possible in England and Wales, 95 same-sex weddings had taken place. By October 2015, around 15,000 new marriages between same-sex couples had been created.[13] Nearly a decade of same-sex marriage has begun to transform the institution. As more and more couples defy the default templates for our proposals, weddings and marriages, the more absurd many of our outdated customs seem and the more liberated we can all feel from the pressures of uncomfortable tradition.

At my wedding, no one received someone else's permission to kiss me. Why should all newlyweds, regardless of sex, not be invited to enjoy their first kiss together as equals? There was no question that a person might possess me enough to give me away. No one expected me to remain silent at my wedding breakfast. I am a wife who feels the burden of domestic and social labour no more than my spouse. My spouse enables, emboldens and empowers me in my career – where sacrifices are to be made for our children, my coparent makes their share. Why should other brides and wives settle for less? Why should grooms and husbands be forced into roles defined and predestined for them? It is clear in the most casual of reflections that gender simply is not the best criteria by which to assign roles and responsibilities within our lives.

New paths are being forged, new traditions continue to spring up, take root and grow. As more and more young people reject gender binaries and identify as neither exclusively a man nor a woman, assumptions are disrupted. A 2021 Ipsos survey found that 4 per cent of Gen Zers globally identified as nonbinary.[14] A 2018 LGBT survey in the UK found that 7 per cent of LGBT respondents identified as nonbinary. The number raised to 12 per cent in 16- and 17-year-olds.[15] In the United States, one in four members of the LGBTQIA+ community are thought to identify neither as exclusively male or female.[16]

It is time to let go of the baggage, the problematic assumptions and narrow expectations that can come with the designation bride or groom, wife or husband. To empower ourselves to make choices relating to our relationships based not on sex or gender but on personalities and preferences, the strengths and interests of the people involved. In recent years, I have heard more wedding speeches delivered by brides, sisters and mothers. I have been a female usher in a wedding party with a male maid of honour. I attended an opposite sex wedding in 2022 in which, in lieu of a giving away ceremony for the bride, the guests were asked as one whether we gave our love and blessing to the couple. I have known more married women hold on to their name. As we continue to reform outdated social structures, we can move further away from the ideas of wifely work that continue to shape women's opportunities.

Today marriage is optional like rarely before. It is an option available to more of us and there are other ways to go. It is not the only safe route to sex, to parenthood or to survival, to long-term companionship or financial security. It is not an alternative to a career or other pursuits. It does not define us. For decades, as some couples campaigned for the right to reject marriage, others fought hard for the right to access it. It is an institution surely better for the choices newly available within it. The choice to enter into it, or not. The choice to shape it around your unique relationship. The choice to end it or keep choosing to stay.

Decade after decade we still choose to take the leap. As we relinquish the practical, social, moral and legal pressures of the past, the desire to marry our partners remains alive and well. For many, the opportunity to make a formal commitment of love and loyalty, to tie the knot in the footsteps of previous generations, feels as relevant as ever. Through our very participation, and our small, everyday choices, we can continue to redefine this most personal of public institutions.

We can choose to reinforce or challenge false illusions of the past, arm or disarm those who would take us backwards. We can shape marriage for the next generation, retaining the traditions that serve us, forging new ones where it is time to let go of bad habits. There is no one authority on marriage and no consensus around any of our relationship choices. As we return, generation after generation to this ancient and almost universally accepted institution, we remember that there is no one way, one right way or one traditional way, to live a marriage.

NOTES

PREFACE

1 The 1918 pamphlet 'Advice on Marriage to Young Ladies', signed by 'A suffragette wife' is on display at the Pontypridd Museum in Wales. It gained widespread attention on Twitter in 2019.

2 Sisterhood and After Research Team, 'Marriage and Civil Partnership', *British Library* (8 March 2013) <https://www-upgrade.bl.uk/sisterhood/articles/marriage-and-civil-partnership>

3 ONS, 'Marriages in England and Wales', *Office of National Statistics* (14 April 2020) <Marriages in England and Wales – Office for National Statistics (ons.gov.uk)>

4 ONS, 'Population Estimates by Marital Status and Living Arrangements, England and Wales: 2019', *Office of National Statistics* (17 July 2020) <Population estimates by marital status and living arrangements, England and Wales – Office for National Statistics (ons.gov.uk)>

5 G. Suneson, 'These States Have the Highest – and Lowest – Percentage of Married People in the US', *USA Today* (2021) <https://eu.usatoday.com/story/money/2019/03/07/marriage-us-states-highest-percentage-married-people/39043233/>

6 Ibid.

7 Reported in K. Hope, 'How Long Should You Stay in One Job?', *BBC News* (1 February 2017). <https://www.bbc.co.uk/news/business-38828581>

8 US Bureau of Labor Statistics, 'Employee Tenure Summary', *U.S. Bureau of Labor Statistics* (September 2020) <Employee Tenure Summary (bls.gov)>.

9 W. Lewis, 'On Average, How Often Do We Move Home?', *Property Reporter* (4 July 2019)

INTRODUCTION

1 C. N. Adichie, *We Should All Be Feminists* (Fourth Estate: London, 2014).

2 *Women's History: The Future, Roundtable Discussion, Followed by Address by Secretary Clinton* (University of Oxford, 26 October 2021) <https://www.youtube.com/watch?v=WiVyTifjwEU>

3 H. Fisher, *Anatomy of Love* (W.W. Norton: New York, 1992), cited in S. Coontz, *Marriage, a History: How Love Conquered Marriage* (Penguin Books: New York, 2006) p. 25.

4 S. Coontz, *Marriage, a History*, p. 36.

5 Ibid.

6 Ibid. p. 35.

7 Ibid.

8   K.E. Starkweather and R. Hames, 'A Survey of Non-Classical Polyandry', *Human Nature*, 23, 149–72 (2012) <https://doi.org/10.1007/s12110-012-9144-x>
9   S. Coontz, *Marriage, a History*, p. 27.
10 Ibid. p. 26.
11 Ibid. p. 30.
12 S.O. Murray, W. Roscoe and M. Epprecht, *Boy-Wives and Female Husbands: Studies in African Homosexualities* (State University of New York Press: Albany, 2021) p. 256.
13 Ibid. p. 253.

POPPING THE QUESTION

1   J. Ballard, 'Do Americans Believe in the Idea of Soulmates?', *YouGovAmerica* (February 10, 2021) <https://today.yougov.com/topics/lifestyle/articles-reports/2021/02/10/soulmates-poll-survey-data>.
2   A. Kalia, 'The Rise of the Proposal Planner: 'It's Not Enough to Get Down on One Knee Any More', the *Guardian*, 17 September 2019 <https://www.theguardian.com/lifeandstyle/2019/sep/17/the-rise-of-the-proposal-planner-its-not-enough-to-get-down-on-one-knee-any-more>
3   N. Stripe, 'Married by 30? You're Now in the Minority', *Office of National Statistics* (1 April 2019) <https://blog.ons.gov.uk/2019/04/01/married-by-30-youre-now-in-the-minority/>.
4   Event Planners Chillsauce interview 10,000 people, 'The Marriage Proposal Survey: Will He or She Say Yes This Year', *Chillsauce* <The Marriage Proposal Survey (chillisauce.com)>
5   Ibid.
6   C. Ritschel, 'Joshua Jackson defends Jodie Turner-Smith over "Racist and Misogynistic" Criticism over her Marriage Proposal', the *Independent* (18 August 2021) <https://www.independent.co.uk/life-style/joshua-jackson-jodie-turner-smith-proposal-b1904755.html>
7   E. Lamont, *The Mating Game: How Gender Still Shapes How We Date* (University of California Press: California, 2020).
8   Ibid. p. 53.
9   Ibid.
10 Statista Research Department, 'Share of Brides Who Received a Diamond Engagement Ring in the United States from 1939 to 1990', *Statista* (2 December 2011) <https://bit.ly/3H86Srr>
11 L. Pressly, 'The Cost of Weddings Spirals in China', *BBC News*, 22 July 2011 <https://www.bbc.co.uk/news/business-14208448>

JUST THE TWO OF US

1   S. Coontz, *Marriage, a History*, p. 5.
2   Ibid. p. 53.
3   Ibid.
4   A. Dhillon, 'Deeply Rooted Tradition': One Man's Long Fight To End Illegal Dowries in India', the *Guardian*, 8 December 2021 <http://bit.ly/3Xffe5R>
5   A. Weikel, 'Mary I', *Oxford Dictionary of National Biography* (23 September 2004) <https://doi.org/10.1093/ref:odnb/18245>
6   Ibid.
7   Ibid.
8   UNICEF, 'Child Marriage', *UNICEF* (June 2021) <https://www.unicef.org/protection/child-marriage>
9   Unchained at Last, 'About Child Marriage in the U.S.', *Unchained at Last* (2022) <https://www.unchainedatlast.org/laws-to-end-child-marriage/>

10 Cited in 'Jerry Lee Lewis and his Child Bride: Inside the Rock Tour That Scandalised Britain', the *Telegraph*, 7 May 2020 <https://www.telegraph.co.uk/music/artists/jerry-lee-lewis-child-bride-inside-rock-tour-scandalised-britain/>

11 Unchained at Last, 'About Child Marriage in the U.S.'

12 Save the Children, 'Covid-19 Places Half A Million More Girls At Risk Of Child Marriage This Year, Warns Save The Children', *Save the Children* (2020) <https://www.savethechildren.org.uk/news/media-centre/press-releases/covid-19-places-half-a-million-more-girls-at-risk-of-child-marrio>

13 S. Neal, et al. 'Childbearing in Adolescents Aged 12–15 Years in Low Resource Countries: A Neglected Issue. New Estimates from Demographic and Household Surveys in 42 Countries', cited in World Health Organisation, 'Adolescent Pregnancy', World Health Organisation (31 January 2020) <https://www.who.int/news-room/fact-sheets/detail/adolescent-pregnancy>

14 J. McNabb, '"She is but a Girl": Talk of Young Women as Daughters, Wives and Mothers in the Records of the English Consistory Courts, 1550–1650' in E. S. Cohen and M. Reeves (eds.), *The Youth of Early Modern Women* (Amsterdam University Press, 2018), pp. 77–96 <https://doi.org/10.2307/j.ctv8pzd5z.6>

15 Ibid.

16 Ibid.

17 Ibid.

18 Ibid.

19 W. Shakespeare, 'Romeo and Juliet' in *The Oxford Shakespeare: The Complete Works*, S. Wells and G. Taylor, (eds.) (2nd ed.) (Oxford: Oxford University Press, 2005) III, 5, 13–14.

20 Romeo and Juliet, III, 5, 160–64.

21 Romeo and Juliet, III, 5, 191–4.

22 'The Marriage Proposal Survey: Will He or She Say Yes This Year', *Chillisauce* <http://bit.ly/3IQJCz1>.

BETTER TO MARRY THAN BURN – OR STARVE

1 J. McNabb, '"She is but a girl".'

2 S. Coontz, *Marriage, a History*, p. 117.

3 S. Coontz, *Marriage, a History*, p. 199.

4 E. Hubbard, 'A Room of Their Own: Young Women, Courtship, and the Night in Early Modern England.' In *The Youth of Early Modern Women*, edited by E. S. Cohen and M. Reeves, 297–314. Amsterdam University Press (2018) <https://doi.org/10.2307/j.ctv8pzd5z.17>

5 Ibid.

6 Ibid.

7 Ibid.

8 S. Coontz, *Marriage, a History*, p. 125.

9 K. Barclay, *Love, Intimacy and Power: Marriage and Patriarchy in Scotland, 1650–1850* (Manchester University Press, 2011) <http://www.jstor.org/stable/j.ctt155j9cf>

10 E. Hubbard, 'A Room of Their Own', p. 301.

11 Ibid.

12 Ibid.

13 S. Coontz, *Marriage, a History*, p. 157.

14 James Woodforde, sometimes called Parson Woodforde, wrote extensive diaries of his life in Norfolk at the end of the eighteenth century. Winstanley and Jamerson, 1999, cited in R. and L. Adkins, *Eavesdropping on Jane Austen's England: How our Ancestors Lived Two Centuries Ago* (Abacus: London, 2013) p. 2.

15 Ibid.

16 Foundling Hospital, 'Poverty in Eighteenth Century London', *Foundling Museum* (*Museum interpretation,* 25 February 2020).

17 S. Coontz, *Marriage, a History*, p. 158.
18 Ibid. p. 127.
19 M. Kaufman, *Black Tudors: The Untold Story* (Oneworld: London, 2019) p. 244.
20 S. Coontz, *Marriage, a History*, p. 127.
21 'Families and Households in the UK: 2016', *Office of National Statistics*, 4 November 2016 <http://bit.ly/3ZU66Fx>

THE USUAL INDUCEMENTS OF WOMEN TO MARRY

1   K. Barclay, *Love, Intimacy and Power*, p. 79.
2   M. Wollstonecraft, *A Vindication of the Rights of Woman*, Project Guttenberg <https://www.gutenberg.org/ebooks/3420>
3   Cited in S. Coontz, *Marriage, A History*, p. 150.
4   Cited in S. Coontz, *Marriage, A History*, p. 150.
5   J. Austen, *Pride and Prejudice* (Chancellor Press: London, 1985.)
6   J. Austen, *Emma,* Project Guttenberg <https://www.gutenberg.org/files/158/158-h/158-h.htm>
7   J. Austen, *Pride and Prejudice.*
8   Ibid.
9   Ibid.
10 J. Austen, *Northanger Abbey*, Project Guttenberg <https://www.gutenberg.org/files/121/121-h/121-h.htm>
11 Cited in S. Coontz, *Marriage, A History*, p. 185.
12 V. Woolf, *Orlando* (Vintage: London, 2016).
13 Ibid.
14 Ibid.
15 Darwin's note was written in pencil in July 1838, the original manuscript is in Cambridge University Library, 'Darwin on Marriage', *Darwin Correspondence Project* <https://www.darwinproject.ac.uk/tags/about-darwin/family-life/darwin-marriage>
16 Ibid.
17 Ibid.
18 Ibid. 11 November 1838.
19 Browning wrote this letter on 10 January 1845, on first reading Barrett's poetry.
20 N. Hawthorne (1840) cited in S. Coontz, *Marriage, a History*, p. 178.
21 K. Barclay, *Love, Intimacy and Power*, p. 90–92.

POLITICAL PROPOSALS

1   T Franks, 'Washington Watch Weekly', FRC, 28 October 2011, <https://www.youtube.com/watch?v=8Sh24eGfeZc>.
2   J Mallif, cited in 'Senior Tory councillor suspended over gay marriage tweet', the Guardian, 11 October 2011, < https://www.theguardian.com/politics/2011/oct/12/tory-councillor-suspended-gay-marriage-tweet>
3   J. Manion, *Female Husbands: A Trans History* (Cambridge University Press: Cambridge, 2020).
4   Ibid.
5   Ibid.
6   Following her visit, on the 3 August, Lister wrote to her lover, Mariana (Belcome) Lawton: 'I cannot help thinking that surely it was not platonic. Heaven forgive me, but I look within myself & doubt. I feel the infirmity of our nature & hesitate to pronounce such attachments uncemented by something more tender still than friendship.' Cited in 'The Ladies of Llangollen', *British Museum* <https://www.britishmuseum.org/collection/desire-love-and-identity/ladies-llangollen>
7   A. Choma, *Gentleman Jack: The Real Anne Lister* (Penguin Random House: London, 2019) p. 152.

8   Ibid.

9   Ibid.

10 Ibid.

11 Ibid.

12 S. Hastings, *Sybille Bedford: An Appetite for Life* (Vintage: London, 2020).

13 Historic England, 'Same sex marriages', *Historic England* <https://historicengland.org.uk/research/inclusive-heritage/lgbtq-heritage-project/love-and-intimacy/same-sex-marriages/>

14 D. Olusoga, *Black and British: A Forgotten History* (Macmillan: London, 2016) p. 110.

15 M. Kaufman, *Black Tudors*, p. 29.

16 Mixed Museum, 'Timeline 1900 – 2021', *Mixed Museum* (2012) <https://exhibition.mixedmuseum.org.uk/museum/timeline>

17 Ibid.

18 'British Nationality and Status of Aliens Act 1914', *UK Public General Acts* <https://www.legislation.gov.uk/ukpga/Geo5/4-5/17/enacted>

19 'The Report of the Select Committee on the Nationality of Married Women' (1923), cited in 'Timeline 1900–2021', *Mixed Museum* (2012),<https://exhibition.mixedmuseum.org.uk/museum/timeline/british-nationality-and-status-of-aliens-act>

20 M.P. Baldwin, 'Subject to Empire: Married Women and the British Nationality and Status of Aliens Act.' *Journal of British Studies*, 40/4 (2001) <http://www.jstor.org/stable/3070746> pp. 522–56

21 Dangerous Women, 'Remembering Chrystal Macmillan – Dangerous Women Project', *Dangerous Women* (24 March 2016)

22 Mixed Museum, 'The Fletcher Report', *Mixed Museum* (2012) <https://exhibition.mixedmuseum.org.uk/museum/timeline/the-fletcher-report>

23 D. Olusoga, *Black and British*, p. 482.

24 Ibid. p. 480.

25 M.C.C. Adams, 'Good War Wives' *Reviews in American History*, 25/1 (1997) <https://www.jstor.org/stable/30030756> pp. 127–31

26 D. Olusoga, *Black and British*, p. 483.

27 *Loving v. Virginia* was decided by a unanimous ruling of the Court on 12 June 1967, *Justia* <https://supreme.justia.com/cases/federal/us/388/1/>

28 R. Nixon, cited in S. Coontz, *Marriage, a History*, p. 256.

A MANOEUVRING BUSINESS

1   S. Varrella, 'Countries Spending the Most on Weddings as of 2019', *Statista* (8 April 2021) <https://www.statista.com/statistics/1226472/countries-spending-the-most-on-weddings/>

2   Ibid.

3   Ibid.; 'The National Wedding Survey: The Average UK Wedding in 2021' *Hitched* (28 February 2022).
    <https://www.hitched.co.uk/wedding-planning/organising-and-planning/average-uk-wedding/>

4   V. Astor, *Invitation to James R. Roosevelt and Helen Astor's Wedding, 1878*, Franklin D. Roosevelt Presidential Library and Museum of the National Archives and Records Administration.

5   M. Weiss, 'The Complete Guide to Planning a Wedding', *Brides* (1 June 2021) <*https://www.brides.com/gallery/how-to-plan-your-own-wedding*>

6   E. Brand, 'Stag Nights and Hen Dos: a Brief History of Bachelor and Bachelorette Parties', *History Extra* (3 April 2020) <https://www.historyextra.com/period/modern/stag-nights-hen-dos-history-bachelor-bachelorette-wedding-party-tradition-origins/>

7   BBC, 'China Cracks Down on Wedding Extravaganza and Extreme Pranks', *BBC* (3 December 2018) <https://www.bbc.co.uk/news/world-asia-china-46423160>

8   B. Montemurro, 'The Modern Wedding', *Aeon* (2014) <https://aeon.co/essays/why-the-traditonal-wedding-isn-t-as-traditional-as-it-seems>

9   C. N. Adichie, *We Should All Be Feminists*.
10 B. Wilson and H. Meyer, 'Nonbinary LGBTQ Adults in the United States', *UCLA School of Law: Williams Institute* (June 2021) <https://williamsinstitute.law.ucla.edu/publications/nonbinary-lgbtq-adults-us/>
11 Government Equalities Office, 'National LGBT Survey: Summary report', *Government Equalities Office* (7 January 2019) <https://www.gov.uk/government/publications/national-lgbt-survey-summary-report/national-lgbt-survey-summary-report>
12 Ipsos, 'LGBT+ Pride 2021 Global Survey', *Ipsos* (2021) <https://www.ipsos.com/en/lgbt-pride-2021-global-survey-points-generation-gap-around-gender-identity-and-sexual-attraction>

MAKING IT OFFICIAL

1   Cited in R.B. Outhwaite, *Clandestine Marriage In England, 1500–1850* (Bloomsbury Publishing: London, 1995).
2   Ibid.
3   In 1234, 60 years before the expulsion of the Jews by Edward I, a recently widowed Jewish woman was denied her dower by Parliament on the grounds that her husband had converted to the Christian faith. The law recognized the marriage, conducted under Jewish rights.
4   CNA Staff, 'Full text: Vatican's Doctrinal Office Response and Note on the Blessing of Same-Sex Unions', *Catholic News Agency* (15 March 2021) <https://www.catholicnewsagency.com/news/full-text-vaticans-doctrinal-office-response-and-note-on-the-blessing-of-same-sex-unions>
5   Ibid.
6   'The Forme Of Solemnizacion Of Matrimonie', *The Book of Common Prayer 1549* <http://justus.anglican.org/resources/bcp/1549/Marriage_1549.htm>
7   R.B. Outhwaite, *Clandestine Marriage In England, 1500–1850*.
8   *The Diary of Samuel Pepys* <https://www.pepysdiary.com/diary/1661/10/>
9   Cited in R.B. Outhwaite, *Clandestine Marriage In England, 1500–1850*.
10 Ibid.
11 Ibid.
12 Ibid.
13 Ibid.
14 Ibid.
15 Ibid.
16 Ibid.
17 Ibid.
18 Robert Elliot took over the running of Gretna Green weddings in 1810 and left this version of the marriage ceremony, *The Gretna Green Memoirs* (London), cited in R. and L. Adkins, *Eavesdropping on Jane Austen's England: How Our Ancestors Lived Two Centuries Ago* (Abacus: London, 2013) p. 14.
19 *The Western Luminary*, February 1815, cited in R. and L. Adkins, *Eavesdropping on Jane Austen's England*, p. 13.
20 J. Austen, *Pride and Prejudice*.
21 S. Marcus traces multiple female marriages of women who lived openly as the wife of another woman in *Between Women: Friendships, Desire and Marriage in Victorian England* (Princeton University Press: Princeton, 2007).
22 A. Choma, *Gentleman Jack: The Real Anne Lister*.
23 Cited in S. Marcus, *Between Women: Friendships, Desire and Marriage in Victorian England*, p. 198.
24 S. O. Murray, W. Roscoe and M. Epprecht, *Boy-Wives and Female Husbands*, p. 254.
25 Ibid.

26 T.D. Parry, 'Married in Slavery Time: Jumping the Broom in Atlantic Perspective'. *The Journal of Southern History*, 81/2 (2015), http://www.jstor.org/stable/43917911 pp. 273–312

27 C. Dickens, *Great Expectations*, Project Guttenberg <https://www.gutenberg.org/files/1400/1400-h/1400-h.htm>

28 'Anger over 'Broomstick' Weddings', *Weekly Dispatch* (London), 12 June 1960, in The British Newspaper Archive <https://www.britishnewspaperarchive.co.uk/>

29 Ibid.

30 Ibid.

31 H.S.Q. Henriques, 'Jewish Marriages and the English Law', *The Jewish Quarterly Review*, 20/3, 1908 <JSTOR, https://doi.org/10.2307/1450891> pp. 391–449

32 A. Khan, *Register Our Marriage* (1 December 2019) <https://registerourmarriage.org/sites/rom.hocext.co.uk/files/2019-12/1%20Dec%202019%20on%20Register%20Our%20Marriage%20%28ROM%29%20campaign%20-%20by%20Aina%20Khan%20%20OBE_0.pdf>

33 Ibid.

34 Ibid.

35 Ibid.

36 K Ghosh, 'Marriages in England and Wales: 2017' *Office of National Statistics* (14 April 2020) <http://bit.ly/3Xipl9W>

37 Ibid.

38 'Number of Non-Religious Weddings Almost Same as Catholic, Figures Show', *Irish Times*, 28 April 2020 <https://www.irishtimes.com/news/social-affairs/religion-and-beliefs/number-of-non-religious-weddings-almost-same-as-catholic-figures-show-1.4240070>

39 Statista Research Department, 'Share of religious and civil celebrant marriages in Australia in 1998, 2008, and 2014 to 2018', *Statista*, (November 2019), <https://www.statista.com/statistics/1155125/australia-share-of-religious-and-secular-marriages/>

40 Law Commission, *Getting Married: A Consultation Paper on Weddings Law* (Law Commission, 3 September 2020) <https://s3-eu-west-2.amazonaws.com/lawcom-prod-storage-11jsxou24uy7q/uploads/2020/09/Getting-Married-A-Consultation-Paper-on-Wedding-Law-web.pdf>

41 'Why Indian Wedding Traditions Could Trump the Pandemic', *BBC The Life Project*, 26 November 2020 <https://www.bbc.com/worklife/article/20201130-why-indian-wedding-traditions-are-powerful-than-the-pandemic>

42 'Coronavirus: How Covid-19 has Changed the "Big Fat Indian Wedding"', *BBC News*, 9 June 2020 <https://www.bbc.co.uk/news/world-asia-india-52892967 – paraphrase?>

43 Law Commission, *Getting Married: A Consultation Paper on Weddings Law*.

44 Ibid.

45 Ibid.

PUTTING ON A SHOW

1 *The Diary of Samuel Pepys* (25 December 1665) <https://www.pepysdiary.com/diary/1661/10/>

2 B. Montemurro, 'The Modern Wedding', *AEON* (5 December 2014) <https://aeon.co/essays/why-the-traditonal-wedding-isn-t-as-traditional-as-it-seems>

3 Rev. W. Holland recorded the wedding on 12 November 1810 (Somerset Archives and Local Studies) cited in R. and L. Adkins, *Eavesdropping on Jane Austen's England: How Our Ancestors Lived Two Centuries Ago* (Abacus: London, 2013) p. 10.

4 Cited in C. Hill, *Jane Austen: Her Homes & Her Friends* (The Bodley Head, 1923) <http://www.digital.library.upenn.edu/women/hill/austen/homes20.html>

5 Ibid.

6   T. Borman (2020). 'Nothing Could Have Gone Off Better': the Wedding of Queen Victoria and Prince Albert. *History Extra*. [online] 9 Feb. [viewed 20 February 2021] Available at: <https://www.historyextra.com/period/victorian/royal-wedding-queen-victoria-prince-albert-dress-cake-1840/>

7   Ibid.

8   C. Bressey, 'Of Africa's Brightest Ornaments: a Short Biography of Sarah Forbes Bonetta', *Social & Cultural Geography* (2005) <https://www.tandfonline.com/doi/full/10.1080/14649360500074675?scroll=top&needAccess=true>

9   Ibid.

10   Ibid.

11   'Sarah Forbes Bonetta, Queen Victoria's African Protégée', *English Heritage* (2021) <https://www.english-heritage.org.uk/visit/places/osborne/history-and-stories/sarah-forbes-bonetta/>

12   C. Bressey, 'Of Africa's Brightest Ornaments'.

13   *The Yemeni Project* <http://www.theyemeniproject.org.uk/4/6/yemeni-and-british-integration.html>

14   S. Devee, *The Autobiography of an Indian Princess, by Sunity Devee, Maharani of Cooch Behar*, 1921, Internet Archive <https://archive.org/details/autobiographyofioosuniuoft>

15   L. Essig, '"All the World Was There" and Other White Lies about the Royal Wedding', *QED: A Journal in GLBTQ Worldmaking* (3/2, 2016) <https://doi.org/10.14321/qed.3.2.0035> pp. 35–55.

16   Ibid.

17   Ibid.

18   *Derby Mercury*, 29 Sep. 1775, cited in R. and L. Adkins, *Eavesdropping on Jane Austen's England: How Our Ancestors Lived Two Centuries Ago* (Abacus: London, 2013) p. 8.

19   *Derby Mercury*, 28 December 1797, cited in R. and L. Adkins, *Eavesdropping on Jane Austen's England*, p. 9.

20   S. Brennan, 'A Natural History of the Wedding Dress', *JSTOR Daily* (27 September 2017) <https://daily.jstor.org/a-natural-history-of-the-wedding-dress/>

21   L. Bates, 'How To Have a Feminist Wedding', the *Guardian* (28 June 2014) <https://www.theguardian.com/lifeandstyle/2014/jun/28/can-a-feminist-be-a-bride-laura-bates>

22   Ibid.

23   T T. Nguyen and R.W. Belk, 'Harmonization Processes and Relational Meanings in Constructing Asian Weddings', *Journal of Consumer Research*, 40/3 (2013) <https://doi.org/10.1086/671464> pp. 518–38

24   K.K. Hersch, 'Introduction To The Roman Wedding: Two Case Studies', *The Classical Journal*, 109/2 (2014) <https://doi.org/10.5184/classicalj.109.2.0223> pp. 223–32

25   D. Vo, 'The Past is Queer' (UK, Alphabet Radio, 30 Sept 2020) <https://www.mixcloud.com/alphabetradio/the-past-is-queer-30092020/>

26   Ibid.

27   Ibid.

28   Ibid.

29   Ibid.

30   Ibid.

31   Ibid.

32   Germaine Greer, *The Female Eunuch* (Fourth Estate: London, 2020).

33   'Dia Mirza on Her Wedding Saree: "Last time I auctioned my attire, this time I got a garment that I could reuse"', *Indian Express*, 16 April 2021 <https://indianexpress.com/article/entertainment/bollywood/dia-mirza-on-simple-wedding-outfit-i-made-sure-to-get-a-garment-that-i-could-reuse-and-wear-again-7275090/>

A CONSUMMATION TO BE DEVOUTLY WISHED

1   C. Wilson, 'Wedding Cake: a Slice of History', *Gastronomica*, 5/2 (2005) <https://doi.org/10.1525/gfc.2005.5.2.69>, pp. 69–72

2   Ibid.

3 R. Hague, 'Marriage Athenian Style', *Archaeology*, 41/3 (1988) <http://www.jstor.org/stable/41730004> pp. 32–36.
4 Ibid.
5 L. Worsley, *If Walls Could Talk: An Intimate History of the Home* (Faber and Faber: London, 2012) p. 68.
6 C. Fisher, 'The Queen and the Artichoke: A Study of the Portraits of Mary Tudor and Charles Brandon.' *The British Art Journal*, 3/2 (2002) <http://www.jstor.org/stable/41614374> pp. 20–27.
7 K. Barclay, 'Women's History Month: Bedding Rituals in Scotland', *Women's History Network* (4 March 2012) <https://womenshistorynetwork.org/womens-history-month-bedding-rituals-in-scotland>
8 Cited in T. Oneill, *Unmentionable* (Back Bay Books: New York, 2016) p. 154.
9 S. Coontz, *Marriage, a History*, p. 190.

WHAT'S IN A NAME?

1 Patricia Highsmith, *Patricia Highsmith: her Diaries and Notebooks*, (Weidenfeld & Nicolson: London, 2021).
2 R. Grossi, *Looking for Love in the Legal Discourse of Marriage* (ANU Press, 2014) <http://www.jstor.org/stable/j.ctt13www3x.1>
3 Sir William Blackstone, *Commentaries on the Laws of England in Four Volumes* (Garland Publishing Inc: New York, 1978), p. 442.
4 A. Adams letter to J. Adams, 31 March 1776, is available at 'All Men Would Be Tyrants if They Could', *Lapham's Quartley* <https://www.laphamsquarterly.org/revolutions/all-men-would-be-tyrants-if-they-could>
5 J. Adams replied to his wife on 14 April 1776, 'All Men Would Be Tyrants if They Could', *Lapham's Quartley* <https://www.laphamsquarterly.org/revolutions/all-men-would-be-tyrants-if-they-could>
6 Ibid.
7 K.K. Hersch, 'Introduction To The Roman Wedding: Two Case Studies'.
8 C. Pettitt, 'Women, Risk, and Intellectual Property: Elizabeth Gaskell and George Eliot in the 1860s', *Patent Inventions – Intellectual Property and the Victorian Novel* (Oxford Academic: Oxford, 2004).
9 J.J. Lewis, 'Marriage Protest of Lucy Stone and Henry Blackwell', *ThoughtCo* (16 January 2020) <https://www.thoughtco.com/marriage-protest-lucy-stone-henry-blackwell-3529568>
10 M. Savage, 'Why Do Women Still Change Their Names?', *BBC The Life Project* (24 December 2020) <https://www.bbc.com/worklife/article/20200921-why-do-women-still-change-their-names>
11 S. Duncan, A.L. Ellingsæter and J. Carter, 'Understanding Tradition: Marital Name Change in Britain and Norway', *Sociological Research Online*, 25/3 (2020) <https://doi.org/10.1177/1360780419892637> pp. 438–55.
12 https://www.washingtonpost.com/world/asia_pacific/japan-names-marriage-women/2021/03/11/0fd38bca-7c30-11eb-8c5e-32e47b42b51b_story.html
13 S. Duncan, A.L. Ellingsæter and J. Carter, 'Understanding Tradition'.
14 Ibid.
15 Ibid.
16 M. Atwood, *The Handmaid's Tale* (Vintage: London, 1996).
17 Ibid.

LOVE, FAIR LOOKS AND TRUE OBEDIENCE

1 *How to be a Good Wife* (Bodleian Library: Oxford, 2008).
2 W. Shakespeare, 'Taming of the Shrew' in *The Oxford Shakespeare: The Complete Works*, S. Wells and G. Taylor (eds.) (2nd ed.) (Oxford: Oxford University Press, 2005) III, 2, 8-9.
3 'Taming of the Shrew, III, 102-04.

4   'Taming of the Shrew', IV, 5, 19-20.
5   'Taming of the Shrew', V, 2, 151-9.
6   'Taming of the Shrew', V, 2, 177.
7   S. Coontz, *Marriage, A History*, p. 121.
8   Ibid.
9   Ibid.
10 Ibid.
11 W.A. Alcott, *The Young Wife, Or Duties of Woman in the Marriage Relation*,(Boston, 1841)
12 T. Oneill, *Unmentionable*, p. 197.
13 Ibid.
14 Ibid.
15 Ibid.
16 'Wife Beating', *The Atlas, London* (15 October 1853) <https://www.britishnewspaperarchive.co.uk/>
17 Ibid.
18 'Wife Beating', *Bell's Life in London and Sporting Chronicle* (30 September 1855) <https://www.britishnewspaperarchive.co.uk/>
19 A.J. Hammerton, 'Victorian Marriage and the Law of Matrimonial Cruelty', *Victorian Studies*, 33/2 (1990) <http://www.jstor.org/stable/3828359> pp. 269–92.
20 Ibid.
21 H. Nelson, '"Nothing That She Could Allege Against Him in Judicious or Judicial Ears": "Consensual" Marital Abuse in Victorian Literature', *George Eliot – George Henry Lewes Studies*, 69/1 (2017) <https://doi.org/10.5325/georelioghlstud.69.1.0089> pp. 89–119.
22 Ibid.
23 S. Hamilton, 'Making History with Frances Power Cobbe: Victorian Feminism, Domestic Violence, and the Language of Imperialism', *Victorian Studies*, 43/3 (2001) <http://www.jstor.org/stable/3829700> pp. 437–60.
24 F.P. Cobbe, *Life of Frances Power Cobbe as Told by Herself* (S. Sonnenschein: London, 1904) p. 592.
25 E. Showalter, 'Killing the Angel in the House: The Autonomy of Women Writers', *The Antioch Review*, 50/1–2 (1992) <https://doi.org/10.2307/4612511> pp. 207–20.
26 *How to be a Good Wife*, p. 21.
27 S. Coontz, *Marriage, a History*y, (2005), p. 223.
28 Advert, 'If Your Husband Ever Finds Out You're Not "Store-Testing" For Fresher Coffee', *Life* (11 August 1952)
29 J. Worth, *Call the Midwife* (Weidenfeld & Nicolson: London, 2002) p. 36.
30 Ibid. p. 36
31 The Law Commission, *Rape within Marriage* (Law Commission: London, 1990) <http://bit.ly/3CTJ4EA>
32 O Bowcott, 'English judge says man having sex with wife is "fundamental human right"', the *Guardian* (3 April 2019) <https://www.theguardian.com/law/2019/apr/03/english-judge-says-man-having-sex-with-wife-is-fundamental-human-right>
33 *Women's History: The Future*, Roundtable discussion followed by address by Secretary Clinton.

FORSAKING ALL OTHERS

1   S. Coontz, *Marriage, a History*, p. 58.
2   Ibid.
3   Ibid. p. 20.
4   Ibid. pp. 20–21.
5   Ibid. p. 20.
6   K.E. Starkweather and R. Hames, 'A Survey of Non-Classical Polyandry'.
7   Ibid.

NOTES

8   Ibid.

9   A. Dreger, 'When Taking Multiple Husband's Makes Sense', *Atlantic* <https://www.theatlantic.com/health/archive/2013/02/when-taking-multiple-husbands-makes-sense/272726/>

10 S. Coontz, *Marriage, a History*, p. 124.

11 E. Fitzgerald et al., *Meaningful Work: Transgender Experiences in the Sex Trade* (2015) <https://transequality.org/sites/default/files/Meaningful%20Work-Full%20Report_FINAL_3.pdf>

12 M. Parker, 'The Married-womans Case: OR Good Counsell to Mayds, to be carefull of hastie Marriage, by the example of other Married-women', *Oxford Text Archive* <https://bit.ly/3GSVoWK>

13 Cited in T. Oneill, *Unmentionable*, p. 212.

14 *How to be a Good Wife*.

15 W. Blake, 'Visions of the Daughters of Albion', in *Romanticism: An Anthology*, W.U. Duncan (ed.), (3rd ed.) (Blackwell Publishing: Oxford, 2005).

16 L. De Salvo and M. Leaska (eds). *The Letters of Vita Sackville-West to Virginia Woolf* (Cleis Press, 2001).

17 'Avvo study examines attitudes around open relationships', *Avvo* (2016) <https://stories.avvo.com/relationships/avvo-study-examines-new-attitudes-around-open-relationships.html>

18 'One Third of Americans Say That Their Ideal Relationships Is Non Monogamous' (31 January 2020), *YouGovAmerica* <https://today.yougov.com/topics/lifestyle/articles-reports/2020/01/31/millennials-monogamy-poly-poll-survey-data>

19 'I Had The Perfect Life Then Both My Husbands Died', the *Guardian* (31 January 2022) <https://www.theguardian.com/music/2022/jan/31/i-had-the-perfect-life-then-both-my-husbands-died-singer-labi-siffre-on-love-loss-and-happiness>

20 'Ethical Non-monogamy: the Rise of Multi-partner Relationships', *BBC Lovelife* (25 March 2021) <https://www.bbc.com/worklife/article/20210326-ethical-non-monogamy-the-rise-of-multi-partner-relationships>

A FRUITFUL UNION

1   'Record Numbers of Women Reach 30 Child-Free in England and Wales', the *Guardian* (27 January 2022) <http://bit.ly/3ZHQYuH>

2   Photography of Mosuo women by Karolin Klüppel is available at *National Geographic* (2017) <https://www.nationalgeographic.co.uk/travel-and-adventure/2017/11/where-women-reign-intimate-look-inside-rare-kingdom>

3   L. Worsley, *If Walls Could Talk*, p. 18.

4   Cited in M. Potts and M. Campbell, 'History of Contraception', *Glob. Libr. Women's Med.* (2009) <https://www.glowm.com/section-view/heading/History%20of%20Contraception/item/375#.YjxX6OrPo2w>

5   R. and L. Adkins, *Eavesdropping on Jane Austen's England*, p. 20.

6   Interview between Toni Morrison and Junot Diaz, *New York Public Library* (12 December 2013) <Toni Morrison | Junot Díaz | The New York Public Library (https://www. nypl.org)>

7   C. Gordon, *Romantic Outlaws: The Extraordinary lives of Mary Wollstonecraft and Mary Shelley*' (Hutchinson: London, 2015).

8   Ibid.

9   Ibid.

10 Ibid.

11 W. Moore, *Wedlock: How Georgian Britain's Worst Husband Met His Match* (Weidenfeld & Nicolson, London, 2009) p. 294.

12 M. Wollstonecraft, *A Vindication of the Rights of Woman*.

13 Cited in H. Lewis, *Difficult Women: A History of Feminism in 11 Fights* (Jonathan Cape: London, 2020) p. 17.

14 Ibid. p. 18.

15 Ibid. p. 18.
16 A. Besant, *Annie Besant: An Autobiography* (CreateSpace Independent Publishing Platform, 2016).
17 H. McCarthy, *Double Lives: A History of Working Motherhood* (Bloomsbury: London, 2020) p. 79.
18 L. Worsley, *If Walls Could Talk*, p. 76.
19 Cited in T. Oneill, *Unmentionable*, p. 175.
20 V.L. Bullough, 'A Brief Note on Rubber Technology and Contraception: The Diaphragm and the Condom', *Technology and Culture*, 22/1 (1981) <https://doi.org/10.2307/3104294> pp.104–11.
21 F. Nightingale, 'Sick-Nursing and Health-Nursing' (1893).
22 M. Roser and H. Ritchie, 'Maternal Mortality', *OurWorldInData* (2013) <https://ourworldindata.org/maternal-mortality>
23 Ibid.
24 J. Worth, *Call the Midwife*, p. 3.
25 Ibid.
26 Ibid. p. 80.
27 S. Coontz, *Marriage, A History*, p. 254.
28 'Women's Rights to Reproductive Healthcare: United States', *UK Parliament* (28 Jun 2022) <https://hansard.parliament.uk/Commons/2022-06-28/debates/75E02BEF-614E-489A-8303-F15015AD83A6/details>
29 B. Friedan, *The Feminine Mystique* (Penguin Classics: London, 2010).
30 'Local Government Act 1988', *UK Public General Acts* <https://www.legislation.gov.uk/ukpga/1988/9/section/28/enacted>
31 D. Rudolph, 'A Very Brief History of LGBTQ Parenting' (20 October 2017), *Family Equality* <https://www.familyequality.org/2017/10/20/a-very-brief-history-of-lgbtq-parenting/>
32 M. George, 'The history behind the latest LGBTQ rights case at the Supreme Court', *Washington Post* (17 November 2020) (<https://www.washingtonpost.com/outlook/2020/11/17/history-behind-latest-lgbtq-rights-case-supreme-court/>)
33 Known as the motherhood penalty and fatherhood bonus.
34 I.B. Wells, *Crusade for Justice: The Autobiography of Ida B. Wells* (University of Chicago Press, Chicago, 2020)

HAVING IT ALL – DOMESTIC, SOCIAL AND PAID LABOUR

1   C. Moran, 'Every few years, I Reread *How To Be A Woman* And Marvel At What I Got Wrong'.
2   Ibid.
3   T. Tusser, *Fiue Hundred Pointes of Good Husbandrie*, Project Gutenberg <https://www.gutenberg.org/files/51764/51764-h/51764-h.htm>
4   'Ballad of a Tyrannical Husband', available at E. Salisbury (ed.) *The Trials and Joys of Marriage* (2002) <https://d.lib.rochester.edu/teams/text/salisbury-trials-and-joys-ballad-of-a-tyrannical-husband>
5   H. McCarthy, *Double Lives*.
6   Ibid.
7   Ibid. p. 31.
8   A. Pochin, *The Right of Women to Exercise the Elective Franchise* (Chapman & Hall, London, 1855), p. 31.
9   L. Garrett Anderson, *Elizabeth Garrett Anderson: 1836–1917* (Cambridge University Press: Cambridge)
10 H. McCarthy, *Double Lives*, p. 71.
11 Ibid. p. 72.
12 Ibid. p. 71.
13 Ibid. p. 82.

14 'Adelaide Knight, Leader of the First East London Suffragettes', *East End Women's Museum* (12 October 2016) <https://eastendwomensmuseum.org/blog/adelaide-knight-leader-of-the-first-east-london-suffragettes>

15 A. Kenney, 'Full Text of "Memories of a Militant"', *Internet Archive* (1924) <https://archive.org/stream/in.ernet.dli.2015.201549/2015.201549.Memories-Of_djvu.txt>

16 'Adelaide Knight, Leader of the First East London Suffragettes'.

17 'Obituary of Winifred Langton', the *Guardian* (1 April 2003) <https://www.theguardian.com/news/2003/apr/01/guardianobituaries.obituaries>

18 H. McCarthy, *Double Lives*, p. 20.

19 Ibid. p. 102.

20 '100 years of Women in the Professions: The Sex Disqualification (Removal) Act 1919', *National Archives* (23 December 2019) <https://blog.nationalarchives.gov.uk/the-sex-disqualification-removal-act-1919/#return-note-46791-6>

21 Annie Errington's story will be shared more widely through *Red Hill's Miner's Hall* in Durham, as part of an ongoing restoration of northeast England's mining heritage <https://redhillsdurham.org/>

22 S. Coontz, *Marriage, A History*, p. 219.

23 Ibid.

24 Ibid.

25 H. McCarthy, *Double Lives*, p. 147.

26 C. Ro, 'Why This Recession Disproportionately Affects Women', *BBC Worklife* (27 October 2020) <https://www.bbc.com/worklife/article/20201021-why-this-recession-disproportionately-affects-women>

27 S. Coontz, *Marriage, A History*, p. 221.

28 Ibid.

29 H. McCarthy, *Double Lives*, p. 167.

30 Ibid. p. 165.

31 Ibid. p. 212.

32 Ibid. p. 218.

33 Ibid. p. 390.

34 S. Coontz, *Marriage, a History*, p. 228.

35 Ibid. p. 217.

36 Ibid.

37 'Sex Discrimination Act 1975', *UK Public General Acts* <https://www.legislation.gov.uk/ukpga/1975/65/enacted>

38 H McCarthy, *Double Lives*, p. 5.

39 J. Brearley, *Pregnant Then Screwed: The Truth About the Motherhood Penalty* (Gallery Books: London, 2021) p. 9.

40 Ibid.

41 Ibid.

42 Ibid.

43 Ibid. p. 10.

44 Ibid. p. 9.

45 'Almost Half of Working-Age Women in UK Do 45 Hours of Unpaid Care A Week – Study', *The Guardian* (31 March 2022) <https://www.theguardian.com/world/2022/mar/31/almost-half-of-working-age-women-in-uk-do-45-hours-of-unpaid-care-a-week-study>

46 'CPP's Latest Report Finds Caring Responsibilities Are Disproportionately Impacting Women In The UK', *Centre for Progressive Policy* (April 2022) <https://www.progressive-policy.net/publications/press-release-cpps-latest-report-finds-caring-responsibilities-are-disproportionately-impacting-women-in-the-uk>

47 B. Friedan, *The Feminine Mystique*.

48 'CPP's Latest Report Finds Caring Responsibilities Are Disproportionately Impacting Women In The UK', *Centre for Progressive Policy*.

49 'Global Gender Gap Report 2020', *World Economic Forum* (16 December 2019) <https://www.weforum.org/reports/gender-gap-2020-report-100-years-pay-equality>
50 J. Brearley, *Pregnant Then Screwed*, p. 10.
51 C. Moran, 'Every Few Years, I Reread *How To Be A Woman* And Marvel At What I Got Wrong.'
52 S. Doughty, 'Why Making Women Retire Later Comes With A Hidden Cost: State Picks Up £5,600 Bill For Care Of Elderly', *Daily Mail* Online (13 April 2021) <https://www.dailymail.co.uk/news/article-9464089/Why-making-women-retire-later-comes-hidden-cost-State-picks-5-600-bill-care-elderly.html>

TILL DEATH DO US PART

1 Fred and Mary are given a 'solid mutual happiness' by G. Eliot at the end of *Middlemarch*, Project Gutenberg <https://www.gutenberg.org/files/145/145-h/145-h.htm>
2 S. Coontz, *Marriage, a History*, p. 22.
3 Ibid. p. 21.
4 'Obituary for Alice Toklas', *NY Times* (8 March 1967) <https://archive.nytimes.com/www.nytimes.com/books/98/05/03/specials/stein-toklasobit.html>
5 *Becoming*, Netflix.
6 'Michelle Obama Shared Some Powerful Relationship Advice: "Marry Your Equal"', *Glamour* (7 July 2019) <https://www.glamour.com/story/michelle-obama-marriage-advice-marry-your-equal>
7 Ibid.
8 B.R. Karney and T.N. Bradbury, 'Research on Marital Satisfaction and Stability in the 2010s: Challenging Conventional Wisdom', *J Marriage Fam*, 82/1 (2020) <https://www.ncbi.nlm.nih.gov/pmc/articles/PMC8186435/> pp. 100–16.
9 Ibid.
10 S. Coontz, *Marriage, a History*, p. 310.
11 University of East Anglia, 'Marriage Could Improve Heart Attack Survival And Reduce Hospital Stay', *ScienceDaily*. (8 June 2016) <www.sciencedaily.com/releases/2016/06/160608100133.htm>
12 T.F. Robles, 'Marital Quality and Health: Implications For Marriage in the 21st century.' *Current Directions in Psychological Science*, 23/6 (2014) <https://www.ncbi.nlm.nih.gov/pmc/articles/PMC4275835/> pp. 427–32
13 S. Coontz, *Marriage, a History*, p. 310.
14 Ibid. p. 310.
15 S. Coontz, *Marriage, a History*.
16 S.Z. Badran and B. Turnbull, 'Contemporary Temporary Marriage: a Blog-analysis of First-hand Experiences', *Journal of International Women's Studies*, 20/2 (2019) <https://vc.bridgew.edu/jiws/vol20/iss2/17> .
17 S. Mahmood and C. Nye, 'I Do ... For Now. UK Muslims Revive Temporary Marriages', *BBC News* (13 May 2013) <https://www.bbc.co.uk/news/uk-22354201>
18 S. Coontz, *Marriage, a History*, p. 22.
19 G.E. Vincent, 'The Laws of Hammurabi', *American Journal of Sociology*, 9/6 (1904) <http://www.jstor.org/stable/2762088> pp. 737–54.
20 Ibid.
21 S. Coontz, *Marriage, a History*, p. 105.
22 W. Moore, *Wedlock: How Georgian Britain's Worst Husband Met His Match*, p. 180.
23 Ibid. p. 305.
24 A.J. Hammerton, 'Victorian Marriage and the Law of Matrimonial Cruelty', *Victorian Studies*, 33/2 (1990) <http://www.jstor.org/stable/3828359> pp.269–92.
25 T. Hardy, *The Mayor of Casterbridge*, Project Gutenberg <https://www.gutenberg.org/files/143/143-h/143-h.htm>
26 Ibid.

27 'Wife for Sale', *North British Daily Mail* (8 November 1856), in The British Newspaper Archive <https://www.britishnewspaperarchive.co.uk/viewer/bl/0002683/18561108/113/0008>

28 Ibid.

29 'The Price of a Wife', *Londonderry Sentinel* (16 May 1907), in The British Newspaper Archive <https://www.britishnewspaperarchive.co.uk/>

30 Ibid.

31 W.M. Thackeray, 'Damages, Two Hundred Pounds', LiteratureApp <https://literatureapp.com/william-makepeace-thackeray/damages-two-hundred-pounds>

32 Ibid.

33 J. Aston, 'Learning from Old Grievances: Revelations from the Court for Divorce and Matrimonial Causes in England and Wales, 1857–1923', paper given at *A Sacred Covenant?* (20 May 2021) <https://asacredcovenant.com>

34 Ibid.

35 E. Acland, *Marriage as the Foundation of the Home* (London, 1902), p. 28–9.

36 S. Coontz, *Marriage, a History*, p. 211.

37 Ibid. p. 211.

38 W. Kuby, *Conjugal Misconduct. In Conjugal Misconduct: Defying Marriage Law in the Twentieth-Century United States* (Cambridge University Press: Cambridge, 2018) p. 150.

39 Ibid. p. 152.

40 Ibid. P. 151.

41 Ibid. p. 152.

42 Ibid. p. 160.

43 Ibid.

44 Ibid.

45 Ibid.

46 L.M. Friedman, 'A Dead Language: Divorce Law and Practice before No-Fault', *Virginia Law Review*, 86/7 (2000) <https://doi.org/10.2307/1073878> 1497–1536. p. 1505.

47 Ibid.

48 S. Coontz, *Marriage, a History*, p. 300.

49 Ibid.

50 Ibid.

51 B. DePaulo, 'Is It True That Single Women And Married Men Do Best?' *Psychology Today* (11 January 2017) <https://www.psychologytoday.com/us/blog/living-single/201701/is-it-true-single-women-and-married-men-do-best>

52 S. Coontz, *Marriage, a History*, p. 261.

53 Ibid. p. 263.

54 Cited in G. Carter (ed.), *Vanity Fair's Proust Questionnaire: 101 Luminaries Ponder Love, Death, Happiness, and the Meaning of Life* (Rodale Books, 2009)

55 @nadiyajhussain, 'Nothing fancy just love … ', Instagram, 18 December 2018 <https://www.instagram.com/p/Brh39sdAXnX/>

KEEPING UP THE FIGHT

1 A. Garza, 'Fight Against Despair and Keep Doing the Work Needed to Change the World', *Forbes* (15 January 2021) <https://www.forbes.com/sites/marianneschnall/2021/01/15/interview-with-blacklivesmatter-cofounder-alicia-garza-fight-against-despair-and-keep-doing-the-work-needed-to-change-the-world/>

2 'Divorce And Matrimonial Causes Bill—Committee', *UK Parliament* (13 August 1857) <https://bit.ly/3XkHXpM>

3 'Current News: For and About Women', *Women's Signal* (21 January 1897), LSE Digital Archive <http://bit.ly/3XAvA8M>

4 O. Hill, 'Women and the Suffrage', *Times* (15 July 1910).

5 Ibid.

6 Cited in S. Duncan and R. Lennon, *Women and Power*.

7 Churchill pasted this private note into an 1874 copy of the Annual Register in 1897.

8   Ibid.
9   Ibid.
10 The anti-suffrage petition was published in the journal *The Nineteenth Century*, in June 1889.
11 Cited in S.S. Holton, *Suffrage Days: Stories from the Women's Suffrage Movement* (Routledge: London, 1996) p. 80.
12 B. Friedan, *The Feminine Mystique*.
13 Ibid.
14 'Mary McIntosh Discusses Financial And Legal Independence', *British Library* (25 August 2011) <https://www.bl.uk/collection-items/mary-mcintosh-financial-and-legal-independence>
15 Ipsos, 'LGBT+ Pride 2021 Global Survey'.

EPILOGUE
1   E. Ortiz-Ospina and M. Roser, 'Marriages and Divorces', *Our World in Data* (2020) <https://ourworldindata.org/marriages-and-divorces>
2   'Population Estimates by Marital Status and Living Arrangements, England and Wales: 2019', *Office of National Statistics*, 17 July 2020. <https://bit.ly/3Frzr1C>
3   B. DePaulo, 'Around the World, Marriage Is Declining, Singles Are Rising', *Psychology Today* (17 August 2019) <https://bit.ly/3h1FwZo>
4   B.R. Karney and T.N. Bradbury, 'Research on Marital Satisfaction and Stability in the 2010s: Challenging Conventional Wisdom'.
5   Widely attributed to Oscar Wilde.
6   B.R. Karney and T.N. Bradbury, 'Research on Marital Satisfaction and Stability in the 2010s: Challenging Conventional Wisdom'.
7   Cited in L. DeFrank-Cole and S.J. Tan, *Women and Leadership: Journey Toward Equity* (Sage: California, 2022).
8   E. Ortiz-Ospina and M. Roser, 'Marriages and Divorces'.
9   Ibid.
10 Two in five trans young people in the UK have attempted suicide. 'The Truth About Trans', *Stonewall* <https://www.stonewall.org.uk/truth-about-trans>
11 C.D. Boateng and R. Kapuku debate dating to marry on their podcast, 'You're Dating to Marry – But is Marriage Even Worth it? The Game Has Changed' *To My Sisters* <https://www.youtube.com/watch?v=FA2CX4ySbdQ>
12 B.R. Karney and T.N. Bradbury, 'Research on Marital Satisfaction and Stability in the 2010s: Challenging Conventional Wisdom'.
13 Stonewall, '2014: I do! Marriage Act means same-sex couples can tie the knot', *Stonewall* <https://www.stonewall.org.uk/our-work/campaigns/2014-i-do-marriage-act-means-same-sex-couples-can-tie-knot>
14 Ipsos, 'LGBT+ Pride 2021 Global Survey'.
15 House of Commons, *Non-binary Gender Recognition: Law and Policy* (House of Commons Library, 2022) <CBP-9515.pdf (parliament.uk)>
16 M. Carlisle, 'Young People Are Taking Control Over Their Gender Identity', *Time* (12 July 2021) <https://bit.ly/3Urd9Bu>

ACKNOWLEDGEMENTS

I have learnt so much in researching this book. As any history that spans such a breadth of time and place, this personal collection of stories owes an enormous debt to so many specialists, researchers, historians, academics, curators and archivists who have worked for years to explore, uncover and shine new light on these past lives.

Wedded Wife would not have been possible without the encouragement and opportunities given to me by Katie Bond, who empowered me to turn my frustrations with traditional and contemporary marriage into a book. A real book.

Thanks too to Phoebe Bath, Claire Maxwell and all the team at Aurum for their patient enthusiasm and support. To the people who made wonderful suggestions to help bring this history to life, including Hannah Squire and Vicky Iglikowski-Broad and the team at Red Hills for preserving and sharing the working-class histories of north-east England. To those who read the first tentative drafts with kindness and generosity, Susan Shanks and Tate Greenhalgh.

An enormous thanks to my extraordinarily talented sister Katherine, who has helped on me every step in the creation of this book, from the earliest ideas to the final drafts. She helped me find structure in garbled imaginings, stories where I found gaps and, most importantly, confidence when I needed it most.

To my parents, particularly my mother, for everything she has sacrificed and achieved for me and my brothers and sister. For giving me with the strong values and stubborn drive that led me here.

Thanks too to my parents-in-law, for providing me with both the time and space to write – particularly for creating an office for my wife and I to work away from the crushing guilt and FOMO that comes with babies. Most importantly, to my wife, for not only sharing the house with this project for the past two years, but, as the woman with whom I walked down the aisle, for being the inspiration behind the whole thing. And to the wonderful children our marriage has created alongside this book, the best little people it is possible to imagine.